Date Due

JUL 28 2005		

Student Affairs

Edited by Lesley Andres and Finola Finlay

Student Affairs:
Experiencing Higher Education

UBCPress · Vancouver · Toronto

15 14 13 12 11 10 09 08 07 06 05 04   5 4 3 2 1

Printed in Canada on acid-free paper

Library and Archives Canada Cataloguing in Publication

Student affairs : experiencing higher education /
edited by Lesley Andres and Finola Finlay.

Includes bibliographical references and index.
ISBN 0-7748-1114-5

1. College students – British Columbia. 2. Education, Higher – British Columbia.
3. Academic achievement – British Columbia. 4. College environment – British
Columbia. I. Andres, Lesley II. Finlay, Finola, 1950-

LB2342.9.S78 2004   378.1'98'09711   C2004-905586-0

Canadä

UBC Press gratefully acknowledges the financial support for our publishing
program of the Government of Canada through the Book Publishing Industry
Development Program (BPIDP), and of the Canada Council for the Arts, and
the British Columbia Arts Council.

This book has been published with the help of the K.D. Srivastava Fund.

UBC Press
The University of British Columbia
2029 West Mall
Vancouver, BC V6T 1Z2
604-822-5959 / Fax: 604-822-6083
www.ubcpress.ca

Dedicated to
Lesley's nieces Claire and Alex
and Finola's twenty-one grandchildren,
who deserve an accessible, affordable, and fair
Canadian post-secondary system

Contents

Foreword
Neil Guppy

Education matters. Indeed, with each passing year it matters more and more. Defined broadly to include such elements as income, morbidity, and civic engagement, life chances depend to an ever larger extent upon an individual's success in the formal education system. Precisely because of that growing importance, this book is timely and thoughtful. Improving the education system for students is the central purpose of each author, and collectively they offer powerful analyses and recommendations.

Education's pivotal role in the modern world is in part a function of increasingly stronger relationships between education, occupation, and income, for which evidence is plentiful. As advanced knowledge drives more and more of local and global trade in goods and services, people and governments want more of what education offers. Nation-states also understand these connections at a societal level, as witnessed by the high levels of education spending that typify countries around the globe, as they also recognize the strong link between a vibrant democracy and an educated society.

In consequence, the more that education matters, the more people need and want access to it. In less than two centuries we have witnessed the creation and expansion of an institutional form virtually unknown prior to the 1800s. Furthermore, the importance of education is not restricted by type of nation-state or economic system. It is everywhere, and everywhere access is a core issue.

Elite access was the hallmark of the earliest examples of formal schooling. Only the privileged few were judged able to benefit from educational instruction. Especially at the elementary and secondary levels access is now far broader. Inclusion of people from divergent backgrounds as defined by class, gender, ethnicity, or ability level is now the norm. But while this inclusion has permeated education for the youngest ages, divergent opportunities and outcomes still characterize significant areas of post-secondary education. At the post-secondary level, access for all remains a goal, not a reality.

Every contribution to this book is a testament to both how much institutional change has occurred in the social organization of post-secondary education as well as how much more change is required to fully meet the challenges of equality of inclusion in access. The pace of this change is asymmetrical, occurring more rapidly in the backgrounds of students attending colleges and universities than in the institutions themselves.

Nevertheless, we are in the midst of a transition away from institutions accustomed to a less diverse population (largely men of privilege) toward institutions more accommodating of differences among students. Institutions still do demand that students change to meet their well-tested policies and practices, but gradually a new institutional responsiveness is emerging in which student diversity is recognized and encouraged. These research studies not only add empirical fuel to the need for change, they also suggest practical ways for creative and effective change to occur.

Increasingly, post-secondary organizations and the educators within them have taken more and more responsibility for the success of students, moving away from an exclusively "sink or swim" approach. By way of analogy, it is not good enough simply to attend the dance, but being rewarded by peers for looking good on the dance floor is imperative. Looking good depends in part upon individual talent and effort, but also on the organizational preparation of the hosts, including their ability to orchestrate the dance floor, the music, the lighting, and the mood of the room. Success depends upon both individual skills and organizational context. Similarly, students from all backgrounds need to enter a context where institutions take responsibility for their success seriously. The authors of these chapters have suggested a myriad of valuable ways to foster and facilitate such action.

Student development is recognized as one of these new institutional responsibilities, at least in more progressive and successful institutions. Beyond coverage of the course content, recognition of broader skills in leadership, communication, critical and moral reasoning, and judgment is now seen as part of the mandate of post-secondary institutions. Long understood as taken-for-granted byproducts of good education, these "meta-skills" are frequently explicit features of quality education. Increasingly students are engaged not as vessels to which knowledge is added, but as people whose diverse experiences and upbringings need recognition. This volume provides reams of illustrations of what works and how much more work needs to be done. These examples include programming in counselling and advising, cooperative education, intercultural communication, disability resources, curricular reform, and the valuing of diverse backgrounds, skills, abilities, and experiences.

Yet another way to understand these studies is through the tension of common but different. The ethos of equality that pervades our thinking about education speaks to common or collective education – a community offering equitable opportunities for all. Simple equality does not often work for people from different, that is unequal, backgrounds. It is hard work to figure out how best to balance these competing themes, but many of these chapters provide sage advice about this tension and its resolution.

This is an important book. Each author cogently addresses themes central to contemporary debates about the future of higher education in North America. The ideas and insights offered in the following pages put students at the centre of the analysis. Across a range of different educational settings and curricular programs the themes return again and again to the importance of getting it right for students. Through both their experiences and their voices, students are the empirical heart of all this work. Significant lessons are here for researchers, educationalists, students, and policy advocates.

Acknowledgments

The production of this book proved to be a model of what a collaborative endeavour can and should be. Although each author was responsible for her or his own chapter, the collective wisdom and energy of the group, from beginning to end, provided the creative milieu within which ideas could be developed, nurtured, challenged, and refined. On many occasions, each chapter was scrutinized by the team of contributors to ensure clarity of themes, voice, and relevance to policy, practice, theory, and further research.

We include Jean Wilson from UBC Press in our definition of "team" and thank her for teaching the group about the publication process, related pitfalls, and strategies for success.

This volume benefited greatly from the careful comments and criticisms from class members of HIED 510 – Foundations of Higher Education, a graduate course within the Adult and Higher Education Program at UBC – who rose to the challenge of being forced to criticize not only the book but also their instructor! We extend special thanks to Jeremy Cato, Karen Gardner, Liz Hammond-Kaarremaa, Ann-Marie Jakobi, Xuehong Liao, Beatrice Lukac, Tricia Rachfall, Chen Shen, Serge Tararensko, Ken Wolgram, and Alina Yuhymets.

In addition, we would like to express our thanks to the Social Sciences and Humanities Research Council of Canada and the British Columbia Council on Admissions and Transfer (BCCAT) for their ongoing financial support of the Paths on Life's Way Project. BCCAT was generous in allowing Finola to pursue this project as part of her work commitments. Also, we gratefully acknowledge the financial support of the province of British Columbia through the Ministry of Education.

Student Affairs

Introduction:
Today's Post-Secondary Students –
Adding Faces to Numbers
Lesley Andres

Expansion of the post-secondary system, increasing evidence of the market and nonmarket effects of education, an emphasis on credentialism as the new rite of passage, and national attention on issues of equality of opportunity have served to promote post-secondary participation in Canada.[1] As a result, provincial systems of post-secondary education have continued to expand and diversify. Between 1984-85 and 1998-99, full-time university undergraduate enrolment increased by 20 percent and full-time enrolment in programs at community colleges increased by 25 percent (Statistics Canada 1984-2001). Much of the growth has been attributed to increased access for nontraditional students, evidenced mainly by higher numbers of women taking part in post-secondary education and, to a lesser extent, students from different ethnic and socioeconomic backgrounds, disabled individuals, and older students. Because these data are disaggregated by gender, comparisons of enrolment and completion rates by women and men in various programs can be determined (Andres 2002; Finnie 2001). However, national databases do not allow for the examination of participation of different age, ethnic/racial, or socioeconomically disadvantaged groups; nor do they permit examination of the experiences and outcomes of these groups. The purpose of this book is to extend current understandings of participation, experiences, and outcomes of today's post-secondary students.

Multiple forces impacting on post-secondary education, including threats to funding, rising tuition fees, labour market restructuring, privatization, and calls for increasing relevance of education to the workplace, have led to growing pressures on post-secondary institutions to pay increasing attention to the quality and relevance of their students' experiences and related educational outcomes. Increased interest is evidenced by activities ranging from national efforts to establish educational outcomes (Canadian Education Statistics Council 2000) to academic (Doherty-Delorme and Shaker 2003) and popular media ratings and rankings of universities (e.g., *MacLean's*, *U.S. News World Report*).

However, in most of the scholarly work to date, theoretical models and empirical studies have focused on student retention and attrition. The most dominant body of research has been grounded on a theoretical model of persistence/dropout developed by Tinto (1975, 1987). Based on this model, persistence and withdrawal behaviour by students has been described as the degree of "fit" between students and their institutional environments. That is, students arrive at a given institution with a range of personal characteristics (e.g., sex, ethnicity), family and community of origin characteristics (e.g., family socioeconomic status, size of community), skills (e.g., intellectual and social), value orientations, achievements, and experiences from prior schooling (e.g., academic ability, secondary school achievement). Each of these characteristics affects the individual's initial formulation of intentions and commitments about future educational activities, which, in turn, influences subsequent experiences within the institution. Ultimately, these experiences determine the individual's integration into the institution. The extent to which academic integration occurs is determined by academic performance and level of intellectual development. Social integration is a result of the quality of peer group interactions and the quality of student interactions with faculty. Levels of social and academic integration lead to second-order commitments toward the institution and graduation. The higher one's level of institutional and goal commitment, the more likely one is to persist at the institution.

Researchers adopting variations of Tinto's model have examined community college students' predisposition to transfer, retention of ethnic groups, and specific constructs of the model such as faculty-student contacts, and predictors of social and academic integration (Chapman and Pascarella 1983; Nora and Rendon 1990). These findings have been used by institutional researchers and planners to assess the fit (or mismatch) between students' initial expectations and actual experiences. By focusing on its various dimensions, interventions have been designed to encourage student persistence, thereby preventing potentially wasted resources associated with post-secondary attrition.

Such approaches, however, are limiting. Originally designed to assess persistence patterns of a young (e.g., the 18- to 24-year-old) residential student population, theoretical developments and empirical studies usually focus on four-year university students and assume full-time attendance. As such, they disregard the demographic heterogeneity of today's student population. Historically, the "traditional" university student meant male and white (Andres and Guppy 1991; Axelrod 2002). Demographic profiles of post-secondary students in the 1990s reveal that students once defined as "non-traditional" are now an integral part of the mainstream student population (Puccio 1995).[2] Although variations of Tinto's model have been devised to assess persistence/withdrawal behaviour of "nontraditional students," these models remain peripheral and continue to deal with the "other."

Moreover, these models locate individuals within a given post-secondary institution and emphasize the effectiveness of the individual to integrate socially and academically into the institution. Concepts within these models are defined and measured in limited ways. For example, the most frequent measures of the concept of academic integration include grade point average or the number of contacts with faculty outside of the classroom setting. As Benjamin (1994) points out, this disregards the complexity of students' lived lives. To extend our understandings of access to post-secondary education and participation and retention once in the system, other individual, institutional, and extra-institutional dimensions are needed. These dimensions include family, society, preparation, situation, institution/program, psychosocial/emotional and socioeconomic considerations, and outside community support (Johnson 1991). Students cannot be examined in isolation from the multiple contexts within which they operate; in other words, it is critical that individuals, environments, and situations remain conceptually and analytically intact. Also, it is important to embrace the complexity of post-secondary institutions and the multiple societal institutions in relation to the quality of students' experiences within post-secondary institutions.

To date, however, existing theoretical models and empirical analyses have not addressed the dynamic relationship between students as agents within societal institutions and institutions as living structures that impact on the lives of students. The relationship between structure and agency has long been acknowledged in the sociological literature (Archer 1982; Coleman 1986; Giddens 1984). Agents (i.e., students) enter post-secondary institutions enabled or constrained by varying levels of competencies, resources, and strategies. As such, they are not without "engines of action," completely constrained and shaped by their environment. However, students also encounter people, policies, and practices within societal institutions, including post-secondary institutions, family, and work, that enable or constrain their ability to integrate socially and academically and to achieve their educational goals. As Bourdieu (1991) indicates, educational institutions can be conceptualized as a "field" within the multidimensional space of the social world. A given institution and the people within it create a *field of forces* and a *field of struggles*, which tend to transform or conserve the field of forces. Students are defined by their *relative positions* in this space, that is, relative to faculty, staff, resources, policies, and practices of a given post-secondary institution. Students' relative positions are also defined by other relevant "fields," such as family and work. Hence, occupants of various positions in each field are oriented, through the network of relations among the positions, to the strategies that may be implemented in their struggles to ameliorate their positions.

Considerable research efforts have focused on access to post-secondary institutions by Canadian women and men. For example, statistics indicate that between 1960 and 1985 enrolment by women in university undergraduate programs increased steadily, and by 1988 women's enrolment had surpassed men's. In 1998-99, the proportion of women in the 18-21 age group enrolled full time in university undergraduate programs in Canada was 35 percent; the comparable figure for men was 26 percent. Since 1976, women's full-time enrolment at community colleges in Canada has exceeded men's and more women students have always participated part-time at community colleges (Statistics Canada 2001). However, women remain underrepresented in mathematics, science, engineering, and technology at both the community college and university levels (Adamuti-Trache and Andres 2002; Andres 2002). Existing national data do not permit an examination of experiences within the post-secondary system by women and men, different age groups, women with multiple responsibilities, students with disabilities, international students who are often visible minorities, or students in alternative programs such as cooperative education. In this volume, we extend the analyses to include the study of access and participation within given institutions and programs. Our chapters focus on participation and experiences of women and men within various post-secondary settings.

This requires an approach to research that permits exploration of the agency-structure nexus. Such an approach allows us to seek answers to the following questions: Who has access to post-secondary education today? At what financial and personal cost? Based on what conditions and criteria? What institutional structures facilitate and constrain successful participation and completion by certain groups? In light of these constraining and facilitating factors, what levels of agency are required for experiences within the post-secondary system? How do various groups of nontraditional and traditional students describe their experiences within universities and the non-university sectors? Now that women are the majority in community colleges and undergraduate education, is gender still an issue?

In this volume, we focus on the experiences of students attending public post-secondary institutions in British Columbia. As such, the British Columbia context provides the specific example of the general case of participation and experiences of students attending Canadian post-secondary institutions. Nowhere has post-secondary expansion and diversification occurred to the extent that it has in British Columbia. In 1963, only one university and a handful of vocational schools constituted the BC post-secondary system. By 1988, the system had expanded to include five public universities, one private university, fourteen community colleges, four public institutes, an Open University and an Open College, and a smattering of small private colleges and trade schools. In 2003, the BC system was composed of fourteen degree-granting institutions (including seven universities, five university colleges, the British Columbia Institute of Technology, and the Emily Carr Institute of Art and Design), twelve community colleges, three public institutes (including two Aboriginal institutes), and a sophisticated network of private post-secondary institutions. In addition, in 1989 the British Columbia Council on Admissions and Transfer (BCCAT) was established as a major initiative to improve access to post-secondary education. The broad mandate of the Council is to provide leadership and direction in ensuring that students can move throughout the network of post-secondary institutions in BC (Andres and Dawson 1998). In other words, in terms of availability and transferability of course credits among institutions, the British Columbia system of higher education provides a vast array of offerings and avenues for successful completion of post-secondary studies.

Because of this great variety of post-secondary offerings, the BC post-secondary system provides an ideal setting in which to study student access, experiences, and outcomes. However, although this volume showcases recent research conducted with students attending BC post-secondary institutions, the studies presented in each chapter will be relevant to post-secondary and secondary educators, educational policy makers, students of higher education, current secondary and undergraduate students, and their parents – within and outside BC – who are interested in the experiences of post-secondary students. Although the BC system has many distinctive characteristics, it shares more similarities than differences with other Canadian provincial post-secondary systems. All Canadian provinces have extensive public post-secondary systems that are controlled at the provincial level. Each provincial system makes provision for open access and highly competitive access to university and non-university programs. The former is fostered through a combined federal/provincial student assistance program in each province. Most provincial university systems include a variety of undergraduate, comprehensive, and medical/doctoral institutions. Although there is variation among provincial community college systems in terms of transfer and terminal programs, all systems offer a mix of developmental, academic, vocational, career, technical, and continuing education programs. In addition, although each province has developed a distinct system rooted in a uniquely Canadian model that is a hybrid of the British and American systems, many aspects of the Canadian system are indistinguishable from state higher education systems in the United States. The transfer systems in BC and Alberta are one example.

As summarized in detail below, the chapters address issues of access and participation by nontraditional and traditional students in programs ranging from community college developmental studies to graduate studies. In the concluding chapter, we will highlight how results, implications, and recommendations offered in each chapter can be transferable to provinces and states within North America and beyond that have post-secondary systems that are similar and dissimilar to that of BC. This volume will provide valuable insights for well- or underdeveloped community college systems, educators and policy makers working in systems with disabled students, a few or many co-op programs, small or large numbers of international, Aboriginal, and nontraditional students, and those interested in improving the transition from high school to post-secondary study and enhancing participation by girls and women in mathematics and sciences. In addition, those interested in the study of systems of higher education – both nationally and internationally – will find the chapters enlightening.

The topics of access and participation are complex and multidimensional. Hence, various approaches to this investigation have been undertaken. In most chapters, the data presented are students' accounts of their experiences. In two chapters, the authors (Adamuti-Trache and Pillay) employ a large longitudinal study of BC young adults to portray patterns over time. In several other chapters, the authors (McGee Thompson, Liversidge, Warick, Lyakhovetska) conducted in-depth interviews with small groups of students to describe, in detail, their experiences in the post-secondary system. Two authors (Hawkey and Grosjean) combined larger-scale survey research and interviews with smaller groups of students. By examining students' participation and experiences at multiple sites and by employing several analytical methods, this collection of research studies is significant in the following ways: From the perspectives of policy and practice, we have been able to document how current admission, tuition, curricular, and institutional policies and practices have an impact on the participation experiences of students. In terms of theory and research, we have extended current thinking on these issues through rigorous conceptual and empirical debate and analysis.

Except for one instance, we have chosen not to reveal the identity of the post-secondary institutional sites. Our intention is not to conceal the identities of the post-secondary institutions. Rather, we felt that readers would be more likely to focus on the stories the authors told instead of the idiosyncrasies of the institutions themselves. However, context remains a central focus of each chapter.

Clearly, we have not been able to address all access and participation issues experienced by BC students. For example, we have not examined experiences of students attending private post-secondary institutions, men in nontraditional programs, students studying part-time, those enrolled in apprenticeship or vocational programs, those engaged in online courses and programs, or specific groups of racial and ethnic minorities, to name a few. In the concluding chapter, we comment on the limitations of this study and suggest directions for further research.

Organization of the Book

In Chapter 1, Maria Adamuti-Trache employs the metaphor of the "leaking science pipeline" to explore the relationship between high school prepared-ness and eventual post-secondary attainment of a large sample of young BC women and men in (and out of) science education and careers over a ten-year time frame. In this study, she employs a structural analysis to deter-mine whether and when women and men with ample high school scientific capital leak out of the science pipeline. After establishing four types of high school graduates – non-science, life science, physical science, and math-ematics – she determines the post-secondary trajectories of these individu-als over time. This study illustrates how girls, and to a lesser extent boys, are filtered away from science beginning at the subject-option level in Grade 12 and continuing throughout their post-secondary years. Results indicate that although post-secondary participation and completion are strongly related to students' high school profiles and only somewhat related to gender, spe-cific fields of study by those graduates from university are strongly related to gender and high school profile. She concludes that young women are more likely to complete studies in a broad range of fields, whereas young men's choices are more narrow and more directly related to their original high school orientation. This pattern is more pronounced for the high school physical science profile, thus leading to a large underrepresentation of women in physical sciences and engineering academic fields. Recommendations reinforce the need to examine the structure of undergraduate and graduate program offerings in science and to increase the link between high school teachers and the post-secondary science departments.

Two chapters focus on the experiences of women attending community college. In Chapter 2, Sharon Liversidge uses the sociology of time lit-erature to inform a study of the experiences of student-mothers who "re/entered" the post-secondary system by enrolling in a community college nursing program. Analyses of in-depth personal interviews and a focus group session conducted with a small group of women in their second year of nursing studies revealed five major themes: time as a scarce re-source, a personal need to achieve, feelings of guilt related to not "being there" for their children, re/entering women as the family organizers, and positive perceptions of their multiple-role status. Liversidge weaves the voices of the women throughout the narrative to reveal their stories. Recommendations from this study suggest ways for post-secondary pro-grams to steer away from being another "greedy institution" in student-mothers' lives. She suggests policies and practices designed to facilitate a balanced approach to post-secondary studies that takes into account stu-dents' other life responsibilities.

In a similar vein, Donna McGee Thompson reports the findings of an investigation of the experiences of mothers of young children attending a community-college-based developmental studies (DVST) program. In Chapter 3, semi-structured interviews were carried out with a small group of women who, while enrolled in this program, simultaneously assumed primary live-in parenting responsibilities for at least one young child. Participation in the DVST program signified a major, and positive, turning point in these women's lives. However, participation required adapting to new time pressures and redefining roles and relationships with children and other family members. In addition, participation entailed vulnerability to childcare and financial crises for which support services may or may not be available. McGee Thompson identifies implications for daycare policy, career counselling, and centralized services for student-mothers receiving welfare assistance. In particular, she concludes that if the goal of government is to move "employable" women from welfare to active participation in the labour force, then policies and practices to support and facilitate this transition are necessary. The identification of barriers and supports could assist women such as those participating in this DVST program in their move from poverty, economic dependence, and social disenfranchisement toward economic and emotional independence and stability.

Three chapters focus on the experiences of undergraduate students attending university. In Chapter 4, the nature of the university experiences of students who are hard of hearing and the impact of this type of disability on their experiences were the focus of Ruth Warick's research. Descriptive categories from Tinto's retention model (1987), along with the use of the agency-structure nexus highlighting the dynamics between an agent and the environment, provided the theoretical framework for the study. Interviews and journal entries of a small sample of hard-of-hearing students attending urban universities provided a detailed account of students' academic, social, transition, and disability service experiences in university, and revealed the impact of students' hearing losses on their university experiences. A key finding from the study is that students who are hard of hearing are similar to other students in many respects, including social patterns, discipline-related differences, and transition experiences. Nonetheless, they have different experiences because of their disability. They make academic decisions based on their hearing loss, such as choice of classes and instructors, seating position in a classroom, and courseload. They often feel like "visitors" in the classroom because of participation barriers, and they experience difficulties in social settings. Recommendations call for a greater emphasis on the classroom participation of students who are hard of hearing, increased disability training for instructors, more support for disability service offices, better classroom acoustics and mentoring programs, and modification of current models of retention.

In Chapter 5, Colleen Hawkey explores how third-year undergraduates sharing the same disciplinary affiliation at a research-intensive university understand and experience "community." The importance of social and academic integration into post-secondary communities has been articulated in the retention literature. Yet the meaning of community, and in particular community bounded by disciplinary affiliation, has not been explored to any great extent. In-depth interviews were conducted with a small sample of third-year students pursuing an undergraduate degree in psychology, and a survey questionnaire designed to explore key aspects of interviewees' experiences was administered to a large sample of this cohort. In this chapter, students' experiences, examined through the lens of a constitutive community framework, form the basis for an exploration of the structural, social, and cultural forces that contribute to community membership, integration, and involvement. The results of this study document the significant influences of disciplinary affiliation on community membership and belonging. Hawkey reveals how issues of community membership, involvement, and belonging were longitudinal processes that entailed complex patterns of participation and modes of exclusion that were influenced by students' aspirations and obligations, as well as by structural characteristics of both the department and the university. Themes emerging from the research included a transition from a social community to integration into the academic community; competency development through enrolment in advanced-level coursework, involvement with faculty research projects, and learning the language of the discipline; research as a mechanism of integration, which included, among other things, a "space" of belonging; and membership status through improved relationships with professors and exposure to cutting-edge research. Recommendations include exploring avenues for increasing student involvement in research, providing physical space to enhance faculty-student interaction, and recognizing that community membership and involvement imply obligations and responsibilities by both the university and students.

In Chapter 6, Garnet Grosjean investigates co-op education programs from the perspective of the students enrolled in these programs. Through survey questionnaires and interview data collected from students, faculty, and staff, he details how students' experiences in co-op programs shape their perceptions of learning and work and how, through these perceptions, they ultimately make meaning of their undergraduate experience. This study focuses on the unique set of social forces and relationships represented in co-op education and investigates them by means of a nested case study that utilizes a variety of data collection methods. Students reported that work placements provided opportunities to apply classroom learning; but more importantly, learning in the workplace had a major impact on subsequent classroom performance and self-confidence. Also, co-op allows students to earn market-rate wages while attending university and to gain employable skills. However, as demand for co-op grows, admissions are becoming increasingly restricted to those with high GPAs, and once in co-op, those with the highest grades are placed in the most coveted work sites. Recommendations emerging from this study include further research and policy to ensure access to co-op remains equitable, the strengthening of knowledge transfer between the workplace and the academy, and the reinforcement of social networks that are fostered during the co-op experience.

The next two chapters focus on graduate students at universities. Any edited collection of work about Canadian post-secondary students would be remiss if it did not address participation by First Nations students. Rather than presenting findings of an empirical study, Michael Marker revisits the four Rs – respect, relevance, reciprocity, and responsibility – originally presented in a classic 1990 article by Verna Kirkness and Ray Barnhardt. This article pondered whether the presence of First Nations students on university campuses led to a genuine change in the academy. Building on this theme, in Chapter 7 Marker points out that although progress has been made in terms of cultural responsiveness to an Indigenous perspective, current emphases on career education in a globalized economy, science as the hegemonic ideology, and compartmentalized, expertized disciplinary-based knowledge present constant challenges to a First Nations epistemology grounded in place and experience-based knowledge. In this chapter, he reviews dominant practices in the university, such as research, methodology, theory, and community, in relation to Indigenous ways of knowing. Marker concludes by describing the Ts`´kel program at the University of British Columbia, an interdisciplinary graduate program providing culturally grounded education for First Nations students, as well as Aboriginal perspectives on and critique of mainstream educational content and goals.

In Chapter 8, Regina Lyakhovetska presents the findings of a qualitative study designed to examine the experiences of international graduate students who were studying in one department in a university faculty of education for at least one term. Individual interviews and one focus group were conducted. The major findings were as follows: students from non-English-speaking countries found it more challenging to survive and progress in their university programs than those students from English-speaking countries. Throughout the course of their studies, few reported being active in the classroom, in extracurricular academic activities, or in social activities on campus. None were active participants in social events at the department and none reported developing more than one or two meaningful contacts with Canadian classmates and faculty. Instead, their connections were with other international students. International students felt neither included nor excluded in the departmental community. Few used student services available on campus. Students who were more proactive, more outspoken about their ideas and concerns, who had more friends among other international and Canadian students, and who were encouraged by their classmates, faculty, and staff to participate in academic and social activities claimed less or no significant challenges in their overall experiences. Students with sufficient financial support and good English skills had the least problems. Despite difficulties, the students in this study developed many connections with other international students and several volunteered to help other international students feel welcome. Although these students reported having struggled considerably, they also learned a great deal from their experiences and became more independent, more outspoken, and more proactive. Lyakhovetska concludes that although international students contribute to the university community in many ways, restrictions in terms of access to financial aid and employment opportunities, insufficient language support, and lack of sensitivity to international student issues among faculty and students present the greatest barriers to integration. Recommendations of this study address how international students can better achieve their educational goals at a host university and how a host university and its community can assist international students in achieving their goals.

Finally, in Chapter 9, Gabriel Pillay analyzes responses to open-ended questions generated from BC longitudinal data collected over a ten-year period to determine young adults' perceptions of the transition from high school to post-secondary destinations and their views about guidance and counselling. Comments provided by respondents illuminate the struggles, challenges, and unexpected realities of young adults as they navigate the transition to post-high-school life. Respondents highlighted the following themes: high school offered inadequate preparation for post-high-school life; high school counsellors and counselling programs did not provide enough accurate information and guidance to students; and success and satisfaction of these young adults with the transition experience were related to their levels of high school planning and preparation. Pillay offers recommendations for high school counselling, career education programs, and the use of the career education curriculum to explore the diversity and uniqueness of the post-secondary system and beyond.

This collection ends with a Conclusion by Finola Finlay. She reminds readers of the importance of moving from research to practice and emphasizes the public and institutional responsibility to make *real* change in order to address the issues raised in the collection. Noting that "nontraditional" students attend institutions that are still for the most part run on traditional lines, Finlay points to the remarkable commonality of concerns that unite many of the chapters. She identifies four themes that emerge from the stories told by the students and researchers: inclusion, engagement, access, and gender. Finally, she suggests areas where further research could address gaps in our current understanding of students' experiences. She concludes by underscoring that only commitment to long-term solutions can lead to transformative change in policy and practice.

Notes

1   The terms "post-secondary education" and "higher education" are synonymous and are used interchangeably in this volume.
2   Bean and Metzner (1985) define the nontraditional student as "older than 24, does not live in a campus residence (e.g., is a commuter), or is a part-time student, or some combination of these three factors; is not greatly influenced by the social environment of the institution; and is chiefly concerned with the institution's academic offerings (especially courses, certification and degrees)" (489).

References

Adamuti-Trache, M., and L. Andres. 2002. Issues of Retention of B.C. Young Women through the Science and Engineering Pipeline. In *Women in a Knowledge-Based Society. Proceedings of the 12th International Conference of Women Engineers and Scientists* (ICWES12), Reference no. 248. Ottawa, Ontario.

Andres, L. 2002. *Policy Research Issues for Canadian Youth: Transition Experiences of Young Women*. Ottawa: Human Resources Development Canada, Applied Research Branch Technical paper.

Andres, L., and J. Dawson. 1998. *Investigating Transfer Project. Phase III: A History of Transfer Policy and Practice in British Columbia*. Vancouver: British Columbia Council on Admissions and Transfer.

Andres, L., and N. Guppy. 1991. Opportunity and Obstacles for Women in Canadian Higher Education. In *Women and Education,* edited by J. Gaskell and A. McLaren, 163-92. Calgary: Detselig.

Archer, M.S. 1982. Morphogenesis versus Structuration: On Combining Structure and Action. *British Journal of Sociology* 33, 4: 455-83.

Axelrod, P. 2002. *Values in Conflict. The University, the Marketplace, and the Trials of Liberal Education*. Montreal: McGill-Queen's University Press.

Bean, J.P., and B.S. Metzner. 1985. A Conceptual Model of Nontraditional Undergraduate Attrition. *Review of Educational Research* 55, 4: 485-540.

Benjamin, M. 1994. The Quality of Student Life: Toward a Conceptualization. *Social Indicators Research* 31, 3: 205-64.

Bourdieu, P. 1991. *Language and Symbolic Power*. Translated by G. Raymond and M. Adamson. Cambridge: Harvard University Press.

Canadian Education Statistics Council. 2000. *Education Indicators in Canada: Report of the Pan-Canadian Education Indicators Program 1999*. Ottawa: Council of Ministers of Education Canada.

Chapman, P., and E. Pascarella. 1983. Predictors of Academic and Social Integration of College Students. *Research in Higher Education* 19, 3: 295-322.

Coleman, J.S. 1986. Social Theory, Social Research, and a Theory of Action. *American Journal of Sociology* 91, 6: 1309-35.

Doherty-Delorme, D., and E. Shaker. 2003. *Missing Pieces IV: An Alternative Guide to Canadian Post-Secondary Education*. Vancouver: Canadian Centre for Policy Alternatives.

Finnie, R. 2001. Graduates' Earnings and the Job Skills-Education Match. *Education Quarterly Review* 7, 2: 7-21.

Giddens, A. 1984. *The Constitution of Society*. Berkeley: University of California Press.

Johnson, D.R. 1991. *Formulating a Conceptual Model of Nontraditional Student Attrition and Persistence in Post-Secondary Vocational Education Programs*. Berkeley, CA: National Center for Research in Vocational Education (ED 332012).

Nora, A., and L.I. Rendon. 1990. Determinants of Predispositions to Transfer among Community College Students: A Structural Model. *Research in Higher Education* 31, 3: 235-55.

Puccio, E. 1995. Developmental Needs of Older Students: Implications for Community Colleges. *Community College Journal of Research and Practice* 19, 3: 255-65.

Statistics Canada. 1984-2001. *Education in Canada.* Ottawa: Minister of Industry.

–. 2001. *Education in Canada.* Ottawa: Minister of Industry.

Tinto, V. 1975. Dropout from Higher Education: A Theoretical Synthesis of Recent Research. *Review of Educational Research* 45, 1: 89-125.

–. 1987. *The Principles of Effective Retention.* Paper presented at the fall conference of the Maryland College Personnel Association, Largo, MD.

1
Equity in Access and Outcomes: Succeeding along the Science Pipeline

Maria Adamuti-Trache

> Ethical axioms are found and tested not very differently from the axioms of science. Truth is what stands the test of experience.
>
> —Albert Einstein (1950)

Increased societal demand for diverse and democratic workforce participation keeps open the debate on equitable access of women to science and engineering fields. For the last several decades, research has documented women's underrepresentation in these sectors, while policy and strategies have been developed to stimulate women's increased participation in the male-dominated fields, both at the educational and labour market levels. There is a unanimous view that conditions have improved over time, especially within particular fields such as biological sciences or medicine (Glover 2000; Luckenbill Edds 2002). Yet, fields such as physical sciences and engineering are more resistant to balanced gender participation (Andres 2002e; Gadalla 2001), thus raising the question whether the desired social change is likely to be effected just by the passage of time.

Researchers have used the imagery of the "leaking science pipeline" to describe the process of training and filtering of scientists. It has been demonstrated that a gender-related "leaking" phenomenon in science manifests itself starting at the subject-option level in high school, continuing through undergraduate and graduate studies, and finally leading to the widely discussed underrepresentation of women in academia, industry, and even science education (Hanson 1996; Glover 2001). Seemingly, the leaking phenomenon is typical for the whole science field in general, but it appears to affect women particularly, their educational and career pathways being more often scattered by a multitude of social, institutional, and personal obstacles.

To document *whether* gender differences in science-related educational and career pathways exist and to find *when* women are likely to abandon their journeys into sciences, systematic, longitudinal research needs to be conducted. Longitudinal research offers valuable data extended over large periods of time and links information on various stages of education and work. It allows testing whether the accumulation of advantages and disadvantages along educational and career pathways would actually lead to successful career outcomes (Zuckerman, Cole, and Bruer 1991). A broad research perspective including the school, post-secondary education, and the labour market would shed light on whether the issue of underrepresentation of women in some academic fields is caused by existing inequity in access (who has access to certain types of education) or inequity in outcomes (who achieves to her or his ability) (Kahle 1996).

When the underrepresentation of women in science is analyzed, the discourse is more focused on the topic of equity in access (i.e., recruitment issues) and less on the topic of equity in outcomes (i.e., retention and advancement issues). I would argue that engaging more strongly in a dialogue about equity in outcomes would correspond to current ethical and social justice goals and could lead to a better return of the investment in education, at both the individual and societal level. It is a legitimate ethical question to inquire whether young women and men who possess the intellectual potential to succeed in science would "get on" and "stay in" this competitive field. By exploring the educational and career strategies adopted by young women and men who received similar formal education in science at the high school level, one can find whether and to what extent academic capital at the high school level is turned into human capital in science and engineering fields. Although the specialized literature on women in science is largely dominated by American and British studies, there is growing interest by Canadian researchers in education and sociology to address this topic from a broad socioeducational perspective. In addition, women in science and professional associations are preoccupied with the debate related to science promotion and career advancement in these fields.

The Leaking Science Pipeline

The Making of a Scientist

Structurally, career pathways in science and engineering are focused, well timed, and continuous (Zuckerman et al. 1991; Wasserman 2000). Students tend to go straight from high school into undergraduate studies. Those who enter teaching or industry careers need to earn additional professional credentials. Those who plan a career in research or academia have to commit themselves to a long journey through graduate and postdoctoral phases. Since these typical paths through the science pipeline require university degrees, well-rounded high school preparedness with a strong emphasis on mathematics and science disciplines is necessary to support these career destinations.

Science seems to be the field in which differences among individuals are accumulated rapidly. Early exposure to science, usually offered by parents through extracurricular activities (Kahle 1996; Zady and Portes 2001), can stir the interest of young children for fun science-oriented activities. An enthusiastic and knowledgeable elementary and/or junior high school teacher who develops a sense of scientific inquiry in his or her students can motivate young people to read more science books, to do hands-on science, and to understand "how things work," at least at the basic level. However, this is just an introduction to a science-related career. Science cannot be learned and practised through stories and excitement only. At some point, and better sooner than later, the student has to reach a level of understanding that requires more abstract thought, as well as an ability to master the mathematical apparatus. In many cases, students lose interest in science when the transition to a mathematical foundation of scientific knowledge is required. In the BC school system, this phase usually occurs at the senior secondary level, when students start to study thoroughly specialized science courses, thus realizing "how scientific reasoning works." To make this qualitative leap, students need the support of knowledgeable and open-minded teachers capable of creating a classroom environment in which various learning styles and assessment practices will be encouraged (Murphy 1996). Not being exposed appropriately to one or more of the above phases diminishes students' chances of following a science-related pathway. This observation raises the issue of whether equal opportunity for all students really exists.

In addition, every science and technological field has its own specificity, each requiring different abilities, learning styles, and levels of persistence. For instance, a career in physics requires mathematics and scientific skills, early and clear career-making decisions, determination to succeed, persistence, and good luck. Although the path toward a physics career requires extensive education, high school students should know that such a background will not limit the individual to this field only, but will open a large range of opportunities in many other fields. Debates continue around why physics is the prototype of the leaking science pipeline and why this phenomenon appears to be true especially in the case of girls and women in science (Wertheim 1995).

An additional question regarding students' preparedness for science-related careers is, "Would it be more beneficial for students to receive broad instruction or a more discipline-oriented one?" Apparently, some career destinations can benefit from a longer and deeper acquaintance with academic disciplines that build the foundation of those particular careers. Mathematics and some sciences, like physics and chemistry, fall into the category of disciplines that require time and persistence. For instance, mathematical skills are developed and consolidated through practice; mastering these skills eases further understanding by following steps in logical connection with previous ones. The BC high school system encourages students to diversify their course selection by trying a large variety of subjects, a practice that supports a broad education approach. However, it may limit the time that science-oriented students can put into excelling in science disciplines and may be a reason why only the best achievers feel encouraged to persevere. Consequently, high school students who may consider a science-related career face the dilemma of focusing mostly on some demanding academic disciplines while suspecting that it will be hard to succeed in the related career paths. This dilemma can raise concerns about the effectiveness of the intellectual and emotional investment involved in planning a science-related career.

An opposite situation occurs when students take mathematics and science courses no matter what their career intentions are, in order to "keep all options open." In general, parents are supporters of this view, which is also embraced by counsellors but less so by math and science teachers, who would perhaps be happier to teach students who have more interest and/or motivation for these academic subjects. This may suggest that course selection in senior high school does not necessarily reflect students' career decisions but represents a strategy to fulfill school graduation, to cover a broader range of post-secondary admission requirements, and to meet parental demands. It is then possible that not all students who make course selections indicating an orientation toward science have the intention to pursue a career in this field.

For the majority of students, the notions of "keeping all options open" and "making early career decisions" may become conflicting. In such cases, the university-transfer option leaves room for the possibility of students getting onto those educational paths that better suit their individual skills and interests. This educational choice suggests that some students experience longer periods of transition after high school graduation and are still in the process of career decision making while starting post-secondary studies.

In the case of science-related professions, a longer career-search process becomes critical. Since successful pathways in science are traditionally linear, continuous, and started at the "right time," there is a possibility that the hesitant or uninformed student will not be able to persist and succeed in the field. For those who intend to pursue science-related careers, "making early career decisions" that would place the student on the appropriate trajectory is imperative. Moreover, most university science departments are still rigid about offering alternative ways for "getting in" and "staying in" programs that can lead to a successful science-related career when the traditional "high-school-calculus-through-PhD" track is skipped for various reasons. This situation makes high school students even more hesitant about committing themselves to science pathways. Particularly, typical gender stereotyping regarding career paths, the multiple-role image of women's lives, and the existence of other societal barriers for women's professional advancement lead to girls' reservations about pursuing scientific careers (Siann and Callaghan 2001; Walz and Bleuer 1992).

Young Women's Participation in Science

Participation and achievement in some academic school subjects such as mathematics and sciences deepen the differences among students by reducing their equal access to career opportunities. Persistence in mathematics and science courses requires a special learning environment that features structured transfer of knowledge, continuous encouragement, as well as recognition and reward for students' achievements. This type of environment is shaped by the action of family (De Broucker and Lavallee 1998; Dick and Rallis 1991; Dryler 1998) and school (Kahle 1996; Parker, Rennie, and Fraser 1996; Scaife 1998), together with societal (Long 2001; Streitmatter 1994) and personal factors (Chiu 1992; Haring and Beyard-Taylor 1992; Kubanek and Waller 1996). To identify the elements that would contribute in creating an appropriate learning environment for all students, science education research focuses on a variety of topics including gendered curricula, class practices, student self-esteem, societal stereotypes, and career decision-making processes.

As shown in the literature (Davis et al. 1996; Hanson 1996), the high school leaking science pipeline has a significant effect in decreasing the number of female students intending to continue in science and engineering programs. Girls who survive in the school science environment start undergraduate studies with a variety of interests. The undergraduate years are a major decision-making stage when young women and men are likely to choose whether to pursue science careers. Female students who finally decide to enrol in undergraduate science courses are above-average achievers in science. Even so, a large number of female students decide to switch to other professional fields at some stage of their educational or career pathway. It is documented that "higher education does not actively discriminate against women; rather, through an acceptance of particular values and beliefs, it makes it difficult for women to succeed" (Thomas 1990, 179). Academic science is one of the strongest in preserving the traditional values that maintain barriers to educational and career success for women (Hyde and Gess-Newsome 2000).

Many studies discuss the effect of academic cultures and institutional structures (Clark 2001) on the rate of noncontinuance of female students in science programs, as well as on women's persistence in the scientific field. Since the culture of the scientific community is masculinist (i.e., teaching and research styles; aggressive, competitive, or indifferent milieu; distancing from social concerns), the feelings of exclusion experienced by women are intensified (Erwin and Maurutto 1998). Brainard and Carlin (2001), who conducted a six-year longitudinal study on undergraduate women in science and engineering at the University of Washington, Seattle, emphasize the importance of specific factors, such as effective teaching methods, stimulating learning environments, knowledgeable advising, and effective role models, as well as sustained career orientation events at the lower level of undergraduate studies.

Some authors express the hope that ensuring a "critical mass" of women in science would help establish a female identity in the field (Byrne 1993) and thus attract more young women toward science. This view is supported by the situation in areas like social sciences, education, arts, or health, where there is a greater participation of women and where a more supportive and open environment is established for both men and women. This friendly atmosphere has recently been created within the area of biological sciences and is cited as a reason why more and more girls feel encouraged to enter the field. New subfields related to biological sciences (e.g., biochemistry, artificial intelligence, or bioelectrical area) also attract a large number of undergraduate female students. Etzkowitz, Kemelgor, and Uzzi (2000, 112) analyze the "paradox of the critical mass for women in science" and demonstrate that issues like group socialization and strategic power attainment are key points of success that cannot be solved by simply increasing a specific minority group numerically. The authors argue that the cause of success in some fields is the rise of central networks developed by "women who are in positions of power"; this change of power contributes to attract more and more young women toward biological-related subfields. "There is a snowball effect: as the numbers increase in the biologically related areas in electrical engineering, chemistry and computer science, they then attract still more women" (112).

Even if all stages of the leaking science pipeline are under scrutiny, there is still a tacit agreement that encouraging more young women to enter the fields of science would create a large supply pool to feed the science pipeline, thus counterbalancing the leaking phenomenon. It follows that as more women penetrate science fields, the result will be a greater number of successful female scientists at the other end of the science pipeline. The pipeline thesis disregards what is actually happening to the large number of women eliminated from the science-related career pathways and whether this waste of talent is harmful for individuals and society (Andres et al. 2002). Following the paths of women who abandon science at various stages can bring a more realistic insight into existing barriers and gender inequities. The above argument leads to the conclusion that research needs to be done from a broader perspective that would include data on all female students who are potential candidates for scientific and technological careers. As long as this issue is not addressed, the rules favouring the "weeding-out" of "persons who are not in the image of those already in the professions" (Etzkowitz et al. 2000, 52) continue to govern the access to higher levels along the pipeline.

Research Design

Purpose of the Study

This is an empirical study that documents educational and career paths of BC high school graduates of the Class of '88 over a ten-year span after high school graduation. It provides descriptive statistics of students' participation in science at various levels (high school, post-secondary) and identifies typical patterns of educational and career pathways for young women and men. Post-secondary educational attainment and career orientation of respondents are correlated to respondents' specific high school preparedness. Post-secondary educational attainment is described by the type and specialization field of the degrees earned by students by 1998.

Science-related educational and career pathways are the focus of this chapter, but these pathways will be discussed in comparison with other career options chosen by respondents. Since science-related careers normally require university instruction, the study will emphasize the university-based route. The research design is based on the assumption that high school preparedness (defined by student interest in science as reflected in the type and number of successfully completed science courses taken for graduation) is a likely indicator of the abilities and interests of students in pursuing specific educational and career pathways. Therefore, senior high school academic orientation will be taken as an initial point on respondents' career trajectories.

The study analyzes the extent to which students' post-secondary choices are consistent with their high school preparedness and reflect career goals made during the high school stage and followed over the years. The study will address the following research questions:

- Are course choices during the senior high school phase an indicator of post-high-school orientations of students? How does this orientation depend on both gender and school curricular differentiation? What is the extent to which young women and men limit their career options through early or late academic course selection?
- What are the educational and career trajectories for women and men who excelled in science during their senior high school years? Are there gender differences in students' persistence in science-oriented educational pathways? How is the rate of completion in science majors influenced by gender and the type of secondary school science preparation (i.e., number and type of courses)?

Description of Data Sets

Longitudinal data have been collected from three surveys conducted by Andres (2002a, 2002b, 2002c, 2002d) on a BC sample of high school graduates of the Class of '88. School records also provide information on Grade 11 and Grade 12 course choices and achievements of study participants. The 1988 data set consists of a selective random sample of about 9,998 students, representing over 40 percent of the 1988 BC high school graduating population. The sample was drawn from all 75 school districts in existence in BC in 1988 (Andres 2002a), and is gender-balanced (52 percent female and 48 percent male). The follow-up surveys were conducted by self-administered questionnaires mailed to the respondents of each previous survey.

The 1998 survey constitutes the core of this study since it contains complete information on post-secondary educational pathways of respondents over the years (i.e., post-secondary academic programs and accomplished degrees). Data from the three surveys are available for N = 1,055 respondents (59 percent female and 41 percent male) representing 5 percent of the entire population of 1988 high school graduates (see Andres 2002a, 2002b, 2002c, 2002d for details of the sample).

Findings

School Participation and Persistence in Science

Many studies in education account for patterns in senior high school course selection and explain these patterns by the effect of influencing factors acting on students from earlier school stages. Observed curricular differentiation in students' course choices appears to be related to student demographics, which include gender, socioeconomic background, and race or ethnicity. In this section, gender differentiation with respect to high school science course selection is discussed.

A preliminary study on science achievement (Adamuti-Trache and Andres 2002) based on the Class of '88 data (N = 9,998) demonstrates that girls are less likely to enrol in hard sciences in senior high school. The data show that overall enrolment rates in Grade 11 mathematics and chemistry courses are not significantly different by gender, although there is a clear orientation of girls toward biology 11 and of boys toward physics 11. Since overall the average number of science courses is 1.56 for girls and 1.64 for boys (only slightly higher), there is no apparent reason for concern regarding gender differences in participation at the Grade 11 level. Moreover, there are no significant gender differences in achievement for Grade 11 mathematics and science courses.

At the Grade 12 level, the rates of persistence in math and science courses show large gender differences. For instance, the noncontinuance rate for

Table 1.1

Participation rates[a] in BC provincial exams for the Class of '88

Grade 12 course	Female (N = 5,168)	Male (N = 4,830)	Total (N = 9,998)
Biology	48%	32%	40%
Chemistry	27%	36%	31%
Mathematics	44%	58%	51%
Physics	7%	28%	18%

a Grade 12 exam participation rate is defined as the number of unique exam writers divided by the number of regular graduates.

biology 12 courses is higher for boys (40 percent) than for girls (35 percent), while the noncontinuance rate for chemistry 12 courses is higher for girls (46 percent) than for boys (37 percent). A different situation occurs for the mathematics and physics courses. Although boys and girls have comparable performances in math 11, about 43 percent of girls did not continue with math 12, as compared with only 28 percent of boys. Physics courses present an even more interesting case. Although girls' achievement in physics 11 is slightly higher than boys' achievement, the noncontinuance rate for girls is spectacular: 76 percent of girls who took physics 11 did not continue with physics 12, while 48 percent of boys dropped out of physics in Grade 12. In addition, physics courses present the highest noncontinuance rates of all courses for both boys and girls.

Underenrolment of girls in physics courses is also demonstrated by their low participation in provincial exams. Table 1.1 shows that male students participate quite evenly in all three sciences exams (28-36 percent); meanwhile, female students prefer to choose biology in a proportion of up to 48 percent to the detriment of physics, which receives about 7 percent participation. Since physics is the most mathematical of all sciences, lower levels of enrolment by girls in physics courses seems to be associated with their tendency not to take math 12 (although required for admission in many post-secondary programs) or high school calculus courses.

High School Profiles
For the purpose of this study, respondents are grouped by their participation in high school science and mathematics courses, as reflected in the type and number of courses taken for graduation. Based on upper secondary school courses, namely Grade 12 biology, chemistry, mathematics, and physics, four high school profiles were developed.

Students in the non-science profile (NONSCI) group did not complete any Grade 12 mathematics and science courses, or in a few cases (1.3 percent) they completed one physics or chemistry course. Since these few respondents did not complete Grade 12 mathematics to ensure a solid foundation for the physical sciences, they were included in the NONSCI group. The mathematics profile (MATH) group contains students who took mathematics but no science courses for graduation. The life sciences profile (LIFESCI) group contains students who took biology (with or without mathematics or chemistry), but no physics courses. Those in the physical sciences profile (PHYSSCI) group have completed courses that include mathematics in combination with at least one of the chemistry or physics courses. Although the purpose of this study is to focus on the last two groups (LIFESCI and PHYSSCI), comparisons with the NONSCI and MATH groups will be made at various stages. In addition, the analysis will include comparisons by sex within each group and for the whole sample.

Table 1.2 shows the high school academic orientation and overall performance of young women and men for the research sample (N = 1,055). The four high school profiles describe the high school academic orientation of students. Although gender differences are not significant for the NONSCI and MATH groups, considerable differences are evident in the LIFESCI (52 percent of female students versus 21 percent of male students) and PHYSSCI (16 percent of female students versus 51 percent of male students) groups. High school performance is assessed by Grade 12 final percentage that would include averages of school and exam marks for all courses taken. Students taking more mathematics and science courses in Grade 12 were also high achievers in all subjects. Previous analyses (Adamuti-Trache 2002) have confirmed that this research sample (N = 1,055) preserves characteristics (i.e., gender and high school profile distributions) of the initial random sample

Table 1.2

Description of research sample by gender and high school profile

High school profiles	Participation			Academic performance		
	Number of students (% in parentheses)			Grade 12 final average mark		
	Female	Male	Total	Female	Male	Total
Non-science (NONSCI)	135 (22)	90 (21)	225 (24)	67	66	67
Mathematics (MATH)	62 (10)	28 (7)	90 (8)	72	68	71
Life sciences (LIFESCI)	323 (52)	92 (21)	415 (39)	72	72	72
Physical sciences (PHYSSCI)	102 (16)	223 (51)	325 (24)	77	76	76
All	622	433	1,055	72	71	72

(N = 9,998). However, higher achievers and more high school science-oriented respondents are present in the research sample, which increases the credibility of study findings.

Post-Secondary Participation One Year after High School Graduation
This section contains findings regarding respondents' post-school orientations one year after high school graduation. Post-school orientation describes whether respondents participated in post-secondary education, and what choices of post-secondary institutions they made. For this purpose, the sample is divided into three groups differentiated by their participation in post-secondary education, namely *nonparticipants*, *non-university participants*, and *university participants*. The influence of the two factors, gender and high school profiles, on students' enrolment in post-secondary education is considered (Figure 1.1). The following findings are the most significant:

- The distribution of students into the three categories is strongly dependent on students' high school profiles. The gender effect is stronger for the NONSCI and MATH groups and less evident for the LIFESCI and PHYSSCI groups.
- For all high school profiles taken together, the rate of post-secondary nonparticipation is lower for women (20 percent) than for men (24 percent). The NONSCI group has the highest rates of post-secondary nonparticipation both for women (35 percent) and for men (57 percent), while the PHYSSCI group has the lowest nonparticipation rates (10 percent for women and 12 percent for men).
- Overall, more women (50 percent) than men (40 percent) enrol in non-university institutions immediately after high school graduation. The highest proportion of non-university enrolment is shown by men in the MATH group (57 percent) followed by women in the NONSCI and LIFESCI groups (54 percent and 53 percent). The lowest rates of non-university participation correspond to men in the NONSCI (34 percent) and PHYSSCI groups (38 percent).
- Overall, more men (37 percent) than women (30 percent) are enrolled in university institutions one year after high school graduation. The PHYSSCI group has the highest rate of enrolment (50 percent) for both women and men, while the NONSCI group has the lowest rates (11 percent for women and 9 percent for men). There is a large gender difference in university participation for the MATH group (40 percent for women and 14 percent for men) followed by the LIFESCI group (29 percent for women and 36 percent for men).

In conclusion, post-school orientations one year after high school graduation appear to depend mainly on students' high school profiles. A large

Figure 1.1

Post-secondary participation one year after high school graduation

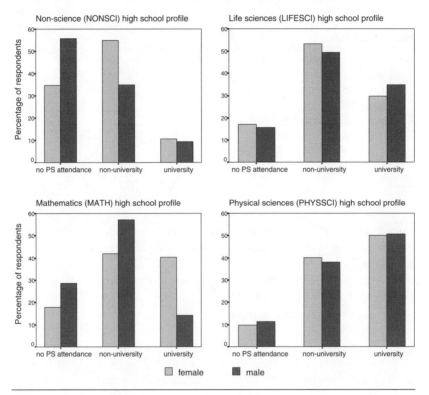

proportion of high school students who continue to post-secondary education immediately after school graduation belong to the category of students
who took science and mathematics courses in the senior years (over 80
percent, excepting men in the MATH group with 71 percent post-secondary
participation). The stronger the math and science preparation (as in the
case of the physical sciences group), the higher the likelihood of participation in post-secondary education, especially at the university level.

Educational Attainment Ten Years after High School Graduation
Post-secondary educational attainment describes whether respondents in
the study ever enrolled in, attended, and/or completed various forms of
post-secondary instruction. Respondents are classified into four groups: students who never enrolled in post-secondary instruction between 1988 and
1998; students who enrolled in various post-secondary institutions (university or non-university) but did not earn any credential; students who attended
non-university institutions (colleges, university colleges, and institutes) and

Table 1.3

Educational attainment ten years after high school graduation, by gender

Educational status	Female		Male		Total	
	N	%	N	%	N	%
No attendance at post-secondary institutions	37	6	29	7	66	6
Post-secondary attendance and no completed studies	62	10	64	15	126	12
Completed non-university studies and obtained credentials	191	31	107	25	297	28
Completed university studies and obtained university degrees	332	53	233	54	566	54
Total	622	100	433	100	1,055	100

earned credentials; students who attended and completed university programs, earning university degrees. Some respondents in the latter group have also completed non-university credentials.

Table 1.3 presents the educational attainment ten years after high school graduation for all respondents. Only 6 percent of all respondents never attended post-secondary institutions, and this proportion is higher for men than for women. Another 12 percent of all respondents attended, but did not complete a post-secondary credential, and again the proportion of men in this category is higher than the proportion of women. About 28 percent of all respondents have completed only non-university studies, with a larger proportion of women than men in this category. Finally, about 54 percent of all respondents in the study have completed university degrees.

Even if overall educational attainment patterns are quite similar for young men and women, different patterns are observed for the four high school profiles that differentiate respondents by their high school preparedness (Figure 1.2):

- Both men and women in the NONSCI group obtained large proportions of non-university credentials (43 percent for women and 34 percent for men) and the lowest proportion of university degrees (30 percent for women and 27 percent for men). About 27 percent of women and 39 percent of men in the NONSCI group, the largest of any of the profiles, did not attend or did not complete their post-secondary studies by 1998.
- The MATH group's educational attainment is less homogeneous by gender. A large proportion of women (about 73 percent) obtained university degrees, while only 36 percent of men completed university studies. In compensation, a larger proportion of men (39 percent) than women (15

Figure 1.2

Educational attainment of respondents ten years after high school graduation

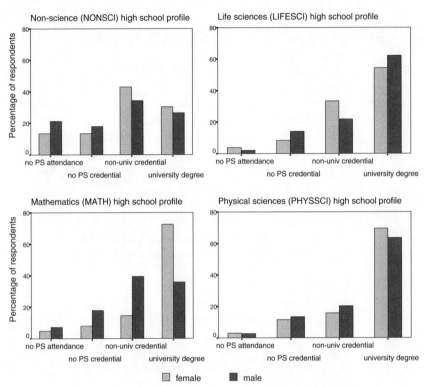

percent) obtained non-university credentials. Less than 7 percent of men and 5 percent of women never attended post-secondary institutions, while 18 percent of men and 8 percent of women attended but did not complete their post-secondary studies.

- The LIFESCI group is more homogeneous by gender regarding both university accomplishments (54 percent of women and 62 percent of men) and nonattendance at post-secondary institutions (4 percent of women and 2 percent of men). However, a larger proportion of women (33 percent) compared with men (22 percent) obtained non-university credentials, and about 8 percent of women and 14 percent of men did not finish their post-secondary studies before 1998.
- Ten years after graduation, the PHYSSCI group obtained a high level of educational attainment for both men and women. Over 64 percent of men and 70 percent of women obtained university degrees, while less

than 3 percent never attended post-secondary institutions. About 20 percent of men and 16 percent of women obtained non-university credentials, while 12 percent of women and 13 percent of men did not complete their post-secondary instruction.

Overall, about 84 percent of all women and 78 percent of all men in the study obtained university or non-university credentials by 1998. Ten years after high school graduation, respondents' educational attainments show a large orientation toward university for both men and women who opted for math and science courses during senior high school years (except the male MATH group). For all three math-and-science groups (MATH, LIFESCI, and PHYSSCI), university attainment rates are higher than the non-university attainment rates (for men in the MATH group these rates are comparable). By contrast, both women and men in the NONSCI group obtained their highest rates of nonparticipation and educational attainment in non-university credentials. When compared with other groups, men in the NONSCI group had completed the lowest proportion of university degrees by 1998. Also, university and non-university completion rates for the math-and-science groups are higher than the rates of nonparticipation or noncompletion.

University Academic Program Choices
The 1993 and 1998 surveys contain valuable information regarding the year-by-year academic programs chosen by all students enrolled in post-secondary institutions between 1988 and 1998. In order to assess whether there is consistency in choices between the secondary and post-secondary study, the respondents' academic orientations, based on their completed degrees, are associated with their high school preparedness.

Respondents indicated a variety of post-secondary academic programs that can be grouped into eight categories, based on the classification of university academic fields used in the report *Education in Canada, 2000* (2001), namely Agriculture and Biological Sciences; Education; Engineering and Applied Science; Health; Humanities; Mathematics and Physical Sciences; Business, Management, Commerce, and Law; and Behavioural and Social Sciences.

A total of 565 respondents in the study (54 percent of the research sample, N = 1,055) completed at least one university program between 1988 and 1998, and obtained a university degree at the bachelor's level. Many respondents also completed graduate studies (mostly after 1993), as well as university professional degrees (e.g., teaching or language certificates) or various non-university credentials. In 1998, about 24 percent of the total number of university graduates were still enrolled in post-secondary studies to complete additional credentials.

Due to the complex educational pathways of study respondents, determining the field of study of university graduates is not an easy task. Students reported the first and second academic programs in which they participated over the years. Their choices combine arts and science, business and engineering, science and health, as well as academic and vocational destinations. It is difficult to assess whether this amalgam of choices is the result of an unfocused career orientation or a lack of persistence in specific academic fields. However, it is definitely possible that, in many cases, the unpredictable post-secondary academic pathways would reflect the variety of educational options offered by Canadian post-secondary institutions (i.e., double majors, degree and nondegree programs, co-op programs). In addition, the opening of the Canadian higher education system to life-long learning allows learners to prolong their studies, to combine school with work, and, thus, to explore a broad range of career destinations.

The fields of study are assessed based on the dominant academic programs attended by students over the years and the type of degree acquired. For instance:

- the Sciences groups (Agriculture and Biological Sciences and Mathematics and Physical Sciences) includes graduates holding bachelor's degrees in Science with or without further graduate degrees;
- the Education group includes graduates holding bachelor's degrees in Education, or a combination of teaching certificates with bachelor's degrees in Arts or Science;
- the Engineering group graduates hold bachelor's degrees in Engineering or Applied Sciences;
- the Health group includes graduates holding bachelor's degrees in Nursing or other medical degrees based on undergraduate science degrees;
- the Humanities group includes graduates holding bachelor's degrees in Arts;
- graduates with degrees in Law, Commerce, and Business are included in the Business group;
- graduates in Behavioural and Social Sciences hold bachelor's degrees in Arts or Science in appropriate fields (e.g., Psychology, Social Work, Sociology, Anthropology).

Since data are accumulated from the 1993 and 1998 surveys, and many respondents completed more than one university degree, the most recent or the highest degree (e.g., graduate degree) was considered. In some cases, university degrees in a specific field were continued with professional degrees (e.g., teaching certificates), indicating the area in which respondents would intend to use their credentials.

Overall,[1] female university graduates populate the fields of Education (25 percent), Humanities (18 percent), Business (18 percent), and Health (17 percent) (Adamuti-Trache and Andres 2002). Small proportions of the total number of women in this research sample went into Engineering (2 percent) and Physical Sciences fields (2 percent). Meanwhile, male university graduates went into fields like Business (24 percent), Engineering (18 percent), Humanities (14 percent), Physical Sciences (13 percent), and Health (12 percent), while Biological Sciences (6 percent) and Social Sciences (5 percent) are the least represented.

Figure 1.3 gives a visual representation of the distribution of university graduates over the above specialization by gender and high school profile. In terms of specialization field destinations, the NONSCI and MATH high school profile groups present some similarity, holding university degrees

Figure 1.3

Fields of study of university graduates ten years after high school graduation

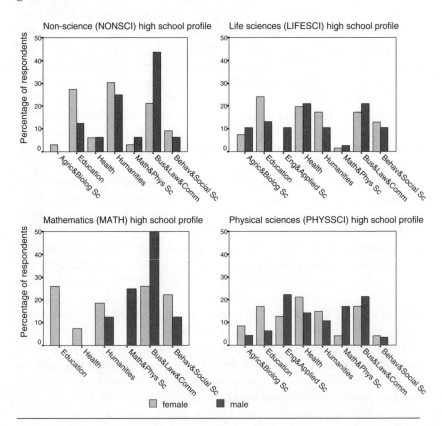

mainly in the field of Humanities, Business, Social Sciences, and Education. For these profiles, degrees in Sciences, Health, or Engineering fields are minimal. The absence of men in the MATH group from the fields of Education and Health should be noted. Meanwhile, women in the MATH group end up in a large proportion (27 percent) in Education, but are absent from the Sciences and Engineering fields. Small proportions of women and men in the NONSCI group are present in Sciences, but none in Engineering.

In contrast, the LIFESCI and PHYSSCI groups cover a broad range of specialization fields. In fact, the PHYSSCI group is represented in all areas, and the most uniform distribution over fields is manifested by women in the PHYSSCI group. However, their low representation in Engineering and Physical Sciences fields, which are supposed to be associated with the PHYSSCI high school profile, is noticeable. Very small proportions of respondents in the LIFESCI group are observed in Mathematics and Physical Sciences, and women in the LIFESCI group are completely absent from the field of Engineering.

Differences in both high school profile and gender are combined to produce specific patterns of academic program choices over the years. However, the relationship between academic program choices and the high school profiles is mostly due to specific distributions of high school groups over post-secondary academic fields, without reflecting a consistent association of the program type at the two educational levels. Even high school students with strong mathematics and science backgrounds do not necessarily go into science-related academic fields. Students in these categories have a broader range of post-secondary choices, both in terms of institutions and in terms of programs (e.g., the PHYSSCI group covers the broader choice of academic programs), than students without mathematics and science backgrounds. Overall, the choices of specific academic programs do not appear to continue a career planning process started in high school, and a net flow of students moving away from science-oriented pathways is noteworthy.

Actually, male university graduates are concentrated in larger proportions in fields related to their high school orientation. Thus, men in the LIFESCI group feed preferentially (about one-third) the Biological Sciences and Health fields; about 44 percent of the men in the PHYSSCI group go into Engineering and Physical Sciences. Men in the NONSCI and MATH groups are oriented toward Business and Humanities. Education and Social Sciences are fed by the LIFESCI and PHYSSCI groups. In the case of female university graduates, the relationship between high school orientation and university academic field is less obvious. Women cover in a large and uniform proportion the Education, Business, and Social Sciences fields, independent of their high school orientation. Differentiations are more distinct in the Biological Sciences and Health fields, chosen by women in the LIFESCI and PHYSSCI groups, and Humanities, chosen by women in the NONSCI and MATH groups. The above discussion suggests that men are more likely than women to keep their initial academic orientation and to persist in fields in which they have accumulated knowledge and skills. Although women with no or little high school preparedness in the physical sciences have no access to Engineering (one field that is highly rewarded financially), some men with the same high school preparedness find their way into this field. Indeed, in many cases, even women with appropriate high school preparedness in the physical sciences do not participate in Engineering and Physical Sciences programs at the post-secondary level.

Findings presented in previous sections demonstrate that post-secondary participation and educational attainment are strongly related to high school profiles, and only slightly influenced by gender. However, the specific field of study of university graduates depends on both gender and high school preparation. High school students who take more science courses (physical sciences, life sciences) are more likely to have their professional orientations evenly distributed across all academic fields, and, thus, they have access to a broader range of career options. Post-secondary academic specializations do not naturally emerge from high school course selection, a fact suggesting that high school course selection does not necessarily reflect consistent planning for future educational destinations. However, men make narrower academic choices at the post-secondary levels and they seem to persist in fields related to their original high school orientation. Meanwhile, women have a greater tendency to cover a broader range of professional fields, independent of their high school preparedness. There is one noticeable exception: science and engineering professions are not likely to be embraced even by women who have excelled in high school math and science courses.

Human Capital in Science and Engineering Fields
In the case of the science and engineering fields, investment in human capital is expensive both at the societal level (i.e., these careers require advanced training and resources) and the individual level (i.e., they involve long, continuous, and focused educational pathways). This subsection explores whether the current situation leads to a loss of human capital for the science and engineering fields.

From the total of 1,055 respondents in the sample, a large proportion of high school graduates had good preparedness in both math and science courses (LIFESCI and PHYSSCI groups with a total of N = 740 respondents) and could have pursued careers in life and physical sciences. A total of 565 respondents (54 percent of the original research sample, N = 1,055) received university degrees ten years after high school graduation. About 79 percent of the university graduates belong to the LIFESCI and PHYSSCI groups, namely 246 women and 199 men. This science-oriented subsample of university graduates (N = 445) with high school preparedness in math and science is large enough to assess the scientific educational paths of BC young women and men, and it will be used for analysis in this subsection.

What are the educational trajectories for women and men who excelled in math and science during their senior high school years? Findings presented in Figure 1.3 show that the LIFESCI and PHYSSCI students' degrees cover almost all academic fields. This is a positive fact that demonstrates that a scientific background would support a broad range of career destinations. However, one can ask whether this wide distribution of human capital does not disadvantage the science and engineering fields that lose potential candidates, especially women, from science-related educational pathways. It takes long, continuous, focused, and expensive effort to create human capital in the science and engineering fields. This large individual and societal investment in science training should be repaid through the wise use of the available human potential for feeding the science professions.

Do high school course selection and students' preparedness match their post-secondary educational specialization areas ten years after high school graduation? Matching the orientation at the two levels is based on the assumption that the life sciences preparedness (based on high school biology) is a "perfect" start for a career in Agriculture and Biological Sciences or Health, while the physical sciences preparedness (based on mathematics and physics or chemistry) is a "perfect" start for a career in Engineering or Mathematics and Physical Sciences. A perfect match of the two educational levels would allow students to focus their energy toward developing and enriching their initial interests, knowledge, and skills along the same direction. This situation would lead to an accumulation of advantages and would increase the chance of a successful and fulfilled career.

Careers in Education, Engineering, Mathematics, and Physical Sciences, or Behavioural and Social Sciences are a "medium" match for the LIFESCI group, while careers in Education, Agriculture, and Biological Sciences or Health would be a "medium" match for the PHYSSCI group. In this case, students use their existing skills only partially and have to acquire additional competencies in a neighbouring field. For some students, this situation may be accompanied by the frustration of having to leave a pathway that was most desirable and to accept a second alternative.

A "low" match would connect the LIFESCI and the PHYSSCI groups to careers in Humanities, Business, Law, and Commerce, or, for the PHYSSCI group, Behavioural and Social Sciences also. In this case, students make a career choice unrelated to their initial high school preparedness. This situation may describe students who took math and science courses under external pressure or due to inadequate information, and chose to switch completely to a new field that would better relate to their interests and abilities.

Figure 1.4 presents the proportion of university graduates who fit their school and university academic orientation ten years after high school graduation at a perfect, medium, or low level. For each high school profile the proportions are compared by gender. The LIFESCI group shows an almost homogeneous distribution of university graduates over the three career-matching categories, with the largest proportion of university graduates (38 percent for women and 37 percent for men) changing their high school educational orientation toward neighbouring fields. About 31 percent of female LIFESCI respondents and 28 percent of male LIFESCI respondents succeeded in keeping their career orientation over the years and may end up working in fields for which they started to prepare in high school. About 31 percent of women and 35 percent of men ended up in fields not related to their initial high school preparedness. For the LIFESCI group, there are no significant gender differences associated with the proportion of respondents matching high school and post-secondary academic choices.

The PHYSSCI group appears to split less homogeneously over the three career-orientation categories, and there are significant gender differences associated with the proportion of respondents matching high school and post-secondary academic choices. While the low-matching category shows proportions similar to the LIFESCI group (39 percent of women and 35 percent of men), the distribution of perfect- and medium-matching categories is different. A favourable distribution is shown by the male PHYSSCI group, with 44 percent of respondents remaining consistent with their initial high school career orientation and only 21 percent of men having a medium connection to their initial orientation. By contrast, the female PHYSSCI group presents the most unfavourable distribution over the specialization areas, since only 13 percent of the women continued in a field directly

Figure 1.4

Matching high school and post-secondary academic choice

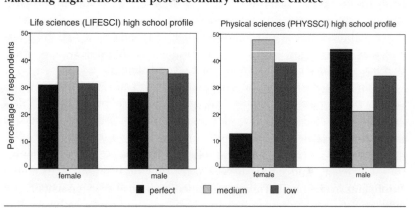

related to their initial high school career orientation. A large proportion of PHYSSCI female students (48 percent) switched to education or biology-related careers.

The above findings show that, independent of gender or high school science profile, more than one-third of the students who succeeded in university have chosen educational and career orientations unrelated to their high school academic preparedness. However, students who succeeded in science-related fields followed a science trajectory beginning in high school and continuing through post-secondary studies. Differences by high school profile and gender occur when the first and second academic matching are compared. In general, men are more likely than women to keep their initial professional orientation and persist in fields in which they consistently accumulate knowledge, skills, and reputation – a tendency that is the most obvious for the male PHYSSCI group. Meanwhile, Figure 1.4 suggests that women in the PHYSSCI group move from the first into the second choice of professions. Obviously, the female PHYSSCI group leaks out of the physical sciences pipeline, a phenomenon that leads to the much-discussed under-representation of women in many male-dominated science and engineering fields.

On the bright side, women appear to be more flexible than men in changing their academic orientation and in accumulating new knowledge and skills within different professional fields. Unfortunately, this ability to change and adjust career plans does not help in a competitive field like science, which requires long-time persistence in accumulating knowledge, building skills, and creating a network of collaborators. The findings of this study are consistent with the specialized literature that emphasizes that, even if a larger proportion of women may "get in" science-related pathways, only a small proportion of women scientists have the chance to "stay on" and "get on" with a scientific profession (Glover 2000, 4).

Discussion

There are two key findings of this study: inequity in access to certain educational pathways and inequity in outcomes. In terms of inequity of access, during the senior high school stage, girls are far less likely to enrol in physics courses, which is aggravated at the Grade 12 level (i.e., less than 10 percent of the Class of '88 female graduates participated in physics provincial exams). Underenrolment can be related to girls' lower rates of participation in mathematics exams (44 percent for girls versus 58 percent for boys). Instead, girls enrol in biology (48 percent) and chemistry provincial exams (27 percent). Boys participate quite evenly in biology (32 percent), chemistry (36 percent), and physics (28 percent) provincial exams, with higher enrolments in chemistry. This gender differentiation at the high school level may limit women's access to certain educational and career pathways.

An appropriate math and science background at the high school level can be beneficial even for students who intend to follow non-scientific educational pathways. This preparation would keep more options open in students' future educational and career pursuits. Even those students who do not go on to science careers will find their skills useful in a wide range of fields. Basic math and science knowledge is an important part of the formation of a well-rounded personality for non-scientists, in the same way that basic preparation in humanities contributes to forming well-rounded scientists.

High school students who took more science courses (i.e., PHYSSCI and LIFESCI) have their post-secondary choices distributed more evenly across all academic fields and thus have access to a broader range of career options. Since there is virtually no movement from non-scientific to science-oriented pathways, one can conclude that the math-and-science-based instruction corresponds to the ideal mode that would support the "keeping options open" strategy emphasized in high school.

Eighty-four percent of all women and 79 percent of all men in the study obtained post-secondary credentials by 1998. About 54 percent of respondents received university degrees. The highest proportion of university degrees (66 percent) was obtained by the PHYSSCI high school profile group for both women and men (213 out of 325 respondents).

Early, continuous, and focused preparation in math and science is demonstrated to be a key to success in science-related fields (i.e., demonstrated by study findings and current practice in science and engineering communities). Students who persist in science-related programs have a good start in high school math and science courses. It may be useful to consider a more specialized and focused high school preparation of students who demonstrate early ability and interest in science.

The notions of "keeping all options open" and "making early career decisions," frequently used in high school, are somehow conflicting, especially in the case of very competitive careers, like science and engineering. Students are in need of specific information and guidance in order to make informed decisions regarding science careers. School counsellors, and especially mathematics and science teachers, should play a significant role in helping students clarify their own options. Before making educational decisions aimed at a specific profession, high school students need to be informed with respect to both advantages and disadvantages of a specific career destination.

Second, inequity in outcomes is strongly determined by gender. From the first year of post-secondary education, the academic program choices of female respondents were highly oriented toward non-science fields. Overall, female students manifested a greater interest for Education, Humanities, Health, and Business, while male students preferred Business, Engineering,

Humanities, Mathematics, and Physical Sciences. Even a large proportion of students with math and science high school preparedness make non-science academic choices.

Male students are more likely than female students to continue their university studies in fields related to their high school academic orientation. In contrast, female students diversify their academic choices at the post-secondary level. As a result, the proportion of women in science and engineering fields at university is even lower than the proportion of female students in high school math and science courses. Female students with science preparedness are among the best high school achievers. They continue and complete post-secondary education, with a large proportion of them opting for non-scientific academic fields.

A scientific background upholds a broader range of educational choices and career opportunity. On the other hand, the fact that many potential candidates for science-related careers are going into unrelated fields leads to a loss of human potential for science and engineering professions. This situation is more critical for women than for men, since the proportion of women is constantly reduced along various educational and career stages. Men who excelled in math and science high school courses are more likely than women to continue in careers that match their initial high school preparedness. Compared with men, young women are more inclined (or forced) to select the second career option that would only partially match their high school preparation.

The job market is rapidly expanding in the science and engineering areas, which creates a large demand for knowledgeable and dedicated scientists, mathematicians, and engineers. In addition, science literacy is becoming a need for every member of our society. Therefore, studying math and sciences in high school and acquiring scientific and technical skills may no longer be optional for the young generation. Meanwhile, since focused preparation in math and science is demonstrated to be a key to success in science-related fields, more specialized high school instruction of students who demonstrate early ability and interest in science may be beneficial. These are challenging demands for the British Columbia school system if it is to offer students a broad education in tandem with guidance and a good start for any future career.

A stronger and more coordinated link between high school teachers and the post-secondary units related to each teacher's subject matter could be beneficial both for keeping secondary school teaching updated and for gathering useful career information to be transferred to students. If general information about post-school pathways can be provided by school counsellors, then knowledge about specific careers has to be provided by subject matter teachers. The training of teachers has to include a mandatory component on "post-secondary education and high school career orientation." This action is meant to improve the *equity of access* to post-secondary pathways for all students.

Post-secondary personnel, and in particular university math and science faculty, need to examine the structure of their undergraduate and graduate program offerings (e.g., the limits placed on studying part-time) in light of the findings of this study. Do individuals with scientific backgrounds choose deliberately to switch their professional destinations or are they forced to do so by actual circumstances that would include the lack of flexibility in science-related programs? While individual agency is one determinant of participation and completion of studies in science and math, the structure of the system is another determinant. The emphasis needs to shift from students choosing science and mathematics programs to these programs choosing and retaining qualified students. The higher education system has to adjust to the needs of a rapidly changing society and to provide more reliable and tempting options to young people in order to ensure the desirable *equity of outcomes* along the post-secondary science pipeline.

A legitimate question is whether math and science education has changed enough over the years to produce outcomes that will differ from the ones obtained in this longitudinal study that originated in 1988. A logical hypothesis is that significant change along the post-secondary pathways can be expected only if the "science pipeline" is leaking fewer men and women at the high school level and/or significant institutional barriers have been removed at the post-secondary level.

Had participation rates in provincial exams changed over years, one would expect that the science-related educational pathways would have also become more open and attractive to young women and men. This is not the case, since mathematics and science courses still receive insufficient attention by students, as demonstrated by steady low participation rates since 1990 (Adamuti-Trache and Andres 2002). Advanced science and math courses that are supposed to open a broader range of post-secondary educational pathways to all students are still considered by less than half of BC high school students. Gender differences are still pronounced and are largely unfavourable for young women.

Clearly, the secondary and post-secondary systems have roles to play in ensuring that girls and boys who excel in science stay in these fields. Grade 12 graduation requirements have remained relatively unchanged over the last fifteen years, being based on Grade 11 and Grade 12 courses and finalized, at minimum, with a single required Grade 12 Language Arts exam. Senior-level mathematics and science courses became important if students intended to continue post-secondary education at institutions or programs where completion of provincial exams in these areas is required for admission. However, recent changes to the BC Grade 12 graduation requirements can be seen as a valuable step in creating a school environment that fosters excellence. The Graduation Program 2004 extends the graduation portfolio to three years, starting with provincial exams as early as Grade 10. Of five required written exams, Grade 10 Mathematics and Science will be mandatory. From the perspective of science literacy, it is expected that this program will give a stronger foundation in science to all students, while offering more choices and a better chance to specialize for those interested in continuing in science-based post-secondary academic programs.

This study has presented empirical evidence that young women are more likely than men to wander off science-oriented pathways at various stages. We need more longitudinal research to document what patterns exist, but also why these patterns are so resistant to change in the case of science and engineering fields. The discourse around the "leaking science pipeline" has to shift from "getting more young women into sciences" to "keeping and developing the available scientific talent." This goal cannot be reached only by women's effort and sacrifice, but should be supported by institutions, science departments, scientists, teachers, and society at large. Otherwise, talented and ambitious women will hardly take the risk of jeopardizing their career plans in fields that offer low retention rates for women. It is definitely accepted that "staying on" a career pathway is more challenging than "getting into" it. If this is the case for science-related careers, individuals and society should combine efforts to make these careers equally accessible to and successful for everybody.

Note
1 These data are based on the distribution of all university graduates across specialization fields.

References
Adamuti-Trache, M., and L. Andres. 2002. Issues of Retention of B.C. Young Women through the Science and Engineering Pipeline. *Women in a Knowledge-Based Society. Proceedings of the 12th International Conference of Women Engineers and Scientists* (ICWES12), Ottawa, Canada. (6 pages, Reference no. 248).

Andres, L. 2002a. *Educational and Occupational Participation and Completion Patterns of the Class of '88. A Ten Year Perspective.* Vancouver: Commissioned report by the BC Council on Admissions and Transfer.

–. 2002b. *Paths on Life's Way: Transitions of British Columbia Young Adults in a Changing Society. Base Line Study 1988 and First Follow-up 1989.* Vancouver: Department of Educational Studies, University of British Columbia.

–. 2002c. *Paths on Life's Way: Phase II Follow-up Survey 1993, Five Years Later.* Vancouver: Department of Educational Studies, University of British Columbia.

–. 2002d. *Paths on Life's Way: Transitions of British Columbia Young Adults in a Changing Society. Phase III Follow-up Survey 1998, Ten Years Later.* Vancouver: Department of Educational Studies, University of British Columbia.

–. 2002e. *Policy Research Issues for Canadian Youth: Transition Experiences of Young Women.* Applied Research Branch Technical paper. Ottawa: Human Resources Development Canada.

Andres, L., M. Adamuti-Trache, E. Retelle, and G. Pillay. 2002. *What Can the Class of '88 Tell Us about Today's Secondary Students?* Report to the Ministry of Education (Sponsored Research Grant Project).

Brainard, S.G., and L. Carlin. 2001. A Six-Year Longitudinal Study of Undergraduate Women in Engineering and Science. In *The Gender and Science Reader*, edited by M. Lederman and I. Bartsch, 24-37. New York: Routledge.

Byrne, E.M. 1993. *Women and Science: The Snark Syndrome*. London: Falmer Press.

Chiu, L.-H. 1992. The Relationship of Career Goals and Self-Esteem among Adolescents. In *Student Self-Esteem*, edited by G.R. Walz and J.C. Bleuer, 181-84. Ann Arbor: Counselling and Personnel Services.

Clark, W. 2001. Economic Gender Equality Indicators. *Canadian Social Trends* 60: 1-8.

De Broucker, P., and L. Lavallee. 1998. Getting Ahead in Life: Does Your Parents' Education Count? *Canadian Social Trends*. Catalogue 11-008-XPE. Ottawa: Statistics Canada.

Dick, T.P., and S.F. Rallis. 1991. Factors and Influences on High School Students' Career Choices. *Journal for Research in Mathematics* 22, 4: 281-92.

Dryler, H. 1998. Parental Role Models, Gender and Educational Choice. *British Journal of Sociology* 49, 3: 375-98.

Education in Canada, 2000. 2001. Catalogue no. 81-229-XPB; ISSN 0706-3679. Ottawa: Statistics Canada.

Einstein, A. 1950. *Out of My Later Years*. New York: Philosophical Library.

Erwin, L., and P. Maurutto. 1998. Considering Gender Deficits in Science Education. *Gender and Education* 10, 1: 51-70.

Etzkowitz, H., C. Kemelgor, and B. Uzzi. 2000. *Athena Unbound: The Advancement of Women in Science and Technology*. Cambridge: Cambridge University Press.

Gadalla, T.M. 2001. Patterns of Women's Enrolment in University Mathematics, Engineering and Computer Science in Canada 1972-1995. *The Canadian Journal of Higher Education* 31, 1: 1-34.

Glover, J. 2000. *Women and Scientific Employment*. New York: St. Martin's Press.

–. 2001. Targeting Women: Policy Issues Relating to Women's Representation in Professional Scientific Employment. *Policy Studies* 22, 2: 69-82.

Hanson, S.L. 1996. *Lost Talent: Women in Science*. Philadelphia: Temple University Press.

Haring, M.J., and K.C. Beyard-Taylor. 1992. Counseling with Women: The Challenge of Non-Traditional Careers. In *Student Self-Esteem*, edited by G.R. Walz and J.C. Bleuer, 185-92. Ann Arbor: Counselling and Personnel Services.

Hyde, M.S., and J. Gess-Newsome. 2000. Factors That Increase Persistence of Female Undergraduate Science Students. In *Women Succeeding in Science*, edited by J. Bart, 115-37. West Lafayette: Purdue University Press.

Kahle, J.B. 1996. Opportunities and Obstacles: Science Education in the Schools. In *The Equity Equation*, edited by C.S. Davis et al., 57-95. San Francisco: Jossey-Bass.

Kubanek, A.M., and M. Waller. 1996. *Confidence in Science: Interpersonal and Institutional Influences*. Ste-Anne-de-Bellevue, QC: College John Abbott Press.

Long, J.S., ed. 2001. *From Scarcity to Visibility: Gender Differences in the Careers of Doctoral Scientists and Engineers*. Washington, DC: National Academy Press.

Luckenbill Edds, L. 2002. The Educational Pipeline for Women in Biology: No Longer Leaking? *BioScience* 52, 6: 513-21.

Murphy, P.F. 1996. Assessment Practices and Gender in Science. In *Gender, Science and Mathematics*, edited by L. Parker, L.J. Rennie, and B.J. Fraser, 105-17. Dordrecht: Kluwer Academic Press.

Parker, L., L.J. Rennie, and B.J. Fraser, eds. 1996. *Gender, Science and Mathematics*. Dordrecht: Kluwer Academic Press.

Scaife, J. 1998. Science Education for All? In *Gender in the Secondary Curriculum: Balancing the Books*, edited by A. Clark and E. Millard, 60-79. London and New York: Routledge.

Siann, G., and M. Callaghan. 2001. Choices and Barriers: Factors Influencing Women's Choice of Higher Education in Science, Engineering and Technology. *Journal of Further and Higher Education* 25, 1: 85-95.

Streitmatter, J. 1994. *Toward Gender Equity in the Classroom: Everyday Teachers' Beliefs and Practices*. Albany, NY: SUNY Press.

Thomas, K. 1990. *Gender and Subject in Higher Education*. Buckingham: Society for Research into Higher Education; Bristol, PA: Open University Press.

Walz, G.R., and J.C. Bleuer, eds. 1992. *Student Self-Esteem*. Ann Arbor: Counselling and Personnel Services.

Wasserman, E. 2000. *The Door in the Dream: Conversations with Eminent Women in Science*. Washington, DC: Joseph Henry Press.

Wertheim, M. 1995. *Pythagoras' Trousers: God, Physics and the Gender Wars*. New York: Random House.

Zady, M.F., and P.R. Portes. 2001. When Low-SES Parents Cannot Assist Their Children in Solving Science Problems. *Journal of Education for Students Placed at Risk* 6, 3: 215-29.

Zuckerman, H., J.R. Cole, and J.T. Bruer. 1991. *The Outer Circle. Women in the Scientific Community*. New Haven and London: Yale University Press.

2

It's No Five O'Clock World: The Lived Experience of Re/entering Mothers in Nursing Education

Sharon Liversidge

> It's a five o'clock world
> When the whistle blows
> No one owns a piece of my time[1]

Re/entering mothers are continuing to enrol in nursing education. Whether they are entering higher education for the first time or re-entering after a period of stopping out, the lived experience of these mothers is reflective of their unique combination of social roles and adult responsibilities. The phenomenon of re/entering mothers in higher education mirrors the increasing number of adult students entering or re-entering some form of educational program.

Adult learners are entering or returning to higher education in unprecedented numbers. In 1998-99, 67 percent of part-time undergraduate students in Canadian universities were older than 25 years (Statistics Canada 2001). Over the past two decades, the number of adult women aged 25 years and older who have returned to higher education has increased dramatically in Canada and in the United States, making this one of the fastest-growing cohorts of students (Barkhymer and Dorsett 1991; Dey and Hurtado 1995). Across Canada, women accounted for 54 percent of full-time and 59 percent of part-time enrolments at community colleges and 56 percent of full-time and 62 percent of part-time undergraduate enrolments in 1998-99 (Statistics Canada 2001). Due to workforce participation, parenting, or both, many re/entering women have been away from the educational sector for some time. Upon re/entering higher education, women do not put aside their current roles and responsibilities but assume the additional demands of student life.

The term "re/entering mothers" is used in this chapter to describe a group of women who are 25 years of age or older, have been away from full-time education for a period of time, and have childrearing responsibilities. Some of these women have previous experience in higher education and are "returning" while others are "entering" higher education for the first time. In the traditionally female-dominated field of nursing, the median age of Canadian nursing graduates is 32 years (Picard 2000).

The purpose of this study was to develop an awareness of the lived experience of re/entering mothers who participate in multiple life spheres while enrolled in a full-time nursing program at a community college. In British Columbia, nursing education is offered within the community colleges, the university colleges, and within the universities.

Characteristics of Re/entering Women

The lived experience of re/entering mothers has remained relatively unexplored, although several recent studies have focused on the phenomenon of multiple social roles and life sphere participations of adult students in higher education (Andres 1999; Hornosty 1998). Within the field of nursing, most pertinent research has focused on diploma-prepared Registered Nurses pursuing a baccalaureate degree in nursing rather than on mothers entering nursing education to obtain their first nursing credential.

Re/entering women do not represent a homogeneous group but are unique individuals with diverse characteristics and life experiences. As these students participate in adult roles reflective of their stage of the life course, their experiences often differ from those of their classmates, the traditional 18-to-24-year-old cohort of students. The complex lives of older women students may include the multiple roles of partners, parents, caregivers, paid workers, volunteers, and students. As re/entering women approach mid-life, they may provide care for elderly parents or grandparents in addition to caring for their own children and dealing with issues such as menopause and launching adult offspring. In a society where women provide most of the care work for elderly family members and other dependants, approximately one million Canadian women were responsible for care of children as well as care/assistance for a senior individual in 1996 (Statistics Canada 2000a, 2000b).

The Influence of Time in Women's Lives

The social construct of time is a major influence for women as they contend with their multiple roles and responsibilities. In his work related to the sociological exploration of time, Zerubavel noted that time "regulates the lives of social entities such as families, professional groups, religious communities, complex organizations, or even entire nations" (1981, xii). "It is *clock time* that is at the basis of the modern Western notion of duration and that allows the durational rigidity that is so typical of modern life" (61).

Moving away from the influence of natural forces, use of a schedule regulates much of human activity (7) and permits individuals to separate their many activities into specific durations of time to ensure that they can participate in each activity while being uninvolved with others (52).

Time is socially structured in a manner that determines social accessibility (Zerubavel 1981, 143). During periods of "public time" one must be accessible to others, as in the role of paid worker or student. Throughout periods of "private time," however, an individual is relatively inaccessible, as in late in the evening or when on vacation. Although these categories of time are not mutually exclusive, this concept has limited application to mothers, who are expected to be accessible at all times for their families. Despite difficulties with meeting simultaneous and perhaps conflicting demands, mothers are expected to be ever-available to a number of different people (Crosby 1991; Zerubavel 1981).

Recognizing the experiences of women in relation to time as they juggle responsibilities of caring work with their families and their responsibilities in the workforce, Davies (1989) contrasted such clock or linear time with cyclical forms of temporality in Western society. Davies described linear time, often considered as chronological time, as unidirectional and leading toward the future. It is this form of temporality that makes up the schedule governing much of our daily activities, including paid labour and post-secondary studies. Cyclical time, however, is reflective of "local and natural rhythms" associated with everyday life, is process oriented, and is based on the nature of the task in hand. For example, care work, such as caring for other people and performing necessary tasks of daily life including laundry or meal preparation, is "characterized by short cycles that are frequently repeated and by the fact that it is *with difficulty* subsumed under strict clock time" (37).

Davies (1989) argues that given the contexts of their lives, women experience time differently than men. Women's time tends to be relational to the time and lives of others, particularly that of their families, friends, and relatives. Women make decisions regarding the use of their time according to the temporal nature of family needs, care work, and other work responsibilities. In addition, women's care work reflects cyclical time, while the lives of men relate more to linear time. During their daily lives, women switch between these two forms of temporality as they juggle care work and other activities such as paid employment and post-secondary participation. As the nature of care work determines the amount of time required to complete it, such work is difficult to schedule within a specified allotment of clock time (Davies 1989).

Also noting that women, not men, were expected to devote most of their time and energy to their family, Coser described the family as a "greedy institution" (1974, 89). Greedy institutions require extensive commitment of time and energy from members, sometimes to the detriment of the member, who is left with little or no time for other activities. In this context, private or personal time is minimal and ever-availability is expected. Within the family home, the time of the mother, "more than any other family member's – becomes others' time" (Davies 1989, 38). When mothers contend with the time demands of two competing "institutions" such as family and higher education, lack of time becomes even more problematic.

Juggling Multiple Roles

For women who juggle family and workforce responsibilities, lack of time is a major issue. These women often feel rushed (Crosby 1991, 24) and some may experience health problems associated with anxiety, lack of sleep, or both. Of the Canadian women who were employed full-time in the workforce in 1998, mothers were almost twice as likely than childless women to feel "time-stressed" (Statistics Canada 2000b, 111).

The nature of certain roles, role combinations, and inter-role relationships contributes to the unique experiences of women who juggle family responsibilities with other activities outside the home. Although inter-role conflict may occur, it is often the quality or nature of the roles, rather than role accumulation, that is a source of stress for these women (Crosby 1991; Verbrugge 1987). For instance, marital stress may occur as some partners resent sharing household tasks.

Despite the effects of time constraints and simultaneous demands, women jugglers experience positive effects when participating in multiple roles (Crosby 1991; Verbrugge 1987). Crosby cites the benefits of multiple-role participation as enhanced self-esteem and well-being and an increase in power. In addition, juggling may act to buffer stress as positive experiences within one role may diminish the negative effects of another (1991, 102). By providing a broader perspective into which events may be placed, buffering may help to protect self-esteem. However, according to Crosby, buffering has limitations. If jugglers cannot maintain control of their time, or if the boundaries between spheres or roles change so the effects of one role do not buffer the other, buffering becomes less beneficial.

Multiple-Role Women in Higher Education

Re/entering mothers add yet another sphere to their social world when they return to higher education. The additional role of student is transitional for such women as they move through the life course, often exiting previous roles in the process. Previous role changes or life event changes are common reasons for re/entering higher education, with divorce often cited (Barkhymer and Dorsett 1991). The role of student may be considered by re/entering women as a bridge or link to new roles in the future (Breese and O'Toole 1994) and as a potential source of status enhancement and increased self-esteem (Gerson 1985).

As re/entering mothers adjust their lives to include the role of student, other roles and relationships often change (Perry 1986). Family members and friends may support or oppose such change and resist changing their own roles and responsibilities to accommodate those of the re/entering women (Lewis 1988; Perry 1986). Lewis explains that "lack of time to devote to family, home and domestic responsibilities can result in a need to develop a wide range of coping behaviors in order to maintain existing relationships and avoid conflict" (1988, 7).

Balancing personal and family needs is a major source of concern for adult students, especially for mothers, and feelings of being overwhelmed by their responsibilities are common (Andres, Andruske, and Hawkey 1996; Hinds, Malenfant, and Home 1995). Noting that balancing multiple roles is characteristic of adult women who resume their education, Lewis describes returning women as "pulled in several (and often conflicting) directions by a seemingly endless stream of demands from work, family, friends and community" (1988, 7). Coordinating childcare, family responsibilities, and schoolwork is a major issue, especially for women with very young children (Hinds, Malenfant, and Home 1995). In addition, when these women become nursing students, they assume a role known to be stressful (Kleehammer, Hart, and Keck 1990).

Despite their many challenges, re/entering women are highly motivated and do well in their studies (Padula 1994; Seidl and Sauter 1990). With a wealth of life experiences, they tend to make skilled professional judgments in nursing and obtain high grade point averages (Seidl and Sauter 1990).

Feelings of Guilt for Not Being There

Regardless of the benefits of juggling multiple roles and responsibilities, feelings of guilt have become prevalent among mothers of the Western world (Forna 1998, 218) and are rooted in one's entrenched ideology of motherhood.

As a social construct, ideas regarding motherhood are created and shaped by cultural and societal values (Forna 1998; Thurer 1994) and are reflective of the way in which children are considered within the culture (Birns and Ben-Ner 1988). Well entrenched in the beliefs and practices of the culture, such ideology becomes accepted as the natural and only way to mother. The ultimate judgment of a woman's ability to mother is how well her children reflect the norms of the society into which they were born (Birns and Ben-Ner 1988). (See Chapter 3 for further discussion regarding mothering.)

In Western society, however, the belief in the biological mother as the exclusive and ideal caregiver of her children has created a conflict for working mothers. This belief of "exclusive mothering" has fostered feelings of guilt when women cannot live up to their own expectations of the "perfect" mother. Still viewed as the central person in their children's lives, mothers, not fathers, are expected to make personal and professional adjustments in their lives to accommodate their children (Crosby 1991; Forna 1998, 226). In 1999, Canadian women in the workforce were absent from work an average of seven days due to family responsibilities, compared with one day for employed men (Statistics Canada 2000b).

Widely communicated by way of the media, the romanticized version of the perfect mother has become the natural image of mothering and has continued to reinforce society's belief regarding how women should mother their children (McCartney and Phillips 1988; Thurer 1994). When mothers cannot attain this unrealistic version of mothering, feelings of guilt arise.

Ehrensaft summarizes the tremendous feelings of guilt that arise in working women who relinquish their full-time mothering responsibilities: "The myth of motherhood takes its toll. Employed mothers often feel guilty. They feel inadequate, and they worry about whether they are doing the best for their children. They have internalized the myth that there is something their children need that only they can give them" (1984, 53).

For some mothers, feelings of guilt stem from role conflicts resulting from dual pressures to stay at home with their children and also to enter the workforce (McCartney and Phillips 1988, 172). Feelings of guilt also arise from the mothers' beliefs that participating in the workforce hinders their observation of the developmental milestones of their children and negatively influences how their ability to mother will be perceived by others. With much attention devoted to mothering, some nursing students experience guilt from perceived neglect of this role (Barkhymer and Dorsett 1991; Hinds, Malenfant, and Home 1995).

Research Design

This qualitative study focused on re/entering mothers who entered full-time baccalaureate nursing education to obtain their first nursing credential during the fall of 1998. The participants were enrolled in two community colleges within the Lower Mainland of British Columbia that offered the first two years of the Collaborative Nursing Program. These colleges were established during the mid-1960s to early 1970s and offered a variety of programs that included two-year diploma programs and university transferable courses. Although considered to be "commuter" colleges with no arrangements for student accommodation, both institutions offered on-site childcare facilities.

This study was designed to determine how re/entering mothers who were first-time students in full-time baccalaureate nursing education perceived their lived experience of participating in multiple life spheres. More specifically, what were the multiple social roles held by re/entering mother students? How did re/entering mothers who occupy multiple roles describe their experiences? What problems and challenges were experienced by re/entering mothers as a result of their multiple roles? How did problems and challenges associated with the multiple roles of re/entering mothers affect their role of nursing student?

A questionnaire and an information letter outlining both the purpose of the study and the criteria for participation were distributed to students in second-year nursing classes at the two community colleges. Of the seventy-one students who returned questionnaires, nine, or 13 percent, identified themselves as mothers. The five English-speaking participants for this study were selected according to the criteria that the women were 25 years of age or older, had been away from full-time education for at least two years before entering the program, were in the second year of their first nursing program, had obtained passing grades in their first attempt in their courses, were responsible for or share responsibility for one or more children, and did not possess an undergraduate degree. Of these five participants, four were Caucasian with English as their first language. One woman was Filipina and, as English was not her first language, experienced difficulty with some of her written work. All were of working or middle social class.

Data were collected over a period of two months from selected participants using two personal focused interviews and a focus group. The interview questions, in the form of an interview guide, were made available to the participants prior to the interviews in order to provide familiarity with the content and an opportunity to reflect upon their experiences. Each audiotaped interview was limited to approximately one hour to respect the interviewee's busy schedule. The second interview was used to clarify and to expand on previously identified data, to share interpretations of certain data (a "member-check"), and to summarize the interview. After participants had been interviewed twice and four of the five participants had taken part in the focus group session, data collection ceased as "saturation" had been reached. In a form of content analysis, concepts generated from the data were analyzed for the presence of emerging themes and patterns.

Findings

The social construct of time in relation to women's lives emerged as a major theme in the lived experience of these re/entering mothers and became a central thread throughout this study. Of the themes evident within the lived experiences of these participants, three were most prevalent. First, time was scarce for these women as they juggled care work with their many other tasks and responsibilities. Second, re/entering mothers maintained their roles as household organizers and, despite little assistance from their partners, juggled family and school responsibilities. Third, these participants experienced a great deal of guilt for not always "being there" for their children and for continuing their education at the perceived expense of their families. Such themes were consistent among the participants, regardless of social class or ethnicity. As certain themes were similar to the findings of Donna McGee Thompson (in Chapter 3 of this volume), those findings will not be described here.

A Portrait of Re/entering Mothers

The participants in this study were deeply motivated to improve the quality of life for themselves and their families and struggled to complete a previously held goal, to enhance meaning in their lives, or to improve their economic status. Considering higher education to be the means to a more fulfilling life, personally and/or financially, the student-mothers sacrificed employment, income, and time with their children in order to study.

Reduced financial income was an issue as four of the five mothers had relinquished their employment in order to increase time for their studies and family responsibilities. For some interviewees, leaving the workforce resulted in a need for student loans, which contributed to feelings of guilt and stress.

Plans to enter higher education were not recent decisions for these women but had been postponed due to other events and circumstances in their lives. Upon resolution of such issues, the need for further education resurfaced. All participants were required to upgrade their education and/or take prerequisite courses in order to enter the nursing program, and, initially, most questioned their ability to succeed.

Fiona, 28 years of age, was a lone parent of a 5-year-old child. While pregnant, Fiona had withdrawn from a Registered Nursing program and worked for several years as a Licensed Practical Nurse (LPN). With a child to support and limited employment opportunities as an LPN, Fiona was determined to complete a program in her chosen field of Registered Nursing. Fiona and her child lived with her parents, who supported them emotionally and financially. Fiona found this transition to be difficult:

> It was hard going from being ... financially independent, on your own, to being dependent on your parents at 28 years old ... is a little bit devastating on your ego.

Gillian, 29 years of age, lived with her husband and her 2-year old daughter. Gillian left school in Grade 11 and, after several years in the workforce, realized her need to complete high school. She encountered difficulties while working toward that goal:

> I took a couple of courses ... which I did really poorly on because I didn't
> have the education ... to do papers and I didn't have the study skills and
> stuff.

Because she moved frequently, Gillian attended several educational institutions throughout the province as she sought to complete her high school
education and the prerequisite courses for nursing.

Helene, 33 years of age, lived with her partner and two preschool children. After she travelled and emigrated to Canada from the Philippines, her
interests changed from computer science to nursing. Helene became pregnant with her first child and chose to postpone her nursing education until
her child was at least 6 months old. Three months after the birth of her first
child, Helene became pregnant again. She chose to enter a Licensed Practical Nursing program (LPN) because

> The LPN course is shorter [than the Registered Nursing program] and I could
> work right away.

After working for about three and a half years, Helene wished to complete
the Registered Nursing program but hesitated, recalling her struggles with
the English language and her experiences while a student with two children
younger than 15 months of age:

> My husband was away for six months, his mom was sick ... waking up at
> four o'clock in the morning ... I was still doing all this breast feeding.

Jackie, 38 years of age, lived with her husband and two teenaged children. Like Gillian, Jackie left high school in Grade 11 and worked at a number of minimum-wage jobs:

> I just made some wrong choices in life. It wasn't that I didn't get good
> grades and couldn't handle it.

Jackie gave birth to her first child just prior to her twenty-first birthday and
spent the next ten years mothering her children and working at different
jobs. As time passed, she became aware of her need to return to school:

> By the time I hit 30 that's when I really realized ... that I had really missed a
> lot by not finishing my education ... I didn't have a lot of self-confidence
> because I had been away from school for so long ... I wanted to go into
> nursing but ... I was afraid to try.

Encouraged by a college counsellor, Jackie spent the next three years completing the prerequisite high school courses prior to entering nursing school. Once in the program, she commuted approximately one to one and a half hours each day.

Kelly, a 45-year-old mother of three, lived with her husband and children aged 18, 16, and 6. Kelly completed high school with plans to enter nursing but, for family reasons, chose to work. During the next few years, she married, and returning to school became an uncertainty:

> I wasn't sure whether I still wanted to go back to school or not, so I just sort of went part-time ... but, I just found with two small kids, it was just a bit much, so I decided to drop that.

After her third child and twenty years in the workforce, Kelly relinquished the security of her well-paid job to pursue her original plan of becoming a nurse. She had misgivings:

> I was absolutely terrified, because I was giving up a very secure job. By this time, I had twenty years seniority, five weeks paid vacation ... it was very scary walking away from that ... But I was really never satisfied there and I always felt I had this void, that I wanted to do this.

In addition to maintaining her childcare responsibilities while a full-time student in nursing, Kelly continued to oversee the care of her mother and her 95-year-old grandmother:

> My mum had fallen and broken her arm ... I had to go grocery shopping for her ... and trying to make some things for her to eat and so between the two of them – Thank God, it was the end of the semester, because I don't know what I would have done otherwise!

A typical week in the lives of these participants consisted of long days filled with family responsibilities and scholarly activity. Classes were held on campus three days per week from 8:00 a.m. to approximately 4:00 p.m., and on some days, did not include a meal break. Two days per week, the students attended hospital practice that usually commenced at 7:00 to 7:30 a.m. Weekends were devoted to family responsibilities, household tasks, and studying.

Beginning at approximately 4:00 to 5:00 a.m., their day often ended after midnight, leaving little time for restorative sleep. Study participants dressed, prepared breakfast and lunches, and packed diaper bags and school bags prior to waking their children. Once the children were dressed, fed, and prepared for the day, the women took them to a baby-sitter or to another individual who would later accompany them to a childcare centre or school that opened at 8:30 or 9:00 a.m. These mothers then travelled for up to an hour to class or to a hospital.

After a day of class or hospital practice, participants picked up their children and returned home to prepare dinner. Following the meal, they cleaned the kitchen, bathed and played with younger children, and put them to bed around 8:00 p.m. Mothers with older children assisted with homework or drove them to extracurricular activities. Once family and household responsibilities were completed, the women studied for several hours, often until the early hours of the morning. Fatigue was prevalent among the participants.

Time as a Scarce Resource

The tasks and responsibilities associated with the student role played a major part in the lives of the interviewees and required large amounts of their time, both in and out of school hours.

> Jackie: There's no time ... for anything else ... And the readings and visits that we have to do ... take up a lot of our time, out of school, too ... I have to rush home and I have a few hours to study for an exam tomorrow.

Given the unpredictable nature of children's needs, the participants experienced conflict when integrating care work (cyclical time) with linear or clock time. A carefully planned schedule was ineffective, especially if they were trying to study when children were in the home. Gillian shared such an experience about her 2-year-old child:

> In the back of my head I've got it all planned out all nice and neat. All those little ... time allotments and then it's unpredictable and sometimes she just doesn't have her nap when she's supposed to or gets cranky ... and then it doesn't work out.

Helene described similar experiences when trying to integrate care work with schoolwork. At times, she was unaware of the amount of time that care work would involve. Given the nature and immediacy of her children's demands, she could focus only on one type of work at a time. Once her children's needs were met, she studied during the late night and early morning hours and went to class the following day without sleep.

> I cannot get my brain to function and get the ideas out when ... they're all around me 'cause ... they're bickering ... I'm just wasting my time, I might

as well sit down with them and enjoy it and then I'll ... put them to bed and then stay up all night and do my stuff and then go to school the next day.

Personal and family time were essential for these women. The participants were angry that nursing faculty did not always understand the complexity of their lives or respect their personal time. Concerned about her time commitments, Jackie believed that her personal time was being infringed upon:

We have to do home visits and write papers ... and you have to do them ... in your own time.

Believing that her instructor did not understand her time conflicts, Gillian described her difficulties with an assigned evening visit to a prenatal clinic that resulted from a lack of available childcare for her daughter during the evening hours:

[The prenatal class] started at 7:00 and Brad doesn't ... get home 'til like 6:30 ... so I didn't go and [my instructor] didn't understand. It was almost like I was being irresponsible. But I couldn't ... just leave home 'cause Lindsay was there.

For the participants, the amount of time and organization required to complete certain nursing assignments outweighed the learning value of the assignments. Family interview assignments usually took place during the evening or a weekend to accommodate the work schedule of the participating families. Given unpredictable situations that occurred with either the students' own families or the assigned family, some of these visits required rescheduling. Students with young children depended on their partners or baby-sitters to care for their own children. Gillian explained that this type of assignment also involved additional childcare arrangements and costs:

I didn't have daycare and my husband was away for a couple of months ... So I would have to just try and work it out with the people ... and my mom ... and then other times, a ... roommate would sometimes baby-sit so that's kind of an extra cost too.

Coping with the time demands of higher education led to health challenges such as fatigue and anxiety. Fiona, mother of one preschool child, described her experience with fatigue:

It's a lot of sleep deprivation ... I started [my homework] at 8:00 or 8:30 at night ... I'm up at like 4:00 or 5:00 o'clock in the morning getting ready for school or for clinical. And I've gone to bed at 12:00 or 1:00 o'clock ... I get frustrated easily, I'm tired.

In an effort to reduce her baby-sitting costs, Helene traded baby-sitting time with friends. Although she saved money, she compensated for less study time by studying all night prior to an exam. Lack of sleep interfered with her exam performance:

I didn't do very well on that exam. I thought I studied well but I was so sleepy and I couldn't think. I read this last night but I couldn't remember 'cause I was so tired ... I couldn't decipher [the exam questions] ... I couldn't [choose] the best one.

Accumulated sleep deficit interferes with mental performance and thinking ability (Coren 1996). Logical reasoning ability and information retrieval from short-term memory are especially affected. In the case of exam performance, sleep deficits can be self-defeating.

Helene spoke of the anxiety and physical distress she experienced since the mid-point of the semester.

[I was] very, very overwhelmed ... I was planning on quitting ... every time I think about two presentations that I have to do ... and exams after that and then I have the paper and I have all these journals and ... my heart just go boom, boom, boom.

Jackie noted a paradox between the philosophy of the nursing curriculum and her experiences:

[Nursing] is supposed to be the caring profession but they don't care about the stress the students are under.

Family Organizers/Jugglers
Like mothers who participate in the workforce, the participants in this study maintained their responsibilities related to organizing the household, doing most of the housework, and caring for young children. Unlike women in the workforce, however, the re/entering students then studied for several hours prior to bedtime. The responsibilities related to their student role were ever-present, invading personal time in a manner unlike their previous experiences in the workforce.

Gillian: When you're working, you can just [come] from your job right, when you're a student, you never can until the semester's done. There's this assignment and you look at the calendar and oh, there's this exam, and when you go home in the evenings, you're not always 100 percent there.

Helene contrasted her previous experience as a mother in the workforce with her current life as a student:

> Whatever happens at work, I leave it at work ... with school, you can't ... You go to the park, you're still thinking about your ... papers to write, exams to write and books to study and the reading to do ... you can't escape ... So you don't have a break.

Although educational pursuits and personal achievements were important to them, these women remained closely connected to their children, placing their student responsibilities second to their children's needs. In order to accomplish the many tasks of the day, the mothers reduced their time for social activities and for sleep.

Despite the increased workload and stress experienced by the participants, husbands and partners provided little assistance, limited largely to performing delegated chores and driving children to activities. While juggling the responsibilities of parenthood, partner, caregiver, and student, these women felt strained by the many demands on their time and energy. A sense of "competing urgencies" (Rubin 1983) was common. Kelly explained:

> I just couldn't spread myself thin enough ... and actually was reduced to tears.

In addition, the women believed that faculty viewed them only as students and not as adults juggling multiple roles and responsibilities. Gillian argued that she had other priorities in her life:

> It just didn't seem to matter, it's like, you are only a student and whatever it takes to get to clinical for twelve hours ... they think that that's your main priority ... But we've got other priorities too.

Having experienced difficulty with rearranging her personal plans to accommodate sudden readjustments in her student schedule, Kelly shared views like those of Gillian:

> More than once we were expected to ... put in a twelve-hour shift with a day's prior notice ... I really got the feeling that they weren't ... viewing us as a whole person, as we're taught to do ... They were just seeing us in the role of a student and ... not taking into consideration what other things might be going on in your lives.

For the mothers who lacked stable arrangements for their young children, childcare responsibilities were a major stressor. Gillian expressed her experience with the unpredictability of current daycare arrangements:

> I never know from day to day if that daycare is still going to be there for me.

Childcare services played a significant role in Gillian's life:

> Daycares are kind of a big problem for me ... if there's a problem with daycare, there's a problem with everything else.

(See Donna McGee Thompson's findings regarding childcare services in Chapter 3 of this volume.)

In order to cope with their many, and sometimes conflicting, demands, the participants became highly organized. With responsibilities waiting at home, the interviewees spent little time at the college after class and tended not to participate in extracurricular activities. Kelly completed assignments prior to deadlines in anticipation of an unexpected event at home that might interfere with her studies:

> That comes with family; you always live with that, what's around the corner ... you're caring for people other than yourself ... that's reality.

Despite their busy lives, feelings of being overwhelmed at times, and continual fatigue, the re/entering mothers believed that the advantages of holding multiple roles outweighed the associated costs, a finding that is consistent with studies by Crosby (1991), Verbrugge (1987), and others. Attaining high academic achievement and positive feedback on assignments was empowering and resulted in increased self-esteem and increased self-confidence. Being a role model for their children was considered to be a positive outcome as well. Gillian commented on such ongoing rewards:

> I go home and I'm like, Wow! I can actually do that ... I get the rewards right away.

Kelly had similar feelings:

> The feedback ... and marks ... it feels very good to succeed and do well.

Feelings of Guilt for Not "Being There"
The interviewees performed well in their studies yet believed that their academic achievements were obtained at the expense of their personal needs and time with their families. Similar to mothers in the workforce, the

re/entering women in this study experienced tremendous feelings of guilt for not "being there" for their families, especially for their children. "Being there" was extremely important for the participants, possibly associated with the concept of ever-availability: always being accessible. Zerubavel explained that "the extent to which one approximates an ideal-typical state of ever-availability is probably still one of the most important criteria for evaluating how good a parent, a child or grandchild, spouse, sibling, relative, or friend one is" (1981, 146) and this sense of ever-availability is strongly cherished within the more traditional spheres of life. As the participants pursued their personal goals, feelings of perceived neglect of their families were common. Fiona explained:

> When [my son] has problems ... I know that I should be there for him to help, to be with him ... I can't give him what he needs and ... he gets really neglected. So that does produce a lot of guilt.

Gillian felt guilty for choosing to return to school instead of remaining at home with her child and for experiencing bouts of anger when her child's needs took precedence over her own:

> When I get home I've still always kinda got other stuff on my mind and I could get pretty annoyed with [my daughter], because she's taking up a lot of my time and I want to do some homework. Yeah, and that makes me feel guilty.

Although the re/entering mothers understood that their children's needs were met, their feelings of guilt persisted. Kelly described her feelings:

> I still think about my son's provincial championships last year and ... I just felt horrible that I wasn't there ... Yes, guilt's a huge thing!

The concept of ever-availability upholds the assumption that the ideal mother is always available for her children. Conversely, ever-availability is an undesirable quality for those who are not mothers, and such individuals attempt to protect their private time (Zerubavel 1981, 146).

Discussion

The findings from this study are consistent with studies of working mothers who balance responsibilities of home, family, and work and with some of the more recent literature related to Registered Nurses who enter higher education to obtain a baccalaureate degree in nursing (Walls and McPhee 2000). In addition to corroborating the findings of other studies, the participants in this study noted that their student status had a greater impact on their lives than did their prior employment. As expected, barriers to higher education such as financial difficulties and responsibility for childcare challenged these re/entering women throughout their studies.

Extremely capable in the face of adversity, the participants in this study were highly motivated and well organized, and coped as well as they could in a society of contradictory expectations and practices and little support. One mother maintained her casual employment status as well. With little family and community support, however, they felt rushed, strained, and chronically fatigued. At times, some were so overwhelmed by their workload that evidence of role strain became apparent.

Family roles continued to be central in the lives of the participants, and not "being there" for their children created an inordinate amount of guilt. Despite the obstacles in their paths, however, they were empowered by their ability to participate successfully in multiple spheres of life.

The lives of the participants were complex as they sought to complete their education despite numerous conflicts and obstacles that existed along their journey. Within the personal spheres of their private lives, these re/entering women struggled with conflicting expectations of themselves as mothers, the prevailing hegemony within their families, lack of time to accomplish their many responsibilities, and resulting personal health issues. Within the public sphere of higher education, the participants struggled with the expectations of higher education, the hegemony within nursing education, and a program that militated against their success.

Conflicting expectations continued throughout their experience. As mothers, they were expected to be ever-available to their families, placing the needs of their families ahead of their own. Conversely, as learners within the public domain, they were evaluated according to the expectations of the institution and an educational system that promotes individualism, motivation, critical thinking, success, and competition.

For these participants, hegemony within their families remained alive and well. The participants continued to be responsible for and carry out the majority of childcare and household tasks while attending school full-time and, for some, participating in paid employment. Again this is reflective of a society where women in family roles hold most of the responsibility for them. Although some of the women spoke of being supported by their partners, their stories revealed otherwise. These findings are consistent with those of studies related to women who work outside the home (Clark 2001; Crosby 1991; Silver 2000; Statistics Canada 2000b). Such studies have determined that, compared with their male partners, working women still carry out most of the housework and activities associated with childrearing. The behaviour of men within the domestic sphere may be partially explained from the perspective of power since housework and rearing of children are not a source of status, power, or money (Polatnick 1984).

The time demands related to juggling family and personal needs with the responsibilities of higher education were considerable. It is of interest, however, that the re/entering mothers in this study believed that they were even more rushed as nursing students than as paid workers.

The health of the re/entering mothers in this study was an issue. There was little, if any, time for leisure activities, and the women could not maintain a balance of work and social/recreational activities. Feelings of being overwhelmed surfaced at certain times during the term due to the amount of work required. Role overload became an issue. Although a certain amount of stress and fatigue is inevitable for students in higher education, the amount experienced by these students was considerable. Anxiety was high. Crying was a common response to stress, and one of the women reported other physical indicators of anxiety. Unlike childless women, one of the participants struggled with childcare services that were inconsistent, inflexible, and costly.

Sleep deficits were common, with resultant blunting of decision-making processes. Most of the re/entering women received five hours or less of sleep per night as they struggled to maintain academic and family responsibilities. Known to impair mental processes such as concentration, memory, reasoning ability, and decisiveness (Coren 1996), sleep deficits are potentially dangerous for nursing students, who must provide comprehensive nursing care. Nursing students must demonstrate clear understanding of written and verbal material, a comprehensive knowledge base, accurate calculation of drug dosages, competent decision-making ability, and the expertise to assess subtle variations in the health status of their clients. How many errors in judgment and drug dosage calculation are related to sleep deficits of nursing students? As continuing sleep debt increases the risk of health problems (Coren 1996), sleep deficit among students must be of concern to educators and decision makers within nursing education.

Within the public sphere of higher education, the nature of the nursing program militated against the success of the re/entering mothers. Although the participants in this study excelled in their schoolwork, they were challenged by heavy workloads, unrealistic expectations of faculty, and lack of respect for their multiple-role status and personal time.

Heavy workloads within the nursing program were problematic for these mothers. While such workloads may result from the increasing amount of knowledge required by nurses, combined with an administrative need to avoid lengthier nursing programs, the participants were vulnerable to the impact of such practices. From the perspective of time, the nursing programs resembled "greedy institutions" (Coser 1974, 89) that demanded much time and energy from students. For instance, the amount of time and energy required to complete certain core assignments was considerable given the learning value of the assignments. The nature of such community and family assignments required the students to travel to various agencies and client homes during the evenings, after class, or on weekends to accommodate the working schedules of the clients as well as their own class schedules. As a result, these assignments required considerable reorganization and negotiation by the re/entering mothers with respect to family schedules and, for women with young children, arrangement of further childcare services with additional cost.

In keeping with the concept of "greedy institutions," the participants believed that their multiple-role status and personal time were not always respected by some of their instructors. Although a college instructor would not expect a recognized guest lecturer or superior to appear on a few days' notice, students were expected to reorganize the schedules of several family members within a similar period of time. Zerubavel indicated that the amount of lead time required reflects one's status within society, and is "regulated by tacit rules of etiquette, varying at regular patterns across relative social status as well as social distance" and that such activity reflects a "symbolic display of social power over someone" (1981, 147). As students, these women felt powerless to resist the demands of a greedy institution that held the power to inflict severe consequences if they did not comply. Given their busy lifestyles, re/entering women cannot commit the majority of their out-of-school time and energy to their studies.

In the workplace, temporal boundaries separate work or public time from personal time. Paid workers are employed for a fixed period of time in a day or week. The purchase of workers' time in return for money is usually controlled closely by the use of collective agreements between employers and the employees, thus protecting workers from "greedy" employers. In the case of students in higher education, however, no such agreements exist and students are not protected from "greedy" programs or faculty. Although course outlines included in the calendars of higher education institutions indicate the amount of time required for formal classes, the amount of homework and out-of-class activities remains within the realm of individual programs and faculty.

In summary, mothering and homemaking responsibilities remained an integral part of the lives of these participants who chose to further their education, yet these roles and responsibilities were not always recognized or respected by faculty. Limited support and chronic lack of time resulted in personal health issues for most of these women. Re/entering mothers participate in the workforce, pay taxes, and assume responsibility for raising a younger generation of society, yet face considerable barriers in order to benefit from a system of higher education to which they contribute. As these women tend to be well organized and have good problem-solving skills and valuable life experiences, they often do well in nursing. Facilitating their journey through nursing education would benefit the profession and society as a whole.

Given the findings of this study, the nature of nursing programs must be considered in light of the student demographics of today. Recognizing the multiple role demands that characterize re/entering women, changes implemented at the institutional and departmental level of educational institutions would reduce some of the conflicts and obstacles faced by these students, thereby facilitating their success. Within the context of the current shortage of nurses, retention of qualified and potentially successful students is paramount.

Awareness of the lived experiences of these re/entering mothers is the initial step toward providing an appropriate learning environment and support for these students. Viewing re/entering mothers from a multidimensional perspective and keeping in mind that the student role is only one of their several major life roles would assist faculty to understand the transitional and stressful nature of the students' worlds. With their lives in a state of flux and their usual coping abilities challenged, re/entering students may feel vulnerable, display behaviours indicative of stress, or both. Listening to what re/entering students have to say and acknowledging their concerns are crucial and contribute to students feeling valued.

By respecting, encouraging, and supporting the efforts of these students, nursing educators and decision makers can facilitate student progress. As faculty are considered to hold significant power, faculty respect and support may be very encouraging for students.

Respect for the personal time of students is essential. Faculty awareness regarding the importance of time and differing forms of temporality in the lives of the re/entering students would facilitate understanding of students' experiences. Recognizing that care work may require more attention and time than expected, faculty might explore the use of flexible or student-determined timelines and due dates for assignments, thus assisting students who are highly involved with care work with their families. Adoption of policies that prohibit changing schedules or assignments once courses have commenced would protect students from additional, unplanned rescheduling arrangements.

Implementation of policies that control, or at least monitor, the number of assignments in nursing programs would prevent excessive workloads for students. Assessment and discussion of the overall number and type of student assignments required per semester could be carried out among involved faculty members prior to the beginning of each term, with consideration given to the amount of time required to complete such work. Fewer time demands would enable students to maintain healthier lifestyles, allowing them to take time for themselves, increase their amount of sleep, participate in family and leisure activities, and, perhaps, partake in social time with their classmates.

Recognizing the importance of time and the need for re/entering mothers to maintain family responsibilities, structural changes to nursing and other post-secondary programs might facilitate student success. Changes that might be incorporated toward this goal include part-time nursing programs, longer periods of time for program completion, apprenticeship semesters, co-op programs (see Garnet Grosjean's chapter in this volume), prior learning assessment (PLA) for certain assignments, independent study courses, distributed learning, and intensive learning practices whereby a course might be delivered in a short yet intense period of time.

These modifications would also address the financial issues identified in this study. For instance, the ability to continue with part-time employment, thereby reducing the necessity of financial loans and the accompanying concern with repayment, might be attractive to potential students. Although such practice may increase the number of roles currently held by some of the women, this possible disadvantage would be offset by the longer period of time in which to complete the requirements of the program while maintaining a certain level of income. An apprenticeship format or co-op experiences could replace the current practice of using hospital preceptors[2] in certain semesters, thus providing an income for the student within the program.

In order to facilitate the transition to higher education, faculty might prepare potential nursing students for the rigours of juggling academic life and family responsibilities. While on the waiting list for nursing programs, applicants could be provided with information that would enable them to expect and plan for the changes that accompany the busy role of nursing student. For instance, a family information session hosted by interested faculty and current nursing students could be scheduled several times per year for applicants and, if appropriate, their families. At this time, information regarding the lived experiences of students and their families in relation to work schedules, the amount of homework, planning and organization, stress, sources of assistance, and the need for family support could be discussed, with an opportunity for questions. This would provide the applicants and their families with the opportunity to plan and prepare themselves, as well as a possible employer, for the upcoming changes in their lives.

The participants in this study were full-time nursing students who continued to juggle the demands of higher education with their many responsibilities and activities of adult life. These re/entering mothers overcame the hurdles of the program by sheer determination to do well and to improve the quality of their lives, but relinquished time with their families, family income, sleep, and a balanced lifestyle to do so. Hindered by the hegemonic ideal of good mothering that has been entrenched by members of society, by institutions, and by women themselves, these re/entering mothers had difficulty sharing their mothering responsibilities and experienced feelings of guilt for not "being there" for their children.

By increasing awareness of and respect for the complex lives of re/entering mothers and modifying the manner in which nursing education is delivered, faculty members/decision makers may facilitate women's access to and success within higher education.

Notes

1 From the Hollies' song "It's a Five O'Clock World."
2 A preceptor is a practising nurse who, concurrently with her/his usual course of duties, supervises/mentors a nursing student for a predetermined amount of time, typically one to three weeks. The preceptor reports to an instructor at the educational institution.

References

Andres, L. 1999. Multiple Life Sphere Participation by Young Adults. In *From Education to Work: Cross-National Perspectives*, edited by W. Heinz, 149-70. Cambridge: Cambridge University Press.

Andres, L., C. Andruske, and C. Hawkey. 1996. *Mapping the Realities of First Year Post-Secondary Life: A Study of Students at Three Post-Secondary Institutions*. Vancouver: British Columbia Council on Admissions and Transfer.

Barkhymer, M., and Y. Dorsett. 1991. *Institutional, Situational and Dispositional Obstacles Encountered by the Re/entering Graduate Woman*. ERIC Document Reproduction Service No. ED 337 068. Rockville, MD.

Birns, B., and N. Ben-Ner. 1988. Psychoanalysis Constructs Motherhood. In *The Different Faces of Motherhood*, edited by B. Birns and D. Hays, 47-72. New York: Plenum Press.

Breese, J., and R. O'Toole. 1994. Adult Women Students: Development of a Transitional Status. *Journal of College Student Development* 35: 183-88.

Clark, W. 2001. Economic Gender Equality Indicators. *Canadian Social Trends* 60: 1-8.

Coren, S. 1996. *Sleep Thieves: An Eye-Opening Exploration into the Science and Mysteries of Sleep*. New York: Free Press Paperbacks.

Coser, L. 1974. *Greedy Institutions: Patterns of Undivided Commitment*. New York: Free Press.

Crosby, F. 1991. *Juggling: The Unexpected Advantages of Balancing Career and Home for Women and Their Families*. New York: Free Press.

Davies, K. 1989. *Women and Time: Weaving the Strands of Everyday Life*. Lund, Sweden: Grahns Boktryckeri.

Dey, E., and S. Hurtado. 1995. College Impact, Student Impact: A Reconsideration of the Role of Students within American Higher Education. *Higher Education* 30: 207-23.

Ehrensaft, D. 1984. When Women and Men Mother. In *Mothering: Essays in Feminist Theory*, edited by Joyce Trebilcot, 41-61. Totowa, NJ: Roman and Allanheld.

Forna, A. 1998. *Mother of All Myths: How Society Moulds and Constrains Mothers*. London: Harper Collins.

Gerson, J. 1985. Women Returning to School: The Consequences of Multiple Roles. *Sex Roles* 13: 77-91.

Hinds, C., B. Malenfant, and A. Home. 1995. Balancing Family, Work and School. *Canadian Nurse* 91, 9: 53-55.

Hornosty, J. 1998. Balancing Child Care and Work: The Need for a "Woman-Friendly" University. In *Illusion of Inclusion*, edited by J. Stalker and S. Prentice, 180-93. Halifax: Fernwood Publishing.

Kleehammer, K., L. Hart, and J. Keck. 1990. Nursing Students' Perceptions of Anxiety-Producing Situations in the Clinical Setting. *Journal of Nursing Education* 29, 4: 183-87.

Lewis, L. 1988. Ingredients of Successful Programming. In *Addressing the Needs of Returning Women*, edited by L. Lewis, 5-17. New Directions for Continuing Education, no. 39. San Francisco: Jossey-Bass.

McCartney, K., and D. Phillips. 1988. Motherhood and Child Care. In *The Different Faces of Motherhood*, edited by B. Birns and D. Hay, 157-83. New York: Plenum Press.

Padula, M. 1994. Re/entering Women: A Literature Review with Recommendations for Counseling and Research. *Journal of Counseling and Development* 73: 10-16.

Perry, A. 1986. Reentry Women: Nursing's Challenge. *Nurse Educator* 11, 3: 13-15.

Picard, A. 2000. Nursing in Canada in a Nosedive: Study. *Globe and Mail*, 10 February, A2.

Polatnick, M. 1984. Why Men Don't Rear Children: A Power Analysis. In *Mothering: Essays in Feminist Theory*, edited by J. Trebilcot, 21-40. Totowa, NJ: Rowan and Allanheld.

Rubin, L. 1983. *Intimate Strangers: Men and Women Together*. New York: Harper and Row.

Seidl, A., and D. Sauter. 1990. The New Non-Traditional Student in Nursing. *Journal of Nursing Education* 29: 13-19.

Silver, C. 2000. Being There: The Time Dual-Earner Couples Spend with Their Children. *Canadian Social Trends* (Summer): 26-29.

Statistics Canada. 2000a. *Education Indicators in Canada: Report of the Pan-Canadian Education Indicators Program, 1999*. (No. 81-582-XPE). Ottawa: Statistics Canada.

–. 2000b. *Women in Canada 2000: A Gender-Based Statistical Report*. (No. 89-503-XPE). Ottawa: Statistics Canada.

–. 2001. *Education in Canada, 2000*. No. 81-229. Ottawa: Statistics Canada.

Thurer, S. 1994. *The Myths of Motherhood: How Culture Reinvents the Good Mother*. New York: Houghton Mifflin.

Verbrugge, L. 1987. Role Responsibilities, Role Burdens and Physical Health. In *Spouse, Worker, Parent: On Gender and Multiple Roles*, edited by F. Crosby, 154-66. New Haven: Yale University Press.

Walls, D., and C. McPhee. 2000. Female Nurses in Post-Secondary Education. *Canadian Nurse* 96, 10: 27-30.

Zerubavel, E. 1981. *Hidden Rhythms: Schedules and Calendars in Social Life*. Chicago: University of Chicago Press.

3
A Tunnel of Hope: The Experiences of Student-Mothers Attending a Community-College-Based Developmental Studies Program
Donna McGee Thompson

Increasing numbers of women today are assuming at least half of the financial obligations for themselves and their families. At the same time that women have an increased need to strengthen their earning potential, the educational qualifications for employment are also increasing. For women with little formal education, the prospects of securing employment with sufficient financial compensation to meet the expenses of a household can seem bleak. Consequently, more women than ever are returning to formal education. Some choose to enrol in a community-college-based developmental studies (DVST)[1] program in order to upgrade high-school-level English or math prior to enrolling in further studies. Many women making this decision return to school while continuing to carry out most of the household and parenting responsibilities for their families.

This chapter reports on a study that explored the experiences of developmental studies student-mothers in a community college. All mothers of young children enrolled in the DVST program, regardless of marital status and income level, were invited to participate in the study. The study not only provided a look into a world of women finding time to do their homework and scheduling their classes around their children's needs; it also cast light on women living in poverty and raising children, mostly alone, while attempting to secure a better future for themselves and their children.

Implications for welfare policy surfaced as an important outcome of this study. Public policy across North America is forcing "employable" women off welfare and into the workforce. As of January 2002, for example, single parents in British Columbia are considered "employable" after their youngest child reaches 3 years of age (down from 7) (Klein 2002). If moving from welfare to work is a worthwhile goal, both in the realm of public policy and for the women themselves, then the best practice would be a series of policies and practices that ensure this transition can be successful. It is therefore important to identify the barriers and supports that will allow women to make this transition. This study addresses some of these issues.

Prior research concerning student-mothers has focused on university- or college-level programs, which assume some level of previous academic success. Other studies have taken place in small community-based programs, which are not linked to larger institutions and are more socioeconomically homogeneous than the DVST classes in the community college sites referred to here. To better inform DVST practices and policies, this study investigated the experience of mothers of young children within the context of the community-college-based DVST program where most program features are designed to meet the needs of both women and men, diverse in age, ethnicity, and educational history.

The study took place in a community college in British Columbia. Participants in the study were enrolled in the DVST program at Lower Mainland College (a pseudonym), which offers upgrading courses in reading, writing, study skills, and mathematics. Adults take these courses to upgrade their skills in these subjects for a variety of personal, vocational, and academic purposes, including preparation for the General Educational Development Test (GED) or for college-level coursework. The college prides itself on its open door policy and its extensive array of support services. Andres, Andruske, and Hawkey (1996) found that the college's attention to student support services was consistent with its philosophy of providing access to all adult members of the community.

This study was based on the premise that mothers of young children participating in DVST face particular barriers in addition to those encountered by most other students. These barriers make returning to formal education a difficult endeavour. According to the literature, student-mothers may face barriers related to the way motherhood is socially constructed; the manner in which public institutions, including educational facilities, embrace many values that contradict those associated with motherhood; and some DVST students face challenges unique to their educational backgrounds.

Motherhood is not merely a biologically induced circumstance. It is also a social construction. Evidence for this comes from historical and sociological examinations of how motherhood has changed to reflect economic currents and prevailing views about the nature of children (Gleason 1999; Hays 1996). In North America today, the responsibilities of motherhood extend well beyond meeting the basic physical needs of the child. Hays characterizes the current mode of mothering as "intensive" (1996, 4) in its requirement that the mother act as primary full-time caregiver and expend a great deal of emotion, time, energy, and money in rearing her young. According to Hays, modern-day mothers are charged with bringing up children who are psychologically balanced, physically healthy, intellectually competitive, independent, responsible, well-rounded individuals. To meet the requirements of this task, modern-day mothers rely upon expert advice, rather than common sense or folk knowledge as they might have in the past. To make matters worse, mothers are meeting their mandate in a society that places a higher worth on marketplace values, such as efficiency and competition, than it does on the values of nurturing. Consequently, mothers who are combining nondomestic with domestic activity operate in two or more conflicting realities. The current motherhood ideal is based on middle-class values. Although all women struggle to some extent in reaching this ideal, it is particularly elusive for working women, poor women, and lone mothers (Gleason 1999; Hays 1996).

Another area of literature that has relevance for this study is that concerning student-mothers in various post-secondary contexts. Although research concerning parent-student role conflict is in its infancy, recent investigations indicate that there are a number of conflicts associated with being both a student and a mother (e.g., Liversidge 2000). Research concerning the experiences of mature women entering college dates back to Mezirow (1978), whose work emphasized the need for colleges to provide women with forums that would allow them to alter their perspectives and assimilate to the new college environment. More recent research has highlighted how difficulties faced by student-mothers stem not from deficiencies within women themselves but from public institutional values and practices that do not accommodate the demands of childrearing, particularly as they are shaped by current mothering ideology (Blackwell 1998; Hornosty 1998).

Even though women are gaining access to all forms of education as never before, most programs fail to consider the realities of many mothers' lives. Women in general, and mothers in particular, face barriers to post-secondary education at the point of entry (Blackwell 1998), then also as they move through their programs (Andres, Andruske, and Hawkey 1996), and again when they attempt to carry their credentials into the labour force (Andres and Guppy 1991). Finances and childcare are particularly crucial to accessing and completing post-secondary studies. Gender segregation in the labour force often prohibits women from fully utilizing their credentials.

Several researchers (e.g., McMahon 1995) have argued that the difficulties faced by adult learners who are also mothers are attributable to a society that has neglected to embrace, in any practical sense, the business of nurturing and rearing our young, or "motherwork," as Hart (1995, 99) has called it. They have maintained that the public settings of paid work and formal education, based on traditional male priorities and realities, reject being upset by the concerns of the private setting of the home, usually associated with childcare and other traditionally female realities.

Mothers attempting to operate in domestic and nondomestic spheres simultaneously may face both emotional and logistical challenges. University student-mothers have expressed feelings of worry, guilt, helplessness, frustration, and inadequacy as both students and mothers, and have felt

alienated and angry at the lack of understanding expressed within the institution (Dalien 1998). Women with low incomes have an especially difficult
time going to school because they can afford fewer resources such as
childcare. They also expend more time and emotional energy dealing with
financial crises (Home and Hinds 2000).

Research also recognizes how public institutions, such as workplaces and
colleges, follow a different type of time than that followed by mothers caring for their children. Public institutions follow linear time, which measures tasks by precisely how long they take to complete and which can be
planned. In contrast, childcare is governed by cyclical time, which does not
follow the clock but is determined by needs as they arise and cannot be
planned. Student-mothers must regularly switch back and forth between
these contrasting temporalities (Liversidge 2000).

A third area of literature relevant to this study is that concerning issues
for learners in DVST and adult basic education (ABE) programs. One of the
crucial ways that DVST differs from other post-secondary programs is that
most other post-secondary programs have academic entrance requirements,
whereas DVST courses typically act as prerequisites for other programs. Therefore, some level of academic success and familiarity can be assumed of students in other post-secondary programs, but such an assumption cannot be
made of students in DVST/ABE programs. Literature in the field of adult
basic education has identified some uneasiness felt by many ABE students
about participating in formal education. This uneasiness has been linked to
previous negative experiences in grade school (Quigley 1992). Low-income
ABE student-mothers in Luttrell's (1997) research avoided formal educational settings because they remembered grade school as a place where they
had been treated as outsiders for being poor and where their commonsense
knowledge was not valued.

In recognition that mothers who are also DVST students face a unique
and complex blend of barriers, several community-based programs have
been developed especially for them. Student-mothers have attributed their
satisfaction with these programs to the overall atmosphere in the classroom,
which validated their emotions and life situations. They were also motivated by the support networks they were able to establish with other women
in the program. In a mixed-gender program, the women, more than the
men, linked the social networks fostered in the classroom with issues around
identity, safety, and knowledge acquisition. They were also more likely to
experience enhanced self-expression as being the basis for new feelings of
empowerment (Malicky, Katz, Norton, and Norman 1997).

Research Design
The research design for this study involved interviewing DVST student-
mothers about their participation experiences. This design decision heeded

the recent program-planning advice of several authors within the field of adult education (e.g., Butterwick 1996). These authors have supported the argument that it is important to understand the educational needs of DVST student-mothers within a context that extends well beyond enrolment, attrition rates, or their performance on educational assessments.

Catalfamo argues that instead of taking the deficit perspective, planners need to be asking themselves, "What social issues must be brought to bear when discussing the educational needs of women who are making transition(s) ... and what are the implications for adult educators who work with these women?" (1998, 23). Some of the issues she has identified include affordable, quality childcare, the incidence of domestic abuse, and spousal sabotage of educational pursuits. Catalfamo maintains that in order for these and other issues to be fully understood, the voices of the participants must be heard.

Participants in this study were eight women holding the primary live-in parenting responsibilities of one or more children aged 12 or younger while taking developmental studies coursework. The site of the study was Lower Mainland College, British Columbia. Information was gathered in the summer of 2001 via semi-structured, in-person interviews, which took place either on campus or in the interviewees' homes. I asked questions about each participant's current and past educational experiences, how the participant's school life impacted on other parts of her life (such as home), and what, if any, supports or barriers to program participation existed in her life, either within or outside the institution. Interview transcripts were analyzed for themes.

This study attempted to address the four criteria for trustworthiness in qualitative research: credibility, confirmability, transferability, and dependability (Marshall and Rossman 1999). Credibility and confirmability were established through the provision of ample, lengthy quotes and follow-up feedback from participants. Confirmability by another researcher may be limited by the assumptions upon which this study was based. This study was informed by certain bodies of literature and was therefore based on the assumptions that motherhood is a social construction characterized by intense demands and contradictions, student-mothering has unique complexities, and DVST participation sometimes follows negative high school experiences. If another researcher who was informed by other bodies of literature had conducted this study, she might have arrived at different findings than I did. The transferability of the findings, or relevance to other settings, of this study might extend to student-mothers in other DVST programs at similar community colleges in British Columbia. They might also extend elsewhere in Canada where similar social programs and funding exist. The dependability of the study was enhanced by my keeping notebooks in which I recorded questions, ideas, and dilemmas as I thought of them.

Findings

Participants

Following are brief descriptions of the eight participants in the study:

Daniella was a 24-year-old divorced parent of a 2-year-old son, taking DVST English and math in preparation for the Nursing Program.

Brooke was a single 22-year-old mother of one son, aged 2½ years, taking DVST English in preparation for the Home Support Program, which would qualify her to work with seniors.

Meesha, originally from the West Indies, was a 44-year-old sole live-in parent of two boys, aged 8 and 10, taking DVST English to meet one of the entrance requirements for the Classroom and Community Support Program. This would qualify her to work as a special-needs teaching assistant in the public school system.

Sunny was a 22-year-old sole parent of a 3-year-old son, taking DVST math and first-year biology through the university-transfer program at the college in preparation for a university teaching degree program.

Mae was a 40-year-old mother of three children, aged 7, 11, and 15, taking DVST English in preparation for the Therapeutic Recreation Program. At the time of the study, she was going through a divorce.

Zahra had recently moved to Canada from Iran and was a married 37-year-old mother of a 12-year-old daughter and a 15-year-old son. Her goal was to complete the Computer Information Systems Program, for which she was taking DVST math as a prerequisite.

Kimberly was a 24-year-old lone parent of a 3-year-old daughter, taking DVST English in preparation for the Child and Youth Care Program.

Marie was 34 years old and the sole parent of a 3½-year-old daughter. She was taking DVST English in preparation for either the Resident Care Attendant or Mental Health Worker Program.

Results

When I analyzed the interview transcripts, six broad themes emerged. First, for all of the women in this study, going back to school signified a major turning point in their lives. Second, participants identified several positive aspects of combining motherhood with their studies. Third, the women in the study were redefining their roles in their relationships with their children and other family members. This redefinition led to feelings of guilt over not living up to cultural ideals. Fourth, participants were adapting to new time pressures. (This finding overlaps considerably with the results of Liversidge's study in Chapter 2 of this volume and is therefore only touched upon briefly here.) Fifth, childcare and finances were key potential barriers to success. Sixth, the women's views about college support services, both positive and negative, related to their needs for childcare, financial assistance, and emotional support.

Developmental Studies as a Turning Point

For the women in this study, the decision to enrol at the college was not a light one, but one full of promise and dread. For all of these women, going back to school was precipitated by life-changing events. For several of them, the decision was made out of a strong desire for a better life for themselves and their children and would mean moving away from rougher times, including "welfare-mom" stereotypes and negative schooling experiences. Several participants talked about the apprehensions they had as they were deciding whether to enrol. Participants were careful to see that reliable support networks were in place before they enrolled at the college. Many of them were also careful to pursue vocations that would allow them to be available for their children. For all of the women, going back to school symbolized independence, for which they all strove.

All of the women in this study returned to school to secure employment that would be meaningful and lucrative enough to support a family and to achieve economic independence from welfare, a spouse, or parents. Without further education, they saw themselves working in jobs with low wages, low levels of satisfaction, and little opportunity for advancement. Kimberly and Mae both remembered employment counsellors telling them that most jobs worth having required some post-secondary education.

> Kimberly: As my Career Links worker says, "You want a career, not a job – something where you wake up every morning and you want to go."

Going back to school also promised to build self-confidence and self-respect. They thought they would feel better about themselves if they could ensure a brighter economic and educational future for their children.

> Kimberly: I don't feel ashamed ... I have changed inside a lot because I feel more pride within myself that I am doing this.

Daniella, Sunny, Kimberly, and Marie expressed similar sentiments.

The five women who were on income assistance were highly motivated to get off the system. Not only did relying on welfare have them in a perpetual state of financial struggle, but it was also associated with a negative stereotype. Catalfamo (1998) describes this stereotype as a societal perception that low-income single mothers rely too heavily on the system. She asserts that, whereas middle-income women are praised for staying home and raising their children, women on welfare are seen as lazy and as leeching off society throughout the time they are home with their children. Several of the women in this study had internalized the negative stereotype people seemed to have of them.

> Daniella: Sometimes I would rather go without milk for a day ... than go in and get a voucher. It's been made really degrading to be on social assistance.

Women receiving income assistance felt unproductive and lacking in direction before they enrolled in school. Even though the women could have, by provincial welfare policy, chosen to stay home until their youngest child was 7 years old,[2] all of the women with toddlers said receiving income assistance was so demoralizing that they were anxious to get going on a career.

> Marie: I guess I shouldn't be embarrassed to say this but I'm on social assistance right now and I want to get off of it ... [Before I came back to school] I was raising my daughter ... on my own and not doing anything ... I just wanted to do something with my life.

The women on social assistance were not the only women who were striving for increased independence. All of the women in this study looked forward to a day when they would not have to rely on someone else economically, whether it was income assistance, parents, an ex-spouse, or a current spouse.

> Marie: That's why I keep saying to myself, "This is why I'm here in school so that I don't have to put myself in that position anymore" – [where I'm] depending on someone for help.

Zahra explains how, now that she is in Canada, she depends on her husband's income:

> In my country ... the economic conditions [are] completely different from Canada – we can invest lots of money in the bank and take from the interest ... and now in this country, I'm not independent.

Six of the eight women remembered high school as a negative experience. Two of these women remembered it as moderately negative.

> Sunny: I was a pretty good student starting in high school; then I got stuck into all the peer pressure. That kind of spiralled me downwards.

The remaining four women remembered high school in intensely negative terms, recalling feeling like an outcast and being teased or bullied. They also could not connect with teachers, feeling too shy or ashamed to ask for help.

Brooke: My first high school that I went to there was a lot of gangs and a lot of violence. So you couldn't talk to the teachers. You would be too afraid to.

Several participants recalled always having difficulty with reading and writing. Mae always had difficulty in school because of a learning disability that went undiagnosed until she was 14.

Of course in the '70s they didn't know anything about [dyslexia] ... So I'm very slow at reading.

Two of the women attributed their inability to integrate into the school environment to very difficult home lives they felt obliged to hide. Kimberly was one of those women:

Kimberly: I had a very complicated ... very rough, rough family life ... [alcoholic mother, verbally abusive stepmother] ... And then ... I was viciously made fun of [at school] ... Basically I had it everywhere around me.

These memories resemble those described by ABE-level participants in Quigley's (1992) and Luttrell's (1997) research, who recalled their previous school as a place where they felt alienated, ignored, and traumatized. However, whereas the people in Quigley's research chose not to go back to school because of their negative past experiences, the women in this study chose to re-enter education despite their histories. Also, whereas the low-income mothers in Luttrell's research chose a community-based ABE program over a closer college-based ABE program in order to avoid the more formal setting, the women in this study described feeling comfortable in the formal college DVST setting (more on that below).

Typically, a life-changing event precipitated the decision to pursue further education. For several of the women, having a baby or going through a breakup triggered the desire to upgrade their education. Newer mothers shared how becoming a mother launched them into adult womanhood.

Daniella: After he was born, I realized that I had to grow up and my husband left and that was really difficult ... And one day I just said that I had to do something.

Sometimes the termination of long-term relationships with the children's fathers sparked a sense of ultimate responsibility for the children. Some of these relationships had been controlling or abusive:

Brooke: My ex was very, very controlling to the fact that he told me what to wear, who to hang out with. It was very, very stressful ... People would just say, "What happened to you? You used to be so happy."

For Mae and Meesha, who both had school-aged children, divorce meant having to stop being full-time mothers and homemakers in order to support themselves and their children:

Mae: Just over a year ago my husband left me for his secretary and I was a stay-at-home mom for thirteen years. And the only thing I ever really did ... before ... was being a cashier.

Zahra had recently moved to Canada, where she learned a new language and culture, stopped being a stay-at-home mother, and suffered a downward economic shift.

Although all but one participant said they wanted to back to school, they worried about the impact their studies would have on their children. They also worried about arranging finances and childcare so that they could go to school:

Marie: At first I thought it was going to be kind of hard because she's so young ... She has to go to daycare and I don't drive, I don't work, so there was kind of barriers ... And a big issue was money.

They further worried about what the college experience would be like – whether they would fit in or be able to keep up with the work:

Meesha: The whole thing was ... am I capable of doing this? Am I able to still retain after doing years of ... organizing ... manual stuff ... and little nursery rhymes.

Meesha's concern that her "nursery rhyme" background (spending a lot of time talking to young children using childlike language) might not transfer well to the formal educational environment echoes a similar notion observed by Luttrell (1997). In her work as a literacy instructor with working-class mothers of young children, Luttrell noticed the women had come to develop a kind of commonsense intelligence that is linked to caregiving activities and is not acquired through formal education.

By the time of the interview, all of the participants had specific career goals. However, choosing a career path was often a very difficult process. Sometimes it involved choosing one that would allow participants to continue to have adequate time for their children:

Meesha: [Going back to school] was not something that I wanted to do. I always thought that I wanted to ... be a mom [so] I was looking at the avenue of ... running a daycare from home.

Mae also thought she would like to study early childhood education so that she could have an in-home daycare and be more available for her children. However, she was advised against this by a career counsellor:

Mae: [The counsellor] said ... "Just sort of picture the future here ... From 6:00 to 6:00 you're gonna be looking after your own kids and then four of other people's kids. And then after 6:00 you're gonna have to deal with your own kids. And you're all by yourself."

Most of the participants had chosen careers in education, health, and social service fields. Zahra was the only woman not going into these fields; she had chosen computer information systems. Education and health fields may have particular appeal to women because they allow for scheduling that is flexible enough to be combined reasonably well with mothering. Schedules within the fields of education, in particular, often match the hours and months that children are in school, so childcare is not as difficult to arrange. Also, education, health, and the social services are "helping" fields, which had appeal for many of the women in this study.

Kimberly: I decided to go through CYCC [Child and Youth Care Counsellor]. I've been through so much experience of being a youth at risk myself.

Prior to enrolling in the DVST program, most participants were careful to have supports in place. Zahra was the only woman who seemed to have very little practical support – she had no family or close friends living in the province. Most of the other women received some practical and/or emotional support from family members. Six of the women were receiving varying degrees of practical help, usually childcare, from their own mothers.

Daniella: I don't know what I would do if I didn't have the support of my family. I have a lot of friends who are truly ... on their own ... and just knowing the struggles they go through.

Kimberly did not have support from family because she had dissociated herself from them. However, both she and Mae had created sophisticated support networks for themselves before they came to the college. Both of them said that these support networks helped them to find their way back to school.

Kimberly: I went to [a job club] and now I've been in a moms' group for almost 2½ years now – ever since my daughter was 1 month old.

Kimberly was also very involved in her church. For Mae participating in an informal "coffee klatch" and seeing a counsellor were just two of her many supports.

Mae: I took a workshop called Divorce Care ... and then I took a course on boundaries ... and I'm very active in my church ... So I have a large network of women that I know and I can count on.

Being a DVST Student-Mother Is a Positive Experience
In general, the women in this study had very positive feelings about being mothers, being DVST students, and combining the two:

Brooke: I feel proud of myself that I can go to school and still have time to go home and spend time with my son.

All of the women described their college experience in positive terms, with only two of them saying their experience was merely "fine." When asked how their college experience had been so far, the remaining six used such phrases as "positive, positive, positive!" "absolutely wonderful," "the light of my person life," and "my getaway."

Kimberly: When I'm in school, I'm in my own little world ... Nothing makes me happier than having that self-fulfillment ... that [I'm] doing something rather than just being a single mom on welfare.

Several women suggested that they felt more competent, comfortable, respected, and willing to express their opinions in the college environment than they ever did in high school:

Brooke: I'm finding that I'm more opinionated now, that I can speak up and say, "Hey, I don't agree with that but what about this idea?" And even if it's a stupid answer, I'm glad I spoke up.

One participant said, "There are a lot of people like me [here]," and another, "I don't feel like an outcast." Participants said they were motivated by their children to go to school. They felt that meeting their educational goals would allow them eventually to better provide for their children.

> Sunny: He's what kind of gets me out of bed in the morning. I'm doing it for myself, don't get me wrong, but in a sense I'm ... doing it for him too ... because I want him to have a better future.

Kimberly said that being a mother causes her to bring a thoroughness to her studies that she has learned from taking care of a child and managing a household:

> Being a mother you're forced to ... maintain the health and safety of your child at home ... and you have to do everything thoroughly ... So when you're doing your homework, you kind of act upon it the same way.

Furthermore, they felt as though the sense of accomplishment they were getting from going to school was bringing a positive energy into the home. They also felt motivated by the sense that they were providing a positive role model for their children.

Redefining Relationships

Not everything about combining motherhood with being a student was positive. Participants with older school-aged children especially shared how they were going through frustrating times with their children:

> Meesha: You know I would be lying if I said, "Oh, it's just so wonderful." Most of it is. There are some days that I lose it. I go, "Rah, I can't take this anymore!"

Taking on the added responsibilities of school alerted some of the women to the need to have children assume some household duties. All three of the women with school-aged children talked about how they were starting to delegate household responsibilities to their children and were working toward their children being more independent.

> Meesha: Last week was when I started delegating more and working on them doing the bathroom and this type of thing, but it's still foreign to them.

Mae's children, who, along with her, were dealing with her recent marriage breakup, were sometimes openly hostile toward her because she required them to change their expectations of her:

They can be very mentally abusive to me ... saying things like I'm not a real mother because I don't wash the boys' clothes anymore and a real mother would wash everyone's clothes.

Mae's ex-husband believed she was going to school just to spite him, and this contributed to conflict with her son:

[My ex-husband is] not very happy with me ... I'm wasting everybody's time and I'm always trying to get him ... by going back to school. And my 15-year-old ... is really buying into that mentality and it's quite difficult at home at times.

Straus (1988) found that divorced custodial mothers face greater parenting challenges than nondivorced mothers. The stress of assuming most or all of the economic, household, emotional, and social responsibilities of the family may temporarily disrupt the dynamics of the mother-child relationship shared previously. However, most mothers get through this period quickly and many find their relationships with their children improve with the waning of marital conflict.

The women with school-aged children expressed regret over no longer being able to live up to ideal mothering images, which often led to feelings of guilt. For example, Meesha felt guilty about leaving her children home alone to supervise themselves when she was away at school. (Recall these interviews took place in the summer months when the children were not in school but the mothers were. None of the school-aged children were with sitters.) Meesha's guilty feelings were not helped by her mother, who apparently also had ideal images of how Meesha should mother:

Mother tends to differ because she raised all six of us; she stayed at home ... She's concerned that I shouldn't be leaving the children at home alone and she rags me about it.

These mothers also felt guilty about not being able to spend time with their children in activities and on outings. They wanted their children to have fun and to be involved in enriching activities, but the time they had for this was limited. This was pronounced for women who had previously been home with school-aged children:

Zahra: Guilty! [Big laugh] Because in my country ... I spent almost [all my] time with my children ... and they want me to participate in their activities. That's why I feel guilty.

Mae said these guilty feelings didn't go away when her children were in school. Whereas she had previously attended all of her children's field trips and assemblies, sat on parent advisory committees, and provided baked gifts for teachers, she was now having to reduce drastically her involvement in these kinds of activities:

> Some of the focus has been taken off [my children] ... I've had to be a lot more selfish about some of my time than I've had to be in the past.

The women with toddlers also felt guilty about being away from their children. For instance, Kimberly felt she was missing some of her daughter's developmental milestones. Sunny talked about how at first it was difficult leaving her son at daycare:

> I felt really bad when I first started school – dumping him in daycare. I didn't want him to feel "Oh, after all this time you're just gonna dump me. Why are you doing this?"

However, all of the women coped with their guilt by reminding themselves of the benefits their schooling would have for their children:

> Zahra: If I get a job, it will help my children as well. I can meet their needs in everything ... It's not just for myself to be independent.

For the women in this study, relationships with other family members also had to be redefined, especially when family members had come to depend on participants too much. For example, Meesha's mother and adult siblings relied on her for many things including transportation to medical appointments and grocery shopping. When she started going to school, she realized that her level of involvement with them was going to have to slow down, but weaning them from her help was difficult:

> I have to really push some of the responsibilities out there, and not feel guilty about doing so ... [My mother] doesn't quite understand that she's making me feel guilty about it.

Zahra, the only married participant, said that while her husband was supportive of her going to school, she noticed their relationship changing:

> He spends a lot of time in front of the TV and I spend lots of time with my desk. Our communication is getting low and low and low.

The women receiving family support said they appreciated all the help they were given; however, they sometimes also worried that the help they were getting would strain their relationships with family members. For instance, Daniella worried that her mother was doing too much baby-sitting for her:

> She's looking after my son all day. And if I need extra time in the evening to study ... I guess it's a little bit stressful for her.

Also, Daniella and Brooke, whose mothers were providing daycare for them, didn't qualify for a daycare subsidy because they had relatives providing their childcare. Consequently, they could not afford to pay their mothers for childcare. They both said they felt they should have been paying their mothers because it was taking them away from time they could have used to make money elsewhere. Daniella said she felt like she was "running a tab" with her mother, and that made her feel guilty.

In addition to redefining their close relationships, participants identified other difficulties of being a student who is also a mother – most notably, adapting to new time pressures. This finding is covered in detail in Liversidge's chapter.

Potential Obstacles to Participation

For the women in this study, the greatest potential obstacles to steady participation were childcare and financial crises. Some of the women with younger children felt that no matter how motivated they were to go to school, they would not be able to continue if reliable childcare were suddenly not available.

> Daniella: If you don't have [reliable quality daycare] then ... you can't necessarily come every day and when you are here you're preoccupied with how your child is doing.

Home and Hinds (2000) found that, because of the strain and energy that had to be put into figuring out how to make ends meet, having a low income was the most important stressor for student-mothers. All of the participants in this study were struggling with their finances. Five of them were receiving income assistance. One was living on wages from her part-time job in a fast-food restaurant. Two of the women were supplementing their incomes with two part-time jobs, and the other relied on grants and a part-time job to supplement her husband's income. Several women told stories of not being able to buy toys for their children or new clothes for themselves when they needed them. Several of them did not have a car and one woman who had a car often did not use it in order to save money.

Meesha: I also look for bargains ... and thank goodness they're right in the vicinity, so I walk. I do have a car, but I don't drive it all the time, so that helps.

A few of the participants lived in quarters that were too small for their families. For example, Zahra's four-person family lived in a two-bedroom apartment and Meesha's three-person family lived in a one-bedroom apartment. Some participants also quite routinely ran out of milk or bread and had relied on friends, family members, or the food bank for more groceries. Marie described how she ran out of paper for her schoolwork but had no money to buy more and so borrowed some paper from a classmate.

Lavell found that single mothers with low incomes faced greater challenges than other students because of having to deal with financial crises and the stressful, time-consuming "foundational work" (1998, 196) involved in meeting the survival needs of themselves and their children. Sunny described the stressful and complicated process she must go through at the end of each semester to set up funding for the upcoming semester:

Going for all the [daycare] subsidy ... registering in school, and filling out Canada Study Grant forms ... I find that at the end of each semester ... for about a week ... during my ... break ... I find that quite a stressful period.

Participants said that grants and other forms of financial assistance have made it possible for them to go to school:

Sunny: [Courses through the school district] ... run about $250 per course, if I'm not mistaken, plus your books. In my situation, that's something that I couldn't have even looked at.

Brooke found that because she lives in her parents' home, she did not qualify for daycare subsidy or other funding:

I find the government is very judgmental ... That ... since you live at home, your parents should pay for everything.

Lochhead and Scott (2000) have also found that welfare and childcare-subsidy policies force women to rely on family members while they are working toward gaining economic independence.

Support Services
As part of the interview, I listed all of the support services available for students at Lower Mainland College and asked participants which of the services they had accessed. In general participants had used very few college

support services. Several women had not even heard of most of the services. Not surprisingly, the women's views about college support services, both positive and negative, related to their needs for childcare, financial assistance, and emotional support. The BC Benefits Office (which provided service to students on welfare), a bridge-in course, and the classroom environment and instructor were identified as the best supports. The Women's Centre, college daycare, and information about funding were viewed as appealing but inaccessible.

The college service identified more than any other as being key to assisting the women to re-enter school was the BC Benefits Office. This office centralized student administrative processes for students on income assistance. Five of the women had used the service extensively, and most of these women had used no other service on campus. Through BC Benefits participants received help navigating the paperwork processes associated with securing funding, applying to programs, course planning, scheduling intake assessments, and other administrative processes. Typically the BC Benefits Office was the first point of contact for these women and helped them make the transition into the college. It was through the BC Benefits Office that many of the women discovered it was even possible for them to go to school:

> Daniella: I would have to say the [BC Benefits Office has] been tremendous support ... Had I not received that support, I don't think I would be here right now.

Marie said that what she appreciated most about BC Benefits was not having to identify herself as being on income assistance when she entered the office, as this was already assumed. In contrast, when she went to other offices for various reasons, she would often have to start by saying that she was on income assistance, which was humiliating and awkward:

> It just makes me feel better that I don't have to go and I don't have to [say] I'm on social assistance ... They already know your situation.

Mae and Meesha were referred by BC Benefits directly into the DVST bridge-in course and found the course excellent for making the transition back to school. Only women who had taken courses at the main campus mentioned this course. Women from the smaller campuses had apparently not heard of it.

> Meesha: It ... was absolutely wonderful ... A lot of us were ... mothers and were going through the same thing. So we spoke with regards to time management, anxiety, what things were bothering us.

The women in this study tended not to integrate too much into the larger college community. Instead, the classroom and instructor were their central focus at the college. Most of the participants described a comfortable, respectful, and supportive social atmosphere in their DVST classrooms. Mae said that when she first came into the program she was relieved to find she wasn't the only person over 35:

I'm not the only person in similar circumstances ... there's been some men and women who for one reason or another have gone back to school.

Classmates supported and shared with each other around issues both related and unrelated to course content. Some of these social networks were starting to extend beyond the classroom. For example, several of the women talked about how they carpooled with classmates. However, not everyone wanted friendships to cross over into their personal lives. Meesha, for example, didn't feel she had the time to devote to friendships that they would require. Sunny said she also preferred to keep to herself but for different reasons:

I don't want anybody to perceive me as the stereotype of a single mother on welfare ... Also, I find it really hard, after being in my relationship with my boyfriend ... where I wasn't allowed to have friends, then making the transition of going back to school and trying to meet people.

Participants described a number of instructor characteristics that they felt helped to promote a supportive classroom atmosphere and a good learning environment. For example, they liked how their instructors demonstrated respect for diverse student opinions on topics discussed in class:

Meesha: He told us what type of environment he wanted to create – he wanted to be respectful of everybody's feelings ... He tries to include everyone in the discussion.

Another quality the women in this study appreciated was how their DVST instructors showed their humanness. One of the ways this was shown was by drawing wisdom from the adult life experiences of students in the class:

Mae: [The instructors] really appreciate our life experience ... It's not just the teacher trying to explain a life experience that maybe she hasn't gone through.

Mae also described how one of her instructors shared her own experiences of being a parent and understood the need to be away from class on occasion to attend her child's school functions:

My teacher, she's a mom too ... so she kind of appreciated what I was going through, said, "You know, you can take time off, you can go and do those things for the kids when it needs to be."

The participants taking math classes appreciated the instructor setting up a lab time after class so that they could work on their homework and get clarification as necessary. This helped to alleviate some of the homework load that had to be done at home, where it was much more difficult to concentrate, especially when the children were awake.

Several women said they wished they were more familiar with what services were available through the Women's Centre. Others said they had wanted to attend Women's Centre workshops but could not because of time conflicts, lack of childcare arrangements, or because they could not make it into the main campus, where the majority of Women's Centre activities were held. (Many of the participants were attending a secondary campus, which has a Women's Centre that operates only a few hours a week in the fall and winter and is closed in the summer.)

Marie: I've actually thought about the Women's Centre ... seminars ... on ... women and self-esteem [but] with the buses being on strike I couldn't really get anywhere. And sometimes my daycare.

Several of the women said they would be interested in participating in a support group for single mothers:

Sunny: It would be nice to meet some other single mothers that are going through the same thing that I'm going through ... to see someone else who is right now seeing things the same way I am.

Dalien (1998) also found there to be demand for student-mother support groups in the university setting. However, Home and Hinds (2000) found that student-mothers did not have enough time to attend extra activities such as support groups.

When I asked participants what else they thought the college could do better for student-mothers, four of the women with toddlers said they wished there were more flexible and affordable daycare available on campus. There is a daycare on campus; however none of the women had their children in it. The college daycare is for 3- to 5-year-olds, which made several of the children ineligible.

Brooke: It shouldn't matter how old your kid is ... I think that would help probably encourage a lot more single moms to [come here].

The on-campus daycare is also more expensive than many private in-home daycares, and although many of the women qualify for a daycare subsidy, they would have to pay extra to have their children in the on-campus daycare. A few women said they had tried to get their children into the daycare on campus, but learned that there is a long waiting list and so made other arrangements.

Sunny: I had two or three months before I started here ... I called them and [they said], "Oh, sorry, we're booked up." ... That was really stressful.

All of these women said they had satisfactory daycare arrangements already in place, but some of them were worried about what would happen if their daycare providers were suddenly unavailable. A few of them had already experienced being without daycare at short notice and had to miss class. They wished there were a daycare on campus or nearby where they could take their children on short notice.

Participants also felt that the college could do a better job of getting information out to low-income women about services and funding options. On the day of our interview, Kimberly had just learned from a classmate about a grant for which she was eligible. If her classmate had not told her about it, she would have missed out on the funding:

You know, what would be really nice? ... To know about all of the services. Where do I go? What do I do? How do I get there? They need to put a big bulletin up saying, "Services for Low Income Students."

Brooke added that more information should be made available to prospective low-income student-mothers:

I think when you're advertising, just say, "We offer this for single moms." Because a lot of people don't know if you go to school you could get so much help.

Discussion

The women in this study faced complexities similar to those that other student-mothers have reported. For instance, participants in this study faced similar time constraints as the nursing student-mothers in Liversidge's research (2000) and likewise felt guilty because they were not always immediately available for their families. However, the women in this study experienced additional complexities.

The participants were going through a noteworthy transition period that would potentially involve economic, psychological, and sociocultural changes in their lives. They were moving from a place of poverty and economic dependence, societal disenfranchisement, and personal dissatisfaction, to a place of economic and emotional independence, societal belonging, and enhanced self-esteem. Participants were highly motivated to make these changes in their lives both for themselves and for their children. However, the successful navigation of this transition depended on the existence of a reliable financial and childcare infrastructure. Grants, daycare subsidies, and income assistance allowed the women in this study to minimally support themselves and their children while they were going to school.

Many of the women were hoping to leave behind negative schooling experiences. Just as the women in this study said they had experienced high school as a place where they felt alienated and incapable, so have participants in research by Luttrell (1997) and Tett (2000). The negative memories the women in this study had of their previous schooling days indicate the need for high school policies and practices that identify and support students who are struggling academically and emotionally. High school career and academic preparation programs (CAPP) are well situated to identify and provide help to students who face barriers to academic and personal success.

The participants faced unique challenges because they were mothers. Some of these women, especially those whose children were school-aged, were also re-evaluating what it meant to be a mother. They were sensitive to current North American messages about "ideal" motherhood and were struggling to define their own experience of motherhood in the face of these messages. They felt pressure to be involved in their children's schools and activities. They made schooling and career choices based on what kind of impact there would be for their children. They felt guilty about being away from their children too much.

Many of the women faced the added challenge of coping with negative stereotypes about low-income single mothers being inadequate parents and citizens. These experiences matched those of the women in Kelly's (2000) research on young single mothers. Furthermore, just as the young women in Kelly's study wanted to be seen as empowered rather than as victimized, so too did the women in this study.

The inner struggle that single mothers face because of negative stereotyping, and that mothers in general face because of societal pressure, is not addressed adequately in the public sphere. In its role as an educational institution, the college would seem to be an appropriate medium for challenging traditional notions of motherhood that serve to oppress women. There are a number of ways in which educational institutions could help to combat oppressive mothering discourse, including the negative stereotypes associated with mothers who are unmarried and poor. For example, course curricula could involve studying alternative (non–North American, pre-twenty-first-century) mothering beliefs and practices. Lavell (1998) argues that institutions could explore ways of more explicitly expressing appreciation for the life experiences that poor lone parents contribute to the institution. Instructors could also be involved in creating language and concepts that make women's work visible (McMahon 1995). Feminist researchers in the social sciences could work to increase the currently scarce research concerning the needs and circumstances of poor and working-class women (Little 1998; Long and Cox 2000). According to Long and Cox, many poor and working-class women face "a complex array of stressors and are the most vulnerable to this stress because of the very limited access they have to resources that ... would help them to respond effectively" (2000, 117). Yet, little is known about their ways of coping with these stressors.

This study confirms the advantages of centralized services for low-income students in post-secondary institutions. When we consider the cumbersome bureaucratic processes required to apply for funding, and how negative stereotypes emotionally impact upon low-income single mothers, it is easy to understand why women would not want to go door to door identifying themselves as "single mothers on welfare," and how having to do this could discourage participation.

Sadly, recent provincial government initiatives have resulted in the closure of the BC Benefits Office and are resulting in a 30 percent increase in tuition fees, reduced daycare subsidies, and reduced income assistance. According to Seth Klein, Director of the Canadian Centre for Policy Analysis (2002), there have been cuts to shelter allowances for families with two or more children and to welfare benefits for single-parent families. Child support and earnings exemptions have been eliminated. "Employable" parents (with children older than 3 years) will receive full benefits for only two out of five years, after which time they will see their benefits cut by 11 percent. Finally, full-time post-secondary students will no longer be eligible for welfare and will have to turn exclusively to student financial assistance.

These cuts follow the disturbing Ontario case of Kimberly Rogers, who died in her sweltering hot apartment in the summer of 2001, eight months pregnant, while on a six-month house arrest for welfare fraud. Ms. Rogers had collected welfare while receiving student loans to attend the social services program at Cambrian College. Even though she had graduated with top marks and had excellent prospects for entering the paid labour force, she was allowed to leave her house only three hours per week and was denied benefits for three months, thus forcing her into destitution during her pregnancy. Subsequently, repayments for her debt were deducted from each welfare cheque, reducing her monthly income from $520 to $468. After paying $450 rent, she was left with $18 for groceries and other expenses (Frenschkowski 2002). The coroner's inquest jury concluded that the Ontario government must change its policy on lifetime bans and adjust social assistance formulas so that they reflect the actual cost of basic needs and housing (Ontario NDP 2002).

The present funding reductions resemble the welfare "wars" Fraser (1989, 144) referred to more than a decade ago. As Fraser (1989) and Gaskell and McLaren (1991) have highlighted, when governments reduce funding for education, health, and social service programs, women are hit hardest. Women are more likely to work, or aspire to work, in these fields than men are. Women are more likely to be poor, to rely on income assistance, and to be lone parents than men are. Also, lone mothers tend to be younger, and consequently have less employment experience and less formal education, than lone fathers (Oderkirk and Lochhead 1992). Furthermore, lone mothers tend to have lower incomes than do parents in two-parent families (Oderkirk 1992). Finally, Townson (2000) and Lochhead and Scott (2000) point out how even women in intact two-parent families may have unequal access to family income. These cuts are likely to have long-term effects for the children of women relying on income assistance while raising children alone.

Since the closure of the BC Benefits Office, students receiving income assistance have been redirected to the Women's Centre, Student Services, or First Nations Student Services. Even when the BC Benefits Office was open, women in this study talked about how they sometimes missed important information about such things as applying for funding. They also spoke about the onerous foundational work they had to do to secure funding for living, educational, and daycare costs. Decentralizing this service would seem to heighten these problems. The BC Benefits Office was a kind of home base for low-income students, where they could ask questions and find out when and where to fill out which form. It will be necessary to consider effective ways of supporting and communicating with low-income students.

Given that the women in this study faced several challenges that were unique to them, it is understandable that they wanted opportunities to connect with women in like circumstances. They wanted to be able to talk about the challenges associated with being a single parent, to explore ways of feeling more empowered, and to share information about such things as funding options. This finding confirmed the demand for women's centre workshops and support groups, particularly at satellite campuses, where such programs are often less available. Also, the fact that many of the women in this study were somewhat disconnected from the larger campus community speaks to a need to involve instructors and their classrooms in the planning of women's centre workshops, support groups, and the like. This might involve integrating these activities into the curriculum.

This study has reinforced findings in other studies (e.g., Andres, Andruske, and Hawkey 1996) that classroom instructors can have a substantial impact on the successful program participation of students. By participant account, their DVST instructors were in tune with the nonacademic issues faced by student-mothers. Participants found their instructors to be sympathetic to their circumstances and to create a respectful learning environment. The classroom represented their primary connection to the college – they did not access a lot of support services or participate in many campus activities outside the classroom. These findings reinforce the prominent role played by DVST instructors and suggest their potential function as conveyors of information, as promoters of support networks, and as links with other services. These findings also highlight the importance of strong relationships between instructors and support service departments.

Other implications for policy and practice coming out of this study relate to the fact that seven out of eight participants were entering careers that were in traditionally female fields, many of which would offer low pay and little chance for advancement. On one hand, the participants in this study are a monument to higher education's potential to enhance quality of life; on the other, however, their experiences are reminders of how only a very narrow and low-paying range of options is available for many women raising young children (Andres and Guppy 1991). Implied again is the crucial role of instructors in empowering women to consider careers that will truly allow them to achieve financial independence. Career counsellors and high school teachers share this responsibility.

This study has revealed the pressing need for more comprehensive daycare on college campuses. None of the women in this study could make use of the daycare on campus because of age restrictions, waitlists, or prohibitive fees. Some of the women in this study had missed classes and other important college events because their childcare arrangements were suddenly not available. Hornosty also found many university daycares to be too restrictive to meet the needs of most women on campus. She has argued that, in order to create a "woman-friendly" (1998, 192) institution, there is a need for affordable daycare centres with flexible hours for children aged newborn to 12 years. Daycare policy and planning must involve student-parents in planning discussions in order to offer services that match their needs.

The results of this study indicate some future research directions. The data from this study could be used to develop a survey for distribution to a wider developmental studies student-mother population. For instance, since women's centre offerings, daycare services, and funding information surfaced as important issues, these could be expanded upon in a survey. Findings from this study could also act as a starting place for discussions in focus groups or support-group action research.

Another important direction for further research would be to look at how the children of the women in this study are impacted by their mothers' decision to participate in further education. Lareau's (2000) research suggests that children raised in working-class homes may have less favourable grade school experiences than children raised in middle-class homes. This is partly because working-class parents have less experience with post-secondary education than do middle-class parents and are consequently less likely to pass "cultural capital" along to their children. It would be worthwhile finding out how the children of the women in this study benefit from their mothers having pursued higher education.

There is a need for research that focuses on mothers who are eligible for developmental studies participation but who have not enrolled in DVST programs. Without such research, the current study provides only half the story at best. The women in this study were remarkably motivated to continue their studies. Most of them also had good support networks in place before they decided to enrol in the program. It could be that other women have thought about enrolling but have not had adequate supports in place, or have had too many obstacles to do so. For similar reasons, it would also be revealing to interview women who have left the program. Finally, it would be worthwhile to follow up with the women from this study in a few years to see what impact education has had on their lives.

Notes

1 Developmental studies is very similar, but not identical, to adult basic education (ABE). Both provide opportunities for adults to upgrade academically. The latter is geared more specifically toward achieving high school graduation, while the former has a broader, less specific aim. Some DVST students have not graduated from high school. Others have graduated but require upgrading before taking college-level coursework.
2 This policy has recently changed. As of January 2002, single parents are considered "employable" after their youngest child reaches 3 years of age (Klein 2002).

References

Andres, L., C. Andruske, and C. Hawkey. 1996. *Mapping the Realities of First Year Post-Secondary Life: A Study of Students at Three Post-Secondary Institutions*. A report prepared for the British Columbia Council on Admissions and Transfer.
Andres, L., and N. Guppy. 1991. Opportunities and Obstacles for Women in Canadian Higher Education. In *Women and Education*, 2nd ed., edited by J. Gaskell and A. McLaren, 163-90. Calgary: Detselig.
Blackwell, J. 1998. Making the Grade against the Odds: Women as University Undergrads. In *Illusion of Inclusion*, edited by J. Stalker and S. Prentice, 60-71. Halifax: Fernwood.
Butterwick, S. 1996. Government Funded Job-Entry Programs for Women: Whose Needs Are Being Addressed? In *Debating Dropouts: Critical Policy and Research Perspectives on School Leaving*, edited by D. Kelly and J. Gaskell, 190-210. New York: Teachers College Press.
Catalfamo, A.R. 1998. Opportunity or Oppression? The Impacts of the 1996 Welfare Reforms on Adult Education. *Adult Basic Education* 8, 1: 18-29.
Dalien, E. 1998. *The Lived Experience of Student Mothers*. Unpublished master's thesis, University of British Columbia, Vancouver.
Fraser, N. 1989. *Unruly Practices: Power, Discourse, and Gender in Contemporary Social Theory*. Minneapolis: University of Minnesota Press.
Frenschkowski, J. 2002. We've Learned Little from Kimberly Rogers's Death. *Globe and Mail*, August 9, A13.
Gaskell, J., and A. McLaren, eds. 1991. *Women and Education*, 2nd ed. Calgary: Detselig.
Gleason, M. 1999. *Normalizing the Ideal: Psychology, Schooling, and the Family in Postwar Canada*. Toronto: University of Toronto Press.

Hart, M. 1995. Motherwork: A Radical Proposal to Rethink Work and Education. In *In Defense of the Lifeworld: Critical Perspectives on Adult Learning*, edited by M. Welton, 39-70. Albany: State University Press.

Hays, S. 1996. *The Cultural Contradiction of Motherhood*. New Haven: Yale University Press.

Home, A., and C. Hinds. 2000. Life Situations and Institutional Supports of Women University Students with Family and Job Responsibilities. *Proceedings of the Adult Education Research Conference*, Vancouver, 181-84.

Hornosty, J. 1998. Balancing Childcare and Work: The Need for a "Woman-Friendly" University. In *Illusion of Inclusion*, edited by J. Stalker and S. Prentice, 180-93. Halifax: Fernwood.

Kelly, D.M. 2000. *Pregnant with Meaning: Teen Mothers and the Politics of Inclusive Schooling*. New York: P. Lang.

Klein, S. 21 January 2002. *Reckless and Unnecessary: CCPA's Analysis, Facts, and Figures for Understanding and Challenging BC's January 17 Budget and Job Cuts*. Vancouver: Canadian Centre for Policy Alternatives.

Lareau, A. 2000. *Home Advantage: Social Class and Parental Intervention in Elementary Education*, 2nd ed. New York: Falmer Press.

Lavell, E.M. 1998. On the Road to Find Out: Everyday Advice for Working-Class Mothers Returning to School. In *Illusion of Inclusion*, edited by J. Stalker and S. Prentice, 194-208. Halifax: Fernwood.

Little, M. 1998. *"No Car, No Radio, No Liquor Permit": The Moral Regulation of Single Mothers in Ontario, 1920-1997*. Toronto: Oxford University Press.

Liversidge, S. 2000. *A Matter of Time: The Lived Experience of Re/entering Mothers in Nursing Education*. Unpublished master's thesis, University of British Columbia, Vancouver.

Lochhead, C., and K. Scott. 2000. *The Dynamics of Women's Poverty in Canada*. Ottawa: Status of Women Canada.

Long, B.C., and R. Cox. 2000. Women's Ways of Coping with Employment Stress: A Feminist Contextual Analysis. In *Coping, Health and Organizations*, edited by P. Dewe, M. Leiter, and T. Cox, 109-23. New York: Taylor and Francis.

Luttrell, W. 1997. *Schoolsmart and Motherwise: Working-Class Women's Identity and Schooling*. New York: Routledge.

McMahon, M. 1995. *Engendering Motherhood: Identity and Self-Transformation in Women's Lives*. New York: Guildford Press.

Malicky, G., C. Katz, M. Norton, and C. Norman. 1997. Literacy Learning in a Community-Based Program. *Adult Basic Education* 7, 2: 84-103.

Marshall, C., and G. Rossman. 1999. *Designing Qualitative Research*, 3rd ed. Thousand Oaks, CA: Sage.

Mezirow, J. 1978. *Education for Perspective Transformation: Women's Re-entry Programs in Community Colleges*. New York: Columbia University.

Oderkirk, J. 1992. Parents and Children Living with Low Incomes. *Canadian Social Trends* (Winter): 11-15.

Oderkirk, J., and C. Lochhead. 1992. Lone Parenthood: Gender Differences. *Canadian Social Trends* (Winter): 16-18.

Ontario NDP. 2002. "NDP Wants Fast Action on Rogers Inquest Findings." 19 December. Available at <http://www.ontariondp.on.ca/news/publish/printer_480.shtml> (accessed 10 June 2003).

Quigley, B. 1992. Resistance, Reluctance, and Persistence: Schooling and Its Effect on Adult Literacy Participation. *Proceedings of the Adult Education Research Conference, University of Saskatchewan*, 205-12.

Straus, M. 1988. Divorced Mothers. In *The Different Faces of Motherhood*, edited by B. Birns and D. Hays, 215-35. New York: Plenum Press.

Tett, L. 2000. "I'm Working Class and Proud of It" – Gendered Experiences of Non-Traditional Participants in Higher Education. *Gender and Education* 12, 2: 183-94.

Townson, M. 2000. *A Report Card on Women and Poverty*. Vancouver: Canadian Centre for Policy Alternatives.

4
Visitors in the Classroom: The Academic Experiences of Students Who Are Hard of Hearing
Ruth Warick

Little is known about the nature of the academic experiences of students who are hard of hearing. Much of what is known is based on empirical studies about students in general, although, of late, a few qualitative studies have contributed knowledge about students' perceptions of their post-secondary experiences (Andres 1992, 1993, 2001; Andres, Andruske, and Hawkey 1996; Hawkey 2000). By focusing on the perceptions of students about their experiences, researchers have gained an understanding that students' views of their experiences are complex and reinforce the need to examine perceptions in relation to the dynamics between individuals and institutions of higher education. This chapter relates findings about the academic experiences of fourteen university students who are hard of hearing. The students were enrolled in one of three universities. Although they differed in age, gender, program of study, and year of study, they all shared in common the experience of being students who are hard of hearing. Through the use of an interpretive research methodology, which was adopted because it emphasizes the importance of individuals' experiences as perceived by the participants themselves (Marshall and Rossman 1999; Smith 1989), the students were interviewed twice; as well, most of them maintained a journal for a three-week period.

Literature Review
The academic integration of students has been the source of much study about students' experiences in university. Academic integration refers to congruency between the "needs, interests, and skills of the individual and those of the communities of the institution" (Tinto 1982, 36). In Tinto's (1987) longitudinal retention model, integration into the academic system of the university is important to persistence, and factors such as academic performance and faculty/staff interactions influence integration. A sense of belonging and being part of the classroom community promotes retention

(Pascarella and Terenzini 1980 and 1991; Tinto 1997). Academic advising enhances student experience (Crocket 1985), and when expectations match performance, students are more likely to be satisfied (Bean and Bradley 1986).

With respect to the experiences of persons with hearing losses in post-secondary education, it is known that students encounter difficulties with hearing instructors and classmates in the classroom, and with participation in social settings such as cafeterias, auditoriums, and campus walkways (Warick 1994). They may encounter instructors who are less than knowledgeable or understanding (Schein 1991; Stinson, Scherer, and Walter 1987; Swartz and Israelite 2000) and have academic content gaps in their learning (Schein 1991). Their style of learning may not match the requirements of the academic environment; for example, a student who relies on textbooks may not fare well when an instructor bases an exam on verbally delivered content (Warick 1998).

Some studies about students who are deaf may be informative about students with hearing losses in general, although caution needs to be exercised in extrapolating from one population to another. Hearing loss ranges along a continuum: the deaf, those with little or no hearing, are generally situated at one end of the continuum; the hard of hearing, placed along the continuum according to their degree of hearing loss, are able to function in the hearing world due to their use of technological equipment such as hearing aids.

Despite differences in the two populations, the difficulties students who are deaf experience in post-secondary education appear to resonate for students who are hard of hearing, albeit for somewhat different reasons. Students who are deaf and use a sign-language interpreter encounter participation difficulties because the interpreting lags behind the speaker (Foster, Long, and Snell 1999). Moreover, they find group work challenging because of the additional factor of the rapid turn-taking in conversation among speakers (Antia, Stinson, and Gaustad 2002). Warick (1998) and Secord (1999) have noted that persons who are hard of hearing experience participation difficulties due to the time it takes to process sound and to fill in missing gaps of verbal content. By the time the person who is hard of hearing comprehends the message, the opportunity for participation may have been lost.

Antia, Stinson, and Gaustad have termed students who do not participate in classes as being "visitors" rather than members of the class. In contrast to being a visitor, being a member means being part of the classroom and school community. Visitors "face greater barriers in obtaining a quality education" (2002, 215). In particular, students who do not participate can face academic consequences such as being marked lower for class participation, in addition to the affective judgments made about them. Furthermore, because classroom participation has been found to be a good predictor of course grades, the inability to participate in the classroom may result in poor academic achievement (Stinson and Antia 1999, 169).

In addition, when students who are deaf or hard of hearing are excluded from informal exchanges among other students regarding instructor expectations, study tips, and unspoken rules for class behaviour and organization, not only do they miss important "unpublished" information, but they are not able to gauge what was missed because they do not know what was not heard, and so they cannot take steps to obtain the missed content.

The provision of disability-related accommodations is intended to overcome the disadvantages of disability, but these accommodations do not level the playing field (Stinson and Walter 1992). Nonetheless, effective communication strategies, and such academic supports as extra instruction, alternative scheduling, reduced courseload, alternatives to exam- and assignment-testing means, and course substitution[1] may promote postsecondary success (Lingen 1993; Warick 1997). Access to services may include assistive listening devices, oral and sign interpreters, notetakers, tape recorders, preferential seating, room changes, and real-time closed captioning (Jones 1993; Killean and Hubka 1999; Lingen 1993; Patterson and Schmidt 1992). The type of accommodation most frequently used by most students who are hard of hearing is that of notetaking services (Warick 1994). Compared with other students with disabilities, students who are deaf or hard of hearing are low users of disability-related accommodations (Killean and Hubka 1999).

Research Methods and Framework

For this research study, Tinto's retention model (1987) provided descriptive categories for identifying a range of academic issues faced by students, with consideration of their level of commitment and individual background characteristics. To deal with a drawback of the model – namely, emphasis on the individual as an independent actor – the concept of agency-structure nexus was used. Based on Bourdieu's (1984) theory of field of forces, an agency-structure nexus (Andres, this volume) recognizes that there is a dynamic tension between individuals and an institution, and offers a way for examining underlying structures that affect students. This chapter focuses on the academic experiences of university students who are hard of hearing, and, in relation to academic experiences, on the extent to which the experiences of students who are hard of hearing are similar or dissimilar to those of other students. An interpretative approach was undertaken to the research; this approach emphasizes understanding students' perceptions and shaping various perceptions into meanings that explain their experiences.

Fourteen students who are hard of hearing participated from three universities in British Columbia. They were interviewed twice, initially in the fall of 1999 and then in the winter of 2000, and were asked to write journal entries of their experiences, both positive and negative, over a three-week period. Eleven students kept journal entries.

Study Participants

Students participating in the study ranged in age from 18 to 58 years; most were single, 9 were female and 5 were male, and 11 were undergraduate students and 3 were graduate students. The area of study was arts for 5 students, and education for another 5, with the rest in science, social work, and commerce. The audiology profiles of the students varied from mild to profound hearing losses, with a third having severe-to-profound or profound losses and a third having moderate-to-severe losses.[2]

The following fourteen students participated in this study:

Charlie, 49, has a severe-to-profound hearing loss and wears hearing aids in both ears. Single and First Nations, his goal is to become an educational counsellor. Presently, he is in undergraduate studies.

Kathy, 27, is a teacher pursuing a master's degree. Recently diagnosed with a mild hearing loss, she is going through an emotional adjustment. She does not wear a hearing aid but does use an FM system with a headphone.[3]

Mark, 21, is a fourth-year commerce student who has a moderate-to-severe hearing loss in his right ear and a severe-to-profound hearing loss in his left ear. He wears hearing aids in both ears. He is single.

Yvonne, 22, is in her fourth year of arts. She has a profound hearing loss and wears hearing aids in both ears. She is single.

Carol, 18, is a first-year arts student who has a moderate-to-severe loss in one ear and a moderate-to-profound loss in the other ear. She wears hearing aids in both ears and uses an FM system. She also has a condition whereby she pulls out her hair. She is single.

James, 18, is in year one of the bachelor of science honours program. He has a moderate-to-severe hearing loss and wears hearing aids in both ears. He also uses an FM system. He is single.

Sarah, 36, single, is in her last year of a master's program to become a teacher of students who are deaf or hard of hearing. She has a moderate-to-severe hearing loss, wears hearing aids in both ears, and is also legally blind.

Gayle, 23, transferred from another university into her fourth year of arts. Single, she lives at home. She wears two in-the-ear hearing aids for her moderately severe hearing loss.

Darcy, in his mid-30s, is in his fourth year, having spent two years at college before coming to university. He has no hearing in his left ear and a severe hearing loss in his right ear, for which he wears a hearing aid. He is married with two children.

Rachel, single and 28, is completing a bachelor of social work degree. Her hearing loss is severe to profound and only recently did she get a hearing aid. After a year on campus, she is now taking all of her classes by distance education.

Ben, 28 years old, is in his third year of science studies. He defines his hearing loss as being moderate and he wears hearing aids in both ears. Ben is single.

Heather, 58, lost her hearing in her early 20s. She has a severe-to-profound bilateral sensorineural hearing loss and has hearing aids. She is married with grown children.

Jennifer, 40, returned to university for a master's degree in a specialized program for teachers of students who are deaf or hard of hearing. She has a moderate-to-severe loss in both ears. She wears hearing aids and also uses an FM system. She lives with her fiancé.

Ann, 24, is in final year in a bachelor of education degree. She only recently got a hearing aid for her moderate-to-severe hearing loss although she has been hard of hearing from birth. She is single.

Findings

The Teaching and Learning Experience

Not surprisingly, given the nature of their disabilities and previous literature findings about hearing difficulties (Stinson et al. 1996; Warick 1994), students participating in the study experienced difficulties hearing instructors when they paced in front of the classroom while speaking and faced the blackboard instead of the class. Hearing difficulties heightened when additional or new information about an assignment or an exam was provided at the end of a class when noise levels were likely to rise in the classroom. However, even in quiet environments, some students had difficulty with certain sounds and with speech comprehension, and especially hearing persons with soft-spoken or accented voices.

> Carol: I think I do hear them, but I don't always understand it in terms that I mistake words for other words, or understand half of a sentence. Usually it's towards the end of the sentence and I make assumptions of the beginning.

Students' hearing strategies included using technical supports, such as FM systems, obtaining notes from classmates or the instructor, and requesting that the professor change his or her communication style. However, as Darcy noted in his journal, it was stressful having to do so:

The professor today spoke whole swaths of information directly to his over-head, looking down or with his back turned to me. I spoke with him after class to once again ask him to please remember to speak looking forward so I can read his lips. He seemed a bit annoyed (but then again, he seems that way *all* the time), but apologized and said he would try to remember that.

Another strategy employed by students was to sit at the front of the class or to carefully select their seat based on their better hearing ear and where the dialogue in the class was likely to be directed. Other strategies employed by students were to select classes based on prior knowledge of the speaking voice of the professor or the acoustical condition of the classroom. How-ever, optimal selections were not always possible if no other section of a course was available.

Nature of Interactions with Professors

The students participating in my study tended to confirm previous research findings about the importance of positive instructor interactions and to rate their interactions with instructors positively. Among those citing posi-tive experiences with instructors was Gayle, who noted that several of her instructors were open and accommodating:

> I feel well respected after notifying my professor [that] I have a hearing impairment. She encourages me to ask whenever I don't hear what she is saying.

Charlie observed that one of his professors made him feel very comfortable:

> She doesn't put me down or anything; she has a way of using her natural humour to make things a lot easier.

Despite the positive reviews, students generally perceived that instructors were extremely busy and had limited time for student interactions. This was particularly felt to be the case for faculty instructing large classes. Some negative experiences were cited, supporting literature findings of difficul-ties with professors wearing an FM system (Warick 1994), singling out of the hard-of-hearing student, treating students in a stereotypical manner (Swartz and Israelite 2000), and having limited knowledge of students with disabilities (Leyser et al. 1998).

Rachel said that she found a lot of her professors were unsupportive and not knowledgeable about hearing loss in many respects. She found them to be very standoffish. [The professor] did not want to deal with me. Felt I was going to make their life difficult.

Charlie had a professor who initially refused to wear the transmitter part of his FM system, and then relented after insistence from the university's Disability Services Office coordinator. Even more offensive, though, was how the professor handled wearing the hearing device. Charlie said that, in a loud voice, the professor told the class, "We have a deaf student in our class. That's the reason why I am wearing this thing." This incident was not the only hurtful experience he had with the instructor. In the presence of a teaching assistant, the instructor talked about Charlie as if he were not present. The instructor also told him that she could not understand why he could not take notes for himself.

Kathy, who was in a class with another hard-of-hearing student with a more pronounced hearing loss, felt that one of her instructors was more sympathetic to the other student. She noted the professor's reaction when she finally got an FM system late in the term:

Because I got my FM so late, it was the first time I wore it to this class. The teacher, quite abruptly, asked me why I was wearing headphones. I was taken back by this comment, but I also realized that this was the prof that forgot I was hard of hearing.

Some students felt that professors tried to be accommodating in the way that they communicated but tended to forget about adaptations. Darcy noted that he found that

they are really good the first couple of times and then they start to forget ... I realized that I was on my own and need to deal with however I can and not worry too much about getting the professor to deal with it.

Several students remarked that the invisible nature of a hearing loss contributed to the tendency to forget about them. Because students who are hard of hearing do not look any different from their hearing peers, it was easy for a professor to interact with and regard them as if they were the same as other students.

Mark: It's their own perception of me. I had people tell me that "I totally forgot you have a hearing loss." I still have my problems and still deal with them, but it's normal for them so they don't think about it anymore.

Not only do instructors "forget" that students have a hearing loss, but they may also assume that students have heard what has been said, when, in fact, they have not. Instructors may not be attuned to cues as to what constitutes reception of the message, or the students themselves may not give any obvious cues.

Charlie: People think hard-of-hearing students understand and we don't because the manifestations of the symptoms of our hearing loss is different. Mine is quite serious because I could sit there and talk to you and then you will say I can understand. "He can understand me." But in fact I don't.

Participants spoke of the need for professors to be willing to spend an extra five minutes or so clarifying class content. For some, this is one of the most important accommodations which helps them overcome not hearing or understanding material presented in class. Mark noted that he regularly approached his professors for help and that frequently he received substantial assistance.

I am practising for the final now. He [the professor] will give me example questions and I work through them and when I run into problems I will say "What has happened here?" and we will go back and he knows exactly why.

However, not all students were comfortable approaching their professors for additional assistance. Some students felt they were not able to follow what transpired verbally, so much so that they felt unable to approach a professor after class. They felt they needed to have some knowledge of exactly what to ask a professor. As well, if they had an initial negative reception they would not be inclined to go back.

Ann: I couldn't follow the lecture enough to be able to ask questions so I would often avoid entirely asking profs questions ... I went to students first. There were a couple of times I went to profs but they were more negative than positive.

Ann's preference to go to students first was echoed by a few other students. They simply found it easier to approach peers. This reinforces findings (Andres, Andruske, and Hawkey 1996) that sometimes students feel most comfortable seeking help from classmates.

One reason for the limited contact with professors could be that students expected that university professors would be extremely busy and not have a lot of time for them. Even students who approached instructors frequently had this view:

Mark: They're busy and have a lot on their plates, so there's not so much time for students. One professor did not even finish my meeting because he had something else. I didn't like that too much but it happened.

A couple of students noted that there was a considerable difference between high school and university in terms of the amount of support provided by the instructor. They did not get the same level of support, nor did they expect to get the same level of support. They perceived that students were expected to be more self-reliant and independent in university than was the case in high school. Their perceptions were confirmed when they found that instructors were less available in university than they had been in high school:

> Carol: When I do go, their office hours are very limited and there's usually a line-up. I have asked a few times to meet at different times and that just [did] not always work out because of scheduling conflicts.

Program differences affected the interaction of professors with students, as found by Hawkey (this volume). Students who found their professors extremely knowledgeable tended to be in a specialized program where the professors had previously worked with hard-of-hearing students. Jennifer, who was in a program to train teachers of the deaf and hard of hearing, said,

> I think I have been fortunate enough to have very understanding professors because of the program I am in.

First- and second-year students were less likely to connect with professors than were students in their senior years. Gayle, a fourth-year student, found one of her professors was very receptive to her. This had more to do with her discipline than her disability:

> She [a professor] is supportive, largely because there aren't a lot of people in that field. There aren't a lot of women who participate in gender work and international development planning. There is real demand for that, particularly women. She wants to see as many women as possible in that area. Is it a political thing? Is it a personal thing? I think it's both. It's not just because I am who I am. I think it's overall.

Ann, a fourth-year student too, noted that

> the first- and second-year courses are really just a mass of students and you are just a face in the crowd, and profs don't have that sort of time to commit to each student.

Some students felt that the size of an institution affected their interactions with professors. Heather noted that she was happy that her university was small, which she felt facilitated more professor-student interactions than would be possible at a large institution.

Providing Specific Accommodations

Professors varied in how they provided accommodations. With respect to getting a copy of the professor's notes, Carol found that one professor gave her notes in advance of the class, whereas another professor didn't give them to her until a few days after the lecture. She found that receiving them later, rather than in advance, made it hard for her to follow the lecture.

Sometimes a professor wanted to provide more accommodations than the student desired. James felt that one of his professors had overstepped matters by arranging for him to write an exam at the Disability Services Office in case he needed extra time. James said that he had not requested such accommodation and wanted simply to write with the class.

Students also faced situations in which it was difficult for them to get accommodations. As previously noted, Charlie had difficulty with a professor refusing to wear his FM system and James almost had a similar difficulty, though based on lack of information, rather than a disagreement. Ben had difficulty getting a professor to understand that being graded for class participation was a problem for him because of his hearing loss:

> I have had trouble with one instructor. Because we had a group presentation and I got marked down for class interaction and I previously explained my problem. Eventually it got worked out, but it was a bit of a pain.

Ben felt it was important for professors to provide accommodations but not to give him preferential treatment. He felt that tended to be the case.

> They don't treat you any different. [Having a hearing loss] doesn't bother me too much. I don't really want to be out of place.

Hearing Classmates

Students experienced challenges hearing instructors, but they faced even more difficulties hearing other students. The difficulties related to two aspects: first, quality of students' voices, and second, positioning, either on the part of the other students or on the part of the students with hearing losses.

Under the category of quality of students' voices, these students had difficulties with accented voices or voices that did not clearly articulate words and project sound. Gayle noted that she found it

> challenging understanding what a girl in my law class says; she has such a strong accent.

Kathy noted the following difficulty in her first journal entry:

> One classmate in particular has been muttering and mumbling in class.
> Perhaps they were side comments but clearly, at one point, it was not. I am
> *extremely* frustrated because all my courses are with this particular classmate
> and I am starting to feel it is on purpose.

Difficulties with positioning could take several forms. Gayle noted that
she had a hard time hearing the people she sat behind in class, especially
when they spoke softly. She said it was

> very aggravating as I cannot hear what is being said; found most often in
> my history class where we sit in rows.

Carol noted another type of positional hearing difficulty. She had been standing in the middle of the hallway and realized too late that someone wanted
to get by her. She was placed in the awkward dilemma of how to explain
what had occurred, while not really wanting to disclose her hearing loss to
the students:

> Since I didn't hear them, I didn't move and they became annoyed and prob-
> ably repeated themselves. I was embarrassed when I turned around because I
> felt like there was someone behind me. If only I had explained then maybe
> they wouldn't think ill of me – but then do I really need to explain?

Hearing difficulties can create tension and feelings such as a sense of ag-
gravation, frustration, or embarrassment. At some point, students tended not
to pursue the matter when accommodating practices were not maintained.

> Gayle: I ask people to speak louder because I am hearing impaired, and
> oftentimes people won't because it's not ingrained in them. They don't
> really think about it. Like practice makes perfect. Because of the fact they
> don't change, I am not going to continuously hound on it. It's not worth
> my time. It means it doesn't matter if I don't hear.

Some study participants were so shy that they were uncomfortable asking
classmates to repeat unheard statements. Ben preferred not to interrupt other
students even if he didn't hear them. "I don't like to intrude," he stated.

Although some students let it go when they could not hear, other students made it a point to remind their classmates to speak up. They felt
comfortable doing so:

Jennifer: I am assertive. It's okay to keep it up, to keep reminding people, to say "Pardon, I didn't hear that." And I've also been told by other colleagues that in my doing so, having people repeat it, help hearing people learn too. They are hearing it again; they are hearing it in a different way. It's really quite beneficial for a lot of people.

Another strategy was for participants to be asked to repeat unheard phrases. Kathy found that classmates were receptive to repeating their names when they started their group discussion, but she also found resistance from the occasional classmate. In her journal she noted that one particular student in her class was quite negative:

I hate to push issues, but a girl in my class continually expresses through facial expression, attitude and body language that it is a nuisance and bother to her that I ask for simple accommodations such as speak slower, don't wave your hands, move something away from my FM mic, etc. I am FED-UP. I don't want to be rude but she is also becoming a teacher of the deaf and hard of hearing. She should have at least a little bit of sympathy.

Participation
Being part of the conversation was an issue for most of the students taking part in the study. Lack of hearing means not only missing what is being said but missing out on the opportunity to take part in the discussion. Students noted that they were at a disadvantage in being able to participate in class discussions. Yvonne said she has to pay attention to find the right moment to jump into a conversation:

Sometimes, I have to wait for an actual quiet when nobody is talking, then I can jump in.

Conversational lag means that students who are hard of hearing have to work at timing themselves to get into a conversation. They can find that they are too late, like James, who stated,

I have to time it really right. When two people are talking at the same time I feel like I did it too late or whatever. I should have just let them go.

Oftentimes study participants simply did not hear what other students stated, and they had no reference point for getting into the conversation. This problem was most predominant in group discussions and led students to feel isolated from classmates. Carol noted in a journal entry:

I met with my tutorial group today as we have to present our research in two weeks. They both were discussing something that they were going to do together and then asked for my opinion. When I said I didn't know what they had been talking about, one of the girls gave me a funny look as if I was intentionally not paying attention. I explained to them that I was hard of hearing but I don't think this helped them to understand.

As indicated by Carol's experience, students who are hard of hearing may be evaluated negatively by other students if they can't respond as others usually expect. Participation carries risks, as Darcy noted in his journal:

I raised my hand to comment on a point I thought was worth mentioning, that the prof had yet to speak about. It turns out that the person who spoke just before me (other than the prof) had just spoken about that very thing; the reason I didn't know about it, other than not hearing it, was that the prof didn't comment on it, but merely said "mmm-mm" or some such. There was a bit of snickering from the back.

Darcy asked permission to skip the classes with group discussions, but the professor felt he could not do that because that would mean missing more than the discussions:

He did promise to try to recap whatever was said, but, and I can understand this, there is simply too much said to repeat.

Two weeks later when a group discussion was scheduled for the class, Darcy skipped the class. He wrote in his journal:

I don't feel good about it, and I hope this doesn't become a habit, but I really dislike the group discussions.

He stayed home and read the play that the class was discussing.

Charlie felt that a different standard than that used for other students was applied to his participation:

I am very sensitive to the fact that I'm hard of hearing and being judged differently and that bugs me.

He noted that he had difficulty jumping into the conversation, and when he got the floor he used the speaking occasion to full advantage. The opportunity to speak may not come again.

I'm treated as if I'm stupid. I do jump in but weigh pros and cons if it is worth it.

Some students required external help getting into the conversation. Even assertive students such as Yvonne found that their participation was easier when there was a discussion leader, the discussion was organized, and rules were applied such as raising a hand to request the floor:

Usually I just raise my hand. I know it's so high schooler; most people don't raise their hands but I do. Not just to be polite but because it's so much simpler because usually when I do try to jump in they don't hear me.

One other way of dealing with discussions was to jump into the conversation first or to initiate the topic of conversation. That way the student avoided having to deal with both the content of what was said previously and the physical challenges of hearing other conversationalists. This strategy was used separately or in conjunction with dominating a conversation.

Some students mentioned that they were the most vocal in their class and tended to lead discussions. Heather noted that she was aware that she could be too verbally active so she consciously tried not to over-participate. Because Yvonne tended to be active, sometimes teachers told her, "Okay, you have already said a lot, so let somebody else talk for a while." The tendency to lead or control the conversation was, in fact, one of the strategies that students with hearing losses adopted to try to be part of the conversation. Leaders of conversations are in control and are able to manage both the content and processes of exchanges.

Course Taking

The nature of the participation of some university students with hearing losses differed from that of their peers in regard to their approach to program and course selection, as well as in the number of courses taken. For example, Kathy, who became hard of hearing in later life, indicated that her hearing loss may have been a factor in her choice of program:

I would probably hesitate to register in law or any other faculty because of the amount of information coming at me. I prefer to be in something that I had to rely on my hearing a lot less and have people understand more. Not that the individuals in other faculties are less sensitive but they are less aware, which makes them essentially less sensitive.

Similar to other students, Kathy selected courses based on room location, size of the class, the vocal qualities of the instructor for the course, and the type of professor. Kathy said that she found out the names of instructors from her academic advisor and then decided which courses to take.

> I also ask her other questions relating to profs and how good they are, if they are the kind of person who can see my changes or see my hearing loss, if they are adapting. That's what helps me in all those areas because I can better choose profs. That will suit my need more, and I have been able to do that for the most part.

Jennifer noted that although she usually did not have to worry about vocal qualities, she would make course decisions based on the instructor's voice:

> Yes, if I heard a teacher had a big moustache and beard and had an accent or anything, and then I say, "I am not going there." This program I assume everybody would speak very clearly because it was a deaf and hard-of-hearing program that I shouldn't have any difficulty.

At registration time, Mark got a list of courses with the names of the teachers and the room numbers for the courses, and then he chose courses based on the best fit for him:

> I know which rooms are good because I have been there for three years now. And I know which rooms are not good.

Gayle noted that

> having a big airy room with high ceilings doesn't call for a sound listening environment, particularly in my instance – fortunately I only have one class in a room like this.

Several students found it easier to hear in lecture format classes than in discussion group classes. However, if it were not for their hearing losses they might have preferred discussion classes:

> Carol: In group discussions I learn more from them in terms of different opinions and give me a chance to participate. It's difficult to follow along in group discussions and know what I am saying is actually relevant whereas lecture instruction type of courses I can just sit and listen and not have to adjust the different speakers and be worried about who is speaking. I really like to take more group discussion courses. If I had to choose what is best I probably stick with the instruction kind of lecture courses.

Yet, there was a limit to how much class change a student could make based on a hearing loss. Preference for a particular subject matter might be more important than the issue around hearing. As well, some courses may be required or are team-taught by several instructors, or the student may feel that having a rapport with the instructor outweighs other factors. For example, James found himself in a class with a professor who was difficult to understand. He considered dropping out of it but stayed on:

> I had a pretty good rapport with my math teacher. We got along and even though I didn't understand some of the things during class, I felt very able to go in and see him and ask him about the questions. That more than made up for it.

When faced with difficulty in the first class, Darcy chose to try a different section of the same class. When several sections are offered, that may be possible to do. Darcy stated:

> In French I had that. The first French class I walked into, the professor spoke really softly so I switched to another professor. He spoke louder.

Several students made a point of assuming a reduced courseload so that they would have sufficient time to devote to their studies, taking into account the extra time required to ensure that missed content was picked up. A number of students stressed the importance of taking classes at a pace that allowed them the time needed to devote to the accommodations required and to simply keep up. For example, having notes taken by someone else requires extra time to read them. Having a tutor demands more time. Reading and writing might all take a little longer because of difficulties related to lack of hearing (Rodda and Hiron 1989; Warick 1994).

Sometimes it took a negative experience for students with a hearing loss to realize they needed to take a reduced courseload. Yvonne found this to be the case after she did not do well in a couple of semesters:

> I didn't do well in two particular semesters, my first semester here and the first semester of my third year, which were difficult ones for me, so I had to drop out of some courses. I am no longer taking four courses a semester. It's too much for me so I am down to three. It will take longer but I will get better grades that way. Kind of makes sense for me to take it at a steady pace instead of trying to rush and finish it all up.

Charlie started off taking two courses, but after a month he was advised to drop these and take two other courses. He did not do well in these courses because of the late start, compounded by not having sufficient time to get accommodations in place. Charlie described the attempt to "fast-track" as a disaster. He ended up withdrawing and starting over in the second year. The university recognized the mistake, refunded him for the year, and gave him a new start; nevertheless, Charlie lost the time invested.

Another student, Darcy, had great difficulty with his French course even after switching to a section where he could better hear the instructor. He dropped the course:

> It was causing me a lot of mental anguish ... a lot of headaches. I was starting to berate myself for not learning the language and the classes were just horrific.

Carol was relieved that she had followed advice to take a reduced courseload. Yvonne had not started with a reduced load but after she failed a class in her first semester, she realized that she needed to scale back. Ben stated that for him, taking a reduced courseload meant that he had "a little bit of extra time, so I can do some extra work. I do a lot more reading just to keep up." For Jennifer, "a lighter load lessens the stress." There is extra strain just from having to hear and compensate for not hearing, she explained. Half of the students took a reduced courseload.

Distance Education

Distance education was not a substitute for classroom learning for most hard-of-hearing students. Other factors besides hearing loss, such as being far away from campus, may be more important in the decision to take distance education classes. Two of the students in this study were taking courses by distance education; however, other students who were asked about this delivery method did not consider it an alternative to classroom learning. They preferred being in classes with other students, regardless of how difficult it was to hear classmates and instructors.

Those students who took distance education courses experienced some difficulties around use of the telephone and receiving materials in accessible format, namely, captioned videos. Rachel also experienced difficulties with a lack of response to her queries, which she felt was the norm rather than the exception.

> Rachel's journal: My research report assignment ... was due on November 27, as well as my summative report. I also had to complete my final paper for [another course] ... and it was due on the same day. Because of my difficulty, I called my Instructor ... to ask for an extension of 1 week. I left 4 messages in 7 days. 3 were verbal and 1 via fax. She did not return my messages. That does not surprise me, they usually never do.

Given the negative experiences and preferences for interactive classes, some caution needs to be exercised in relation to promoting distance education courses as the solution to overcoming in-class hearing difficulties for hard-of-hearing students.

Academic Advising

Academic advising is stressed as being important to retaining post-secondary students (Crockett 1985). But just as other studies (Andres, Andruske, and Hawkey 1996; Guppy and Trew 1995) reported mixed experiences with academic advising, so, too, did the participants in my study. This is not to suggest that academic advising is not important. On the contrary, the experience of Charlie supports the literature on the importance of good academic advice. Just because the experience of students is mixed does not negate its importance.

In Charlie's case, his advisor suggested that he switch into different courses a month after the start of the term. Charlie did so, but he was not able to recover from the delayed start. His departure from university was prevented due to extraordinary efforts.

Several students who received academic advising spoke about discussing with an advisor the courses they were supposed to be taking and about ensuring they had sufficient credits to graduate. In some cases it was not a specific person assigned to them but, rather, a pool of advisors for a faculty. One student got the information from the registar's office. Those without a declared major felt at a disadvantage in getting academic counselling; there was less likely to be someone to go to see.

Several students were aware of advising services but did not use them. Rachel said that she handled her course schedule herself. "I just do that on my own," she stated. Ben said that "they have an academic advisor in the Faculty; I don't keep in contact with them." Gayle cited her difficulties in seeing an advisor at a previous university:

> I can't tell you how many times in university ... that I went to go to talk to an advisor. I was faced with the sign that said "Come back another time" and I didn't declare my major until the end of third year. It took me a long time. Obviously it could have been done a little bit earlier.

Some of the students were part of a cohort of students who were taking a graduate program that specified course requirements. They had a program advisor and had fewer program difficulties than other students.

Only one student, Mark, referred specifically to asking his advisor for advice related to his hearing. Besides being concerned about course requirements, he was concerned about how his professors would respond to him as a student with a hearing loss:

I also asked [my advisor] other questions relating to professors and how good they are – if they are the kind of person who can see my hearing loss, if they are adaptable. That's what helps me because I can better choose professors that will suit my needs more and I have been able to do that for the most part.

Commitment

Students' commitments or motivations to higher education are important factors influencing retention (Tinto 1982). Finishing a university degree program requires a considerable amount of effort and, therefore, commitment to the goal of university completion (Hackman and Dysinger 1970; Tinto 1982). It also is influenced by the nature of the experiences students have while they are students; if these are negative experiences, students may withdraw (Terenzini, Lorang, and Pascarella 1981; Tinto 1982).

Students were asked to rate their level of commitment to university on a seven-point scale with 1 representing the low end of the continuum and 7 the highest end. Only two students did not say that their commitment was at the highest level, a 7. One of these two students would have given a 7 instead of a 5 rating if he could have attended a university closer to home, which would have abated his homesickness. The other student selected a 4.5 rating, citing financial difficulty as possibly influencing her level of commitment.

The degree of commitment did not appear to be related to difficulties experienced in university or to the students' grade point averages. However, the level of commitment may help students deal with difficulties encountered. Carol felt that the high level of commitment was necessary to overcome the difficulties she had experienced:

> If I was not committed then there would be difficulties that would overrun my commitment. If I don't have a commitment then the difficulties just override that.

Reasons for the level of commitment varied for students, from motivation to get the degree, to a love of learning, to contentment with university. For example, one graduate student stated that she was committed to her present institution because she was not able to transfer credits elsewhere, but she was planning to do a PhD elsewhere. Another student was one course short of graduation; this meant that the commitment was for only a little while longer.

The nature of the institutional commitment to students affects students' level of commitment. Tinto addressed this issue when he explained that some students may depart from university because of the nature of their university experience. As noted by Tinto, "such departures are more a reflection of experiences following entry" than predispositions of the students (1982, 35).

Three students in this study could well have been drop-out statistics due to their university experiences. Their retention was due to extraordinary intervention; their own commitment to university was a factor, but that would not have been sufficient without substantial intervention. Rachel was one of the three students who had a difficult time with her university. The event that almost led to her dropping out was that the faculty had not registered her in classes. She said the faculty had committed to do this based on a fax she sent because she could not register by telephone. Faculty members told her they had not received the fax. To resolve the difficulty, she had to make several long distance calls and had great difficulty following the automated voice system and reaching people. Then she ended up being listed as registered in two courses when she was in five courses, and the bank called in payment of her student loan. She wrote the following in her journal:

> Because record services disagrees, I have to start making my student loan payments, even though I am a full-time student. I GIVE UP. Sometimes, I just think there is no hope or no point when you are a student with a hearing disability and you are just trying to get through life and educate yourself to fully employ yourself. I am not asking for special privileges, I am asking for a little help with the things I can't do.

Rachel was close to quitting at that point. However, she persisted because of the help of an advocate for deaf and hard-of-hearing students who worked for a service delivery agency outside of the university. As well, Rachel was near graduation. Asked where she would put herself on the seven-point scale, after having been registered, Rachel stated, "Right now I'd say 'seven.' I'm right at the end of the tunnel."

Another student, Jennifer, had also been on the verge of dropping out because of a negative experience during her first semester in which she took two difficult courses and did not pass one of them. Even so, one of her professors took an exceptional interest in her, and without her intervention Jennifer would have dropped out of the program:

> I was seriously thinking of not coming back. It was such a devastating experience for me. I think because of the persistency on the phone and just hearing that they really wanted me. "Please don't quit, come and talk to us." ... a couple of things that one of the instructors said on the phone, almost like a guilt trip, manipulative, that made me hang on ... through the support of my two advisors, I felt like they rolled out the red carpet and they said, "What will work for you? Let's work out something that will work for you."

In Jennifer's case, her advisors not only encouraged her to come back but modified her program so that she could do it on a part-time rather than a full-time basis. As a result, Jennifer persisted; as of this writing she has successfully graduated.

Charlie was the other student whose initial experience was almost a disaster. Interventions by a disability service coordinator prevented him from dropping out.

The above three students exemplify how student commitment alone is insufficient. The importance of institutional behaviour and commitment, along with individual commitment, is underscored in these examples. These situations illustrate that student experience is characterized by a dynamic tension between agents (students), the institution itself, and other players within the institution, in keeping with the agency-nexus concept.

Academic Performance

The commitment of the study participants to university seemed unconnected to their grades. The range of grades was from C to A, but level of commitment was not any lower for students receiving lower grades than for their peers who received higher grades. A student with a C average was just as committed as an A student.

Dissatisfaction with performance does not mean a lack of commitment if the student has sufficient hope to expect that he or she can improve. It can serve to heighten the student's commitment to improve performance. Several students in my study thought that they could be doing better. Carol, who expected a grade drop from high school, where she got As and Bs, was getting marks in the C⁺ range:

> I am discouraged by some of the marks but I think I have been given enough encouragement by tutors and professors.

The encouragement appeared to help her deal with the change in grades.

James, whose grades had dropped from As to Bs, would have liked to do better. Darcy, who got As in college, was also disappointed with getting mostly Bs:

> At first I thought it was just adjusting to a new school, figuring out how things work in a big university, but after being here for long enough and still getting B in the summer, I am a little disappointed in myself. I am not doing all that well this semester.

When students' grade expectations match results, they are likely to be content (Bean and Bradley 1986). Mark exemplified this. He was getting mostly Bs in university, whereas in high school he often got Cs. "I have certain standards and I guess I have been meeting most of my standards, which is good," he said. He has one course in which he is not doing well, but accepts that sometimes that happens. Heather described herself as a "B student" with a dream of getting an A⁺ one day. The second time I interviewed her she had achieved this dream and was ecstatic. Ann maintained an A⁻ average, both before and after getting hearing aids. With her hearing aids, she said,

> Like it's easier now so I don't have to work as hard. So that's where the difference is. The marks have kept the same. If I had worked as hard as I did before without my hearing aids with my hearing aids I would probably have got higher marks. Definitely. Like sometimes I don't catch important details so there would definitely be an improvement in certain situations.

Jennifer also felt her grades were affected by her hearing loss in that her writing skills were weak. Carol referred to having to modify her approach to studying so that she concentrated more on the instructor's comments than on the written text. Darcy was concerned about how he would do in French, which he had to repeat. However, some students felt that their hearing losses did not affect their grades. Sarah, whose grades were As, said her "hearing loss had nothing to do with my grades."

Discussion

Instructors are central to a positive learning experience for students with hearing losses. A positive relationship with instructors promotes course completion and academic retention (Pascarella and Terenzini 1991; Tinto 1982). In one respect, the nature of faculty interaction is different for students with hearing losses than it is for other students, namely, in relation to the additional communication challenges and students' accommodation needs. For example, instructors need to face the class when providing verbal information, rather than looking down at papers or speaking while writing on a blackboard. As well, there may also be additional accommodations that instructors need to provide, such as writing out any verbal instructions during examinations or providing copies of their lecture notes to students.

When students who are hard of hearing feel instructors are receptive, they are more likely to disclose their disabilities and to negotiate necessary disability-related accommodations, such as for exams and copies of lecture notes. They are also likely to remain steadfast in their academic pursuits if they feel welcome in the classroom. Furthermore, as a result of receptive attitudes, students who are hard of hearing are more likely to seek one-on-one discussions about course content with instructors than if they find their instructors to be intimidating.

Most students in my study described their interactions with faculty as being positive. However, students also discussed the lack of understanding of their hearing losses and the lack of attention to their needs on the part of a few faculty members. Students perceived that instructors were extremely busy and had limited time for student interactions. This was particularly felt to be the case for faculty instructing large classes.

Supporting findings from Hawkey (this volume), upper-year and graduate students were found to be more likely to have faculty contact and a connection to their discipline than first- and second-year students. This was particularly the case for the three graduate students in my study who were in the same master's program for educating teachers of students, who are deaf and hard of hearing. Furthermore, because of the nature of the program, these students expected and found that their instructors were sensitive to their hearing-related needs. Academic advising also appeared more utilized by students in upper levels or in the graduate programs.

A few students had discriminatory or extremely negative experiences when interacting with instructors. In one case, a faculty member refused to wear an FM transmitter required by the student to amplify sound. In another case, a student taking a distance education course was unable to hear the instructor and was refused a request to be provided the information in writing. In a third case, a student was refused acceptance into a work study program of the faculty because of the quality of his speaking voice. There were severe consequences for the students in each case: withdrawal from the course, failure in the course, and denial of a learning opportunity, respectively.

Distance education was not found to be a substitute for classroom learning for most students who are hard of hearing. It may suit some students, but predominately for reasons other than hearing loss. Other factors, such as being far away from campus, may be more important in the decision to take distance education classes. Two of the students in my study were taking courses by distance education; however, other students who were asked about this delivery method did not consider it an alternative to classroom learning. They preferred being in classes with other students, regardless of how difficult it was to hear classmates and instructors. Furthermore, those students who took distance education courses experienced some challenges; telephone conversations proved difficult in one case and videotapes were not captioned initially, causing delays in getting classroom material. Thus, some caution needs to be exercised in promoting distance education courses as the solution to overcoming in-class hearing difficulties for students who are hard of hearing.

The commitment of students to staying in school is important to completion (Hackman and Dysinger 1970; Tinto 1982). The retention model depicts a link between commitment and a student's grade point average (GPA),

while recognizing that a student's expectations play a large part in acceptance of GPA results. Thus, a student does not necessarily need to have a
high GPA to be committed to university but does need to feel that the grades
received are in accordance with expectations. In my study, the level of commitment of participants seemed unconnected to their grades. Students with
lower grades expressed a commitment as strong as those with higher grades,
as long as their grades matched their performance expectations. As well,
students who had hopes of improving their grades could accept low grades
as an interim step to better performance. If they were encouraged by their
instructors, low grades were viewed as a temporary state; these students
anticipated improving their grades and, therefore, were motivated to continue with their studies. Andres (2001) also found this to be the case.

My findings support the contention that goal commitment is related to
expectations. However, an additional factor at play for these students was
an ability to cope with adversity. Students noted that their experiences with
handling the difficulties of their disabilities built up their internal capacity
to manage difficulties encountered in university. They demonstrated ex-
ceptionally high levels of commitment to persisting in university, even in
the face of severe difficulties or, in some cases, having to contend with double
disabilities or other factors.

However, at times, even positive personal attitudes were insufficient to
overcome difficulties. Three students would have been drop-out statistics if
it were not for substantial program adaptations and supporting personnel.
Two of these students faced discriminatory practices. In one case an instructor refused to wear the transmitter of a student's FM system. This discriminatory behaviour, combined with other difficulties, resulted in the university
refunding the student's tuition and giving him a fresh start for the following year. This result occurred after the intervention of the university's Disability Services Office coordinator; that intervention was essential to this
particular student's retention. In the second case, a disability service provider external to the university was pivotal to the student's success. For the
third student, who was at risk of dropping out after doing poorly in two
tough courses during her first term, direct intervention by her academic
advisor turned the situation around. This student was so discouraged and
fearful that the rest of the program would be the same that she contem-
plated exiting from it. Her advisor restructured her full-time program to
enable her to take it on a part-time basis.

As noted, in two cases there were programmatic changes to the institution's
usual way of doing things. In other words, there were structural changes
that did not compromise the academic standards of the university. This suggests that, for some students, simply making programs and processes "equally"
available is insufficient for their retention. The institution needs to look at its
own structures and processes. In this respect the agency-structure concept

has meaning. The individual as agent is engaged in a struggle within the institution and reshapes the institution; at the same time, the individual is reshaped by the institution .

Students who are hard of hearing are both similar to other university students in many respects and different from other students. It is not contradictory that these two dimensions coexist because individual experience can be affected by a multitude of factors.

In terms of similarities, students appeared to experience university in the same way that other students did, depending on their previous life experiences, their expectations, their identity, the nature of their program, and the nature of their university. Although there is considerable variation among students who are hard of hearing, the participants in this study exhibited some general patterns found in studies of other university students related to age, year of study, and type of program. They also had similar experiences with respect to initial change in grades, and the nature of academic advising. Thus, in many respects, this study reinforced research findings about students in general, namely, that their grades often drop in the first year of university (Andres 2001; Andres et al. 1996); academic advising is important but not always available (Crockett 1985; Guppy and Bednarski 1993); and their level of involvement varies according to year of study (Hawkey 2000).

At the same time, students with hearing losses were different from other students. They differed in how they chose classes, taking into account instructor and classroom characteristics. Another factor in class choice was the nature of the class, namely whether it was lecture-based or discussion-oriented. Once a student was in a class, seat choice was influenced by hearing loss. The study participants also had different levels of participation in the class than other students, based on their ability to hear. Their ability to participate in informal conversations was impaired due to hearing difficulties, and certain types of milieus, such as cafeterias and coffee places, tended to be avoided. Students with normal hearing do not face such constraints.

The students participating in this study adapted to their university environment. They endeavoured to fit in, some of them using university disability-related resources. As persons who are hard of hearing, they are already predisposed to "fit" into a hearing world and to accommodate themselves to the demands of the hearing world. This may put students in the position of wanting to fit into the system and not expecting the system to change or be different on their account. They did not feel that they should impose significant change on the dynamics of the learning environment. Furthermore, their university environment tended to expect the same as well. To be sure, some accommodations and adjustments were made, but no evidence emerged from the research of a dramatic change in the system to ensure full hearing access for the students. However, there were examples that demonstrated that the post-secondary system shows capacity for change and modification on a retroactive basis. Two students would have been dropouts without institutional intervention.

The foregoing emphasizes the importance of considering the dynamic between structure, namely, the post-secondary institution, and the players within it, including students. The agency-structure nexus provides a framework for doing so. Based on Bourdieu's (1984) field of forces concept, it depicts the dynamic between the individual and the social system and recognizes that there are underlying structural influences that impact the individual. The concept acknowledges that students are agents with different degrees of competencies, resources, and strategies as they proceed through university. Although students may act, they also encounter people, policies, and practices, inside and outside the institution, that may constrain their ability to act (Andres, Andruske, and Hawkey 1996).

Retention models would benefit from the agency-structure nexus concept to ensure that the focus of retention activity is not solely aimed at individuals, in isolation from the larger social dynamics at play. Without this type of consideration, retention strategies may be unlikely to get at the systemic nature of difficulties and solutions, namely, those that are larger than the individual student and individual institution.

This study found that one of the key systemic challenges facing students who are hard of hearing is to become full members of the classroom community. The dynamic of wanting to fit in places students who are hard of hearing in the role of visitors to the classroom. Because instructors are key figures in promoting the involvement of students so that they are not visitors in the classroom, two recommendations are framed on this issue. The first recommendation calls for university senior administrators to ensure that faculty interaction with students is incorporated as part of faculty job descriptions and evaluation processes. Through these means, faculty-student interaction would be incorporated as an expectation of faculty.

The second recommendation to promote faculty-student interaction calls for university faculty development centres that would offer courses to faculty members on teaching methods fostering classroom participation, student development theory, and disability awareness. In particular, disability awareness should incorporate content about the nature of a hearing loss, its impacts on classroom learning, and strategies to promote communication and student involvement. Such courses should be mandatory for all university instructors. Such courses should incorporate follow-up opportunities for reinforcement and further training.

An additional implication of the present study is the need for educational institutions to design programs and courses that allow for a flexible courseload. A large number of the students interviewed for this study were taking a reduced courseload; the nature of their disability often meant a greater workload in dealing with courses and accommodations than experienced by other students. As a result, by taking a reduced courseload, they were more likely to be successful. Several were aware of their heavy investment and anxious to do well and succeed on account of it. Recommendations in this area call for extra time for course completion. For example, doctoral programs usually have a six- to seven-year limit; this should be adjusted for students taking a reduced load because of their hearing disability, or because of any other disability for that matter. In addition, institutional awards programs should not evaluate the longer completion time negatively.

Awareness-raising and education should also be aimed at students so that they have an understanding of the agency-structure dynamics at play in post-secondary education vis-à-vis the identity of being hard of hearing and trying to fit into the institution. They also need to be aware of their rights and responsibilities as students and the range of services and resources available to them. They are not alone in facing the challenges of university participation.

The findings of this study suggest several areas for further research, such as a participant observation study to explore whether, and the extent to which, students who are hard of hearing are visitors in the classroom. Such a study might include the examination of conversational timing and interactions with instructors and classmates, and would assess the students' participation in class discussions, engagements with other students during formal and informal class times, and interactions with instructors.

A study focused on instructors and other students would shed light on their perspectives of issues raised by students who are hard of hearing. The extent to which some accommodations are universal for all students, and others are specifically tailored for students with disabilities could be explored.

Comparison studies between students who are hard of hearing and other students could help ascertain the commonalities and differences the students share. In this respect, it would become more possible to delineate aspects of post-secondary experiences that may be disability-related versus those that apply to all students.

Students who are hard of hearing strive to fit into the university, to behave as if they were hearing students. But the very nature of their disability often results in their being unable to hear instructors and other students in the classroom and, thus, affects their ability to be full classroom participants. Instead, they are often visitors to the classroom and thus not fully integrated.

Hearing loss also results in a differential pattern of participation for students who are hard of hearing. They choose classes based on their hearing loss, and many of them study on a part-time basis to better manage their disability and studies.

Regardless of pattern of participation and difficulties encountered, students were highly committed to university life. However, even that commitment would have been insufficient without exceptional intervention by others on their behalf.

The agency-structure nexus enables a fuller understanding of the dynamics at play between students, the institution, and other players in the institution. The incorporation of this framework into retention models would add to our understanding of retention dynamics.

Notes

1 A different course may be substituted in place of a conversational language course due to a student's disability affecting the learning of a language. In the case of hard-of-hearing students, difficulties hearing a foreign language may qualify them for a course substitution.

2 Categories of hearing loss are organized as follows:

Profound – 91 decibel loss and greater often requires signing, oral interpreting, or captioning.

Severe – 71 to 90 decibel loss means students hear loud noises at close distances and require individual hearing aids, intensive auditory training, and specialized instruction in language development.

Moderate to severe – 56 to 70 decibel loss means that without amplification students with this degree of loss can miss up to 100 percent of speech information. Full-time use of amplification is essential.

Moderate – 41 to 55 decibel loss means classroom conversation from 3 to 5 feet away can be understood if the structure and vocabulary are controlled. Hearing aids and/or personal FM systems are considered essential.

Mild – 26 to 40 decibel loss means a student may miss up to 50 percent of class discussions, especially if voices are soft or the environment is noisy.

Minimal loss – 16 to 25 decibel loss means students may have difficulty with faint or distant speech and conversation that proceeds too rapidly. (BC Ministry of Education 1994, 3)

3 An FM system includes a receiver worn by the user to amplify sounds that are being broadcast or reflected from the speaker's transmitter.

References

Andres, L. 1992. *Paths on Life's Way: Destinations, Determinants, and Decisions in the Transition from High School*. Unpublished doctoral dissertation, University of British Columbia, Vancouver.

–. 1993. Life Trajectories, Action, and Negotiating the Transition from High School. In *Transitions: Schooling and Employment in Canada*, edited by P. Anisef and P. Axelrod, 137-57. Toronto: Thompson Press.

–. 2001. Transfer from Community College to University: Perspectives and Experiences of British Columbia Students. *The Canadian Journal of Higher Education* 31, 1: 35-74.

Andres, L., C. Andruske, and C.L. Hawkey. 1996. *Mapping the Realities of First Year Post-Secondary Life: A Study of Students at Three Post-Secondary Institutions*. Vancouver: University of British Columbia, Centre for Policy Studies in Education.

Antia, S.D., M.S. Stinson, and M.G. Gaustad. 2002. Developing Membership in the Education of Deaf and Hard-of-Hearing Students in Inclusive Settings. *Journal of Deaf Studies and Deaf Education* 7: 214-29.

Bean, J.P., and R.K. Bradley. 1986. Untangling the Satisfaction-Performance Relationship for Colleges. *Journal of Higher Education* 57: 393-412.

Bourdieu, P. 1984. *Distinction. A Social Critique of the Judgement of Taste*. Translated by R. Nice. Cambridge: Harvard University Press.

British Columbia Ministry of Education Special Education Branch. 1994. *Hard of Hearing and Deaf Students: A Resource Guide to Support Classroom Teachers*. Victoria, BC: BC Ministry of Education Special Education Branch.

Crockett, D.S. 1985. Academic Advising. In *Increasing Student Retention*, edited by L. Noel, R. Levitz, and D. Saluri and Associates, 244-63. San Francisco: Jossey-Bass.

Foster, S., G. Long, and K. Snell. 1999. Inclusive Instruction and Learning for Deaf Students in Postsecondary Education. *Journal of Deaf Studies and Deaf Education* 4: 225-35.

Guppy, N., and V. Bednarski. 1993. *Enhancing Student Retention in Higher Education: A Literature Review*. Report for the British Columbia Council on Admissions and Transfer. Vancouver: University of British Columbia, Department of Anthropology and Sociology.

Guppy, N., and M. Trew. 1995. *Graduate Student Experience at UBC: An Assessment*. Vancouver: University of British Columbia.

Hackman, R., and W.S. Dysinger. 1970. Commitment to College as a Factor in Student Attrition. *Sociology of Education* 43: 311-24.

Hawkey, C.L. 2000. *Patterns of Participation, Modes of Exclusion: Undergraduate Students' Experience of Community at a Research-Intensive University*. Unpublished doctoral dissertation, University of British Columbia.

Jones, L. 1993. *Education and Deaf and Hard of Hearing Adults: A Handbook*. Leicester, UK: National Institute for Adult and Continuing Education.

Killean, E., and D. Hubka. 1999. *Working toward a Coordinated National Approach to Services, Accommodations and Policies for Post-Secondary Students with Disabilities: Ensuring Access to Higher Education and Career Training*. Ottawa: National Educational Association of Disabled Students.

Leyser, Y., S. Vogel, A. Brulle, and S. Wyland. 1998. Faculty Attitudes and Practices Regarding Students with Disabilities: Two Decades after Implementation of Section 504. *Journal of Postsecondary Education and Disability* 13, 3: 5-19.

Lingen, P.D. 1993. Post-Secondary Planning for Integrated Deaf and Hard of Hearing Students. *Vibrations* (Summer): 10-11.

Marshall, C., and G.B. Rossman. 1999. *Designing Qualitative Research*, 3rd ed. Thousand Oaks, CA: Sage.

Pascarella, E.T., and P.T. Terenzini. 1980. Predicting Freshman Persistence and Voluntary Dropout Decisions from a Theoretical Model. *Journal of Higher Education* 5: 60-75.

–. 1991. *How College Affects Students. Findings and Insights from Twenty Years of Research*. San Francisco: Jossey-Bass.

Patterson, K., and M. Schmidt. 1992. Preparing the College Student with Hearing Loss for Success. *Volta Review* 194: 47-57.

Rodda, M., and C. Hiron. 1989. Postsecondary Educational Services for Deaf and Hard of Hearing Students in Canada: A Survey of Need. *ACEHI Journal* 15, 2: 45-56.

Schein, J.D. 1991. Postsecondary Education for Alberta's Students with Impaired Hearing. In *Postsecondary Education for Deaf Students*, edited by E.G. Wolf-Schein and J.D. Schein, 144-68. Edmonton: University of Alberta.

Secord, S. 1999. It's All a Matter of Timing. *Listen* 7, 3 (Spring): 18.

Smith, J.K. 1989. *The Nature of Social and Educational Inquiry: Empiricism versus Interpretation*. Norwood, NJ: Ablex.

Stinson, M.S., and S.D. Antia. 1999. Considerations in Educating Deaf and Hard-of-Hearing Students in Inclusive Settings. *Journal of Deaf Studies and Deaf Education* 4: 163-75.

Stinson, M.S., M.J. Scherer. and G.G. Walter. 1987. Factors Affecting Persistence of Deaf College Students. *Research in Higher Education* 27: 244-58.

Stinson, M.S., and G.G. Walter. 1992. Persistence in College. In *Deaf Students in Postsecondary Education*, edited by S.B. Foster and G.G. Walter, 43-60. London: Routledge.

Swartz, K., and N.K. Israelite. 2000. *Negotiating the University Environment: Perspectives of Students Who Are Hard of Hearing.* Paper presented at the International Congress on Education of the Deaf, Sydney, Australia, July.

Terenzini, P.T., W.G. Lorang, and E.T. Pascarella. 1981. Predicting Freshman Persistence and Voluntary Dropout Decisions: A Replication. *Research in Higher Education* 15: 109-27.

Tinto, V. 1982. Limits of Theory and Practice in Student Attrition. *Journal of Higher Education* 53: 687-700.

–. 1987. *Leaving College. Rethinking the Causes and Cures of Student Attrition.* Chicago: University of Chicago Press.

–. 1997. Classrooms as Communities: Exploring the Educational Character of Student Persistence. *Journal of Higher Education* 68: 599-623.

Warick, R. 1994. A Profile of Canadian Hard of Hearing Youth. *Journal of Speech-Language Pathology and Audiology* 18: 253-59.

–. 1997. *Hearing the Learning: A Post-Secondary Education Handbook for Students Who Are Hard of Hearing.* Ottawa: Canadian Hard of Hearing Association.

–. 1998. *Classroom Hearing Accessibility in Post-Secondary Education: A Student Perspective.* Paper presented at the symposium of the Institute of Hearing Research Accessibility, University of British Columbia, Vancouver, February.

5
Disciplinary Affiliation and the Experience of Community among Undergraduate Students
Colleen Hawkey

A hallmark of the contemporary university is its disciplinary-based organizational structure and curricular focus. Disciplinary differences are deeply entrenched and significantly influence students' experiences, both within and outside of the classroom. Although the influence of discipline on learning, integration, and student success has been acknowledged (e.g., Hativa and Marincovich 1995; Kolb 1981), little work has focused on the discipline as a learning community. Indeed, the meaning of *community* itself and the numerous ways in which students experience community, has been little explored, even though it often informs empirical investigation in higher education and shapes fundamental assumptions about educational practices for researchers and educators alike. This chapter reports on a study that examines the parameters and meaning of the academic discipline as a community for a group of third-year undergraduate students enrolled in a research-intensive university. In-depth interviews (N = 23) and a survey (N = 75) were administered to psychology students pursuing either a bachelor of arts or a bachelor of science degree at a large research-intensive university. The study explores the role of disciplinary affiliation in students' sense of community – the structural, social, and cultural forces that contribute to community membership, integration, and involvement.

Literature Review
Cultural differences associated with disciplinary affiliation have long been recognized as creating distinctive teaching and learning communities within a university setting. King and Brownell identify a discipline as an interest community characterized by a concern with the pursuit of knowledge, with the "ultimate task ... [of] the gaining of meaning" (1966, 68). Specifically each discipline may be considered a unique community, the members of which "share a domain of intellectual inquiry or discourse" (68). Evidence of distinctive disciplinary communities based on ways of knowing is supported by the empirical work of Becher, who writes that "there are identifiable

patterns to be found within the relationship between knowledge forms and their associated knowledge communities" (1989, 150). Kolb argues that "for students, education in an academic field is a continuing process of selection and socialization to the pivotal norms of the field governing criteria for truth and how it is to be achieved, communicated, and used, and secondarily, to peripheral norms governing personal styles, attitudes, and social relationships" (1981, 233).

Identifying a congruence between students' learning styles and academic interests and the "learning demands" of particular disciplines, Kolb presented data in support of the hypothesis that over time "selection and socialization pressures combine to produce an increasingly impermeable and homogeneous disciplinary culture and correspondingly specialized student orientations to learning" (234). The combination of these factors contributes to a greater degree of "fit" between individual students and their particular discipline. Conversely, a lack of fit results in increased alienation and greater risk of academic failure.

The importance of integration into social and academic communities for student persistence is articulated by Tinto (1975, 1993), who developed a theory of student withdrawal based on rites of passage and community membership. Tinto (1993) proposed that students who were more fully integrated socially and academically would be less likely to withdraw from university. Successful integration involved movement through a series of stages (separation, transition, and incorporation) from one community or set of communities (e.g., home or work) to the communities of the university. The failure or unwillingness to "become integrated as competent members" (1993, 104) of the social and intellectual communities of the university would increase the likelihood of voluntary withdrawal. The initial utility of Tinto's community integration model for traditional-age undergraduate students has been confirmed (e.g., Bean 1982; Pascarella and Terenzini 1991), and Tinto (1997) later expanded this work to explore the influence of classrooms as communities on student retention and integration.

It is assumed in this study that the definition of community could be extended to a learning community bounded by disciplinary affiliation. This option is rarely explored in the research literature even though evidence of the strength of disciplinary ties is reported by Kolb (1981), and disciplinary influences on the undergraduate student learning environment have been reported by a number of researchers (Donald 1997; Hativa and Marincovich 1995; Kuh and Whitt 1988). Disciplinary ties are rooted in an established approach to knowledge production and dissemination, and in the structural organization of universities. It makes sense, then, to come to an understanding of the processes and mechanisms of student membership and integration within a disciplinary community. Accordingly, the purpose of this study was to explore the experience of community for a group of students who share a disciplinary affiliation; it is assumed this approach will be a valuable first step in understanding the possibilities for community in the discipline-based, research-intensive university.

A number of questions were of interest in this study: How do third-year students experience the disciplinary community? What mechanisms facilitate or inhibit students' integration within the community? As Kolb (1981) suggests, what "socialization pressures" shape students' community involvement? How do students become members and what is their "status" within the community?

Research Methods, Study Participants, and the Research Site

This study employed two complementary strategies. First, twenty-three in-depth interviews were conducted with third-year psychology students;[1] second, a survey based on findings from the interviews, and from previous research on undergraduate students and community, was administered to third-year psychology students enrolled the following year. Interview volunteers were recruited from January to April 1998 using posters, in-class invitations, and snowball techniques. The gender distribution of interviewees was identical to the actual eligible third-year cohort, with women comprising 74 percent and men 26 percent of interviewees. Interviews, which lasted between forty-five minutes and two and a half hours, were conducted in a meeting room on campus, were audiotaped, transcribed, and inductively coded. Interviewees were given a $10 honorarium. Third-year psychology students were surveyed[2] beginning in January 1999; a reminder letter followed by a second questionnaire was sent out in early and late February 1999. The questionnaire, consisting of both open-ended and Likert-type questions developed from interviews and relevant literature, was pilot tested with the interviewees from the first phase of the study. The adjusted response rate was 62 percent, with 75 questionnaires returned from 122 eligible respondents.

At the research site, psychology is dominated by women at the undergraduate level, but in this study, women survey respondents (85 percent) were slightly overrepresented compared with the actual population of women (78 percent) and the women interviewees (74 percent). Although it is not uncommon for women to be more likely to respond to survey questionnaires than men, it is important to bear in mind the overall number of respondents and the relatively small number of potential male respondents. There were 28 (23 percent) eligible males in the survey sample and 13 (17 percent) male survey respondents; only 6 of the 23 interviewees were male.

The study was conducted at what is being called RIU (research-intensive university), the largest university in the province in terms of physical space and in terms of enrolments. In 1997-98, over 26,000 undergraduate students and approximately 5,000 graduate students were enrolled. Most undergraduate students (73 percent) attended full-time. Slightly over half of all full-time undergraduate students at RIU were women (54 percent), and 90 percent of all undergraduates were between the ages of 18 and 26 years old.

Conceptual Framework

A constitutive conception of community provides a framework for this study. The constitutive conception of community assumes a strong sense of unity between members; it implies "commonly situated subjects discovering their identity" (Corlett 1989, 21) through their participation in the community. One's identity is established by the subjective position each member inhabits within the community; a member's position is both enabling and constraining, depending on his or her location in relation to other members in the field (Howard 1997). This notion of community implies an agent acting within boundaries established by her or his position within a community. As the literature suggests, students form identities as community members over time and in relation to their experiences. Their perception of their status and the perceptions others hold of their status within the community has an impact on their opportunities, level of involvement, and the nature of their social interactions.

Cohen suggests that a reasonable interpretation of the word community implies that "members of a group of people (a) have something in common with each other, which (b) distinguishes them in a significant way from members of other putative groups" (1985, 12). This is perhaps an obvious statement, but the implications of it are frequently masked by the very word signified: *community* evokes images of consensus and commonality, but ultimately that commonality is expressed in opposition to some other. A community necessarily separates the "pure" from the "impure," authentic from inauthentic, because the "essence sought receives its meaning and purity only by its relation to its outside" (236). This oppositional dynamic also operates within the community itself insofar as it serves to differentiate between core and peripheral members. Membership "implies marginalization of those on the periphery inside and exclusion of others outside the community" (Atkinson and Cope 1997, 203). Similar "splitting" of communities into parts was noted by Brent, who demonstrated how "unacceptable parts within" (1997, 80) could be denied full membership benefits.

Findings

The purpose of this study was to explore and report on students' experiences within a particular community, in the case of this study, the disciplinary community of the psychology department at RIU, from the point of view of students. Four key concepts were identified from interviews and further explored in the survey: transition, competency development, research as a mechanism of integration, and membership status. Each theme is discussed below in detail.

Transition

A key element of students' experiences is the transition from integration in the social communities of the university to integration in the academic community. This transition is characterized by a general pattern of movement away from social preoccupations toward more academically oriented activities. When students first enrol, post-secondary education signals a time to enjoy newfound freedoms, including, for many, social activities associated with drinking alcohol. "Partying" and "clubbing" were noteworthy activities for a number of students, even among those students who lived at home with parents. In addition to "partying," being involved in a variety of other social activities was a significant aspect of students' experiences in first year. These activities included joining one or more campus clubs, participating in intramural sports, or using the fitness facilities on campus. Both types of activities began to diminish in importance by third year. One student commented that "it was good to party, have a good time, fit in with the first-year crowd" but at some point it was imperative to stop: "you've got to ... draw the line." Almost all interviewees talked about undergoing a social-to-academic transition. Two students described the social-to-academic shift in terms of percentages. One student said if she were to "make a ratio out of them, extracurricular was 60 percent, and studying was 40, whereas now it's more like extracurricular 40, studying 60." Another identified the same "60-40 split ... [It] was 60 in the first year, then it sort of bumped down to 50 last year" and so on. He continued: "you just started realizing ... going out Monday, Tuesday, Wednesday, Friday ... wasn't so beneficial!"

Astin (1984) points out that the amount of energy (mental and physical) that one devotes to a particular endeavour contributes to one's integration and an enhanced sense of belonging. The gradual reduction of intensive involvement in the social communities of the university was an integral first step toward giving more energy to academic involvement and the eventual integration into the disciplinary community that would result. Interviewees expressed less interest in socializing with friends than they did in the first two years. In contrast, they expressed a desire to engage more intimately and meaningfully with the course material and with their professors. This was also prompted by greater academic demands:

> The stuff that we're doing ... in third year or fourth year, it's really time consuming, so unless you're doing exactly the same thing it's really hard to find time to spend time together.

Findings elicited through a survey questionnaire support the comments made by interviewees. Although survey respondents indicated they were more engaged socially (mean[3] of 4.31), social activities on campus had become less important (mean of 3.96). Academic interests (mean of 5.05) and engagement (mean of 5.38) had both become considerably more important. These changed patterns of participation within the social communities of the universities signalled the development of conditions that contributed to further integration into the disciplinary community and the development of an "academic affinity" with it.

Competency Development

Building a knowledge base was an integral step in the process of developing competencies associated with community membership. Advanced-level coursework and involvement with research played key roles. There were two main aspects to the knowledge-base development of students. One was cultural, the other intellectual. Both interacted to produce a nascent identity as psychology student or even psychologist. Greater distinction between students as participating members of the disciplinary community and their awareness of their position within it was ever more apparent. Socialization is an act of production and reproduction that enables a community to renew itself over time. Only a few undergraduate students will eventually pursue an advanced degree, and of those, even fewer will aspire to a PhD in psychology, thereby reproducing the disciplinary community. However, in the shorter term, the socialization process contributes to student involvement in the disciplinary community insofar as it defines boundaries of discourse between faculty and students, and enables their interaction. Within the psychology department, research was an integral element of the undergraduate curriculum. Participating in research projects provided a reason to frequent the psychology building, and offered a window through which students could "see what [was] going on" in the department. Participation contributed to students' awareness of the culture of their discipline and provided a point of contact between undergraduate students and graduate students and faculty members.

The integration of students into the research culture of their discipline was evidenced by the language used throughout the interviews. One student who was involved in a research project with a faculty member in which they were studying human development talked about going to the psychology building between classes in order to "run a baby at the lab." This meant the "subjects" were "run through a couple more of the studies" and the data entered in a statistical database on a computer. Running experiments, testing hypotheses, filling in questionnaires, and measuring causal relationships were all common phrases used by students when discussing their involvement with research or when discussing psychology in general. Students learned the language specific to their discipline from textbooks, faculty, and graduate students. One student relayed a story about being corrected for using "inappropriate" language in relation to animal experiments:

> I said "kill" once, because ... I mean I'm really blunt and I said kill, the animal dies, you kill it. And the graduate student I work with, she got really offended, she said, "Sacrifice!" And I know with even "depriving" I used to say "starving" them and she said "No! Depriving them."

Learning the language of their discipline was one aspect of developing a broader knowledge base in psychology, which also included learning the history of the discipline, foundation theories all core members of the community knew, and accepted procedures for knowledge generation and validation. As another student pointed out, it was important for students to "get the technical lingo down to understand what's being developed" in terms of ideas in class. This student was skeptical that students had achieved this ability before third year, "maybe in second year, but in first year, definitely not." Others confirmed that students needed "that background" in order to participate in the disciplinary community in the area of research and in classroom discussions. It was suggested that "first or second year of study [was] quite general and students [were] not quite expected to ... really go that deep." Similarly, another student argued that in first year courses students were "not really learning anything ground-breaking. Sort of the stuff you need for your foundations." Part way through, third-year students had taken sufficient numbers of courses specifically related to their discipline to accumulate a substantial body of knowledge.

Research as a Mechanism for Integration
For psychology students, research is a key mechanism for involvement within the academic community. There are several ways a student can become involved as a researcher or research assistant in the psychology department at RIU. One is as part of a credit course. Bachelor of science psychology students were required to enrol in a course that, as one student put it, "incorporated a large chunk of [their] mark into helping out with research." Students are expected to "get hooked up with a prof" who would supervise them on a small project that was usually a part of the professor's larger research program. The student was required to engage with the research process from conceptualization of a research question and the development of appropriate hypotheses, through data collection, analysis, and finally the writing of a research report. The students were involved in a wide variety of projects, all of which entailed working closely with an assigned professor. Arts psychology students were not required to take the course described

above or an equivalent, but one arts interviewee had enrolled in a directed studies course that allowed him to conduct a research project of his own, under the supervision of a professor. According to the survey respondents, 9 percent of arts psychology students had worked under the supervision of a professor on a research project as part of their degree, compared with all of the BSc psychology students.

A second way that students could be involved in research in the psychology laboratories was to volunteer as research assistants. This was something both bachelor of science and bachelor of arts students did. Becoming a volunteer could be the result of having established a relationship with a professor from class, and being in the right place at the right time, as was the case for this student:

> I was sitting in a lab doing whatever the day's thing was and I saw my psychology professor from last year, and she recognized me ... And she said "This is very similar to what I do in my lab," and I was like "Oh, hey, can I volunteer?" And she said, "Sure come on in."

Other students had to be much more proactive if they wanted to volunteer. One student, who wanted to get into graduate school, visited several counsellors to ask their advice and was told "it's a good idea if you have some background in doing laboratory work."

> So, I printed out a whole bunch of letters and stuff and then I sent it to all the profs and to ... assistants in their labs. So, some called back, so I'm in two labs right now.

There was a third group of students comprised of arts students who either did not know about the research opportunities, were not interested in them, or were certain that they would be excluded from participating and so did not pursue the possibility of volunteering in a professor's lab. According to one interviewee, this kind of work was for "other" students. Another interviewee noted that if students wanted to do research outside of the course requirements, they had to "push" a bit. "You have to approach the profs, and be interested and get them to let you do studies with them."

For those students who did engage in research, either as part of their course or on a volunteer basis, the rewards were substantial. In addition to gaining greater access to professors, students who were involved as researchers or research assistants felt privileged and developed a strong sense of belonging to the disciplinary community. Among survey respondents who participated in these types of research projects, 75 percent strongly agreed and 13 percent somewhat agreed that their participation had made them feel more a part of the psychology department. One factor that contributed to students' sense of belonging was access to a physical place to "be" on campus where students were known and knew other people – access to a place where they "commanded" the attention of others (Rosenberg and McCullough 1981). Several interviewees commented that giving undergraduate students keys or codes so they could gain access to research labs was a sign of respect and trust. One student felt a sense of privilege and responsibility that resulted from the task with which she was entrusted:

> And feeling respect, though as an undergrad ... you do get that sense of trust as well. Like Dr. A. gave me the code to get into her lab any time. And she said any time you feel like, you know [come in] ... And for one of her experiments I made, sort of like a fluid, which was necessary ... to run her equipment. And it's hard, I mean if I contaminate it, that's it. Like you're in trouble, the machine will get contaminated, everything. And she let me do it ... And that really, you know, meant a lot to me.

Another key aspect of feelings of belonging was articulated by a student who pointed out that she had the opportunity to contribute meaningfully to the research project:

> I'm doing research, I'm actively involved in the department, like I'm actually contributing to what they're doing there ... I leave and I feel I've done something and it's good.

Most survey respondents who had participated in this type of research strongly (38 percent) or somewhat (50 percent) agreed that they had made important contributions to the research project. When assuming the active role of researcher or "experimenter," students felt they learned a great deal about their discipline (100 percent) and their participation contributed to feelings that they were "more a part of the psychology department" (87 percent agreed or strongly agreed that this was so).

One of the most frequently identified benefits to result from participating in research projects as a researcher was the increased interaction with professors, teaching assistants, or laboratory assistants:

> I liked getting to know the prof and the other students working on the project. It was also valuable experience on research. I enjoyed conducting the experiment.

> It let me experience firsthand what research is really all about. It also showed me how research is conducted for studies heading for publication. It was good to interact with professors and grad students.

Some study participants recognized that students who were involved with this type of research were a privileged group. As one of them said, as a result, her undergraduate experience was qualitatively different from other students' experiences:

> I totally think that if I didn't have this, it would be very much a different experience ... If I hadn't forced myself to, like, actively seek out what I want, if I had just been really lackadaisical and just, been like "Whatever, what comes, comes" ... then I think you'd be talking to somebody quite different.

Students' participation in the disciplinary community as researchers and as research assistants highlights both the benefits they derived from their participation and the inability of the department to afford the same privileges to all students. It was interesting to note that although 10 percent of arts students had worked or were working under the supervision of a professor on a research project, 43 percent expected to be able to do so in the future. Although it was an experience all bachelor of science psychology students would eventually have, arts students were required to find some way to actively participate in this significant aspect of the community.

Closely related to the opportunities for research for select members of the psychology community was the notion of physical space. In contrast to those who had access to the psychology building because of their volunteer or work commitments, many students did not have easy access to "psychology space" in which they could meet other psychology students or faculty. The contrast between those who did and those who did not have such access to a "home base" demonstrated that the spatial aspect of community is of great significance for undergraduate students. Place is a customary meaning of the word community, and although an incomplete conceptualization, it is nonetheless important; as Poplin points out, in the day-to-day activities of people it is impossible to "transcend space" (1979, 11). This is evident for students who spoke about the importance of places for them to gather and talk. In the absence of such places, students are isolated and sometimes lonely. According to a survey respondent,

> RIU does a pathetic job at building a good student atmosphere. I know of many people who didn't know where to go and ate lunch in their cars alone. I've seen many people sitting in the hallways because there's nowhere else to go.

Other survey respondents suggested it would not be difficult to "create better meeting places," preferably lounge spaces with such things as kettles and microwave ovens, more comfortable furniture, and less "harsh fluorescent lighting." Being in a place, or as one student said, "having somewhere to hang out," develops a sense of belonging and contributes to the creation of disciplinary identity.

At the same time, place is a defining characteristic of membership status. Discussions of space and place began to bring into focus the relative status of undergraduate students compared with other community members – graduate students, students in other disciplines, and faculty. According to interviewees, the psychology building was equipped with a lounge, but it was restricted to graduate students. Unlike other buildings that had cafeterias or lounges, there was no "social space" in the psychology building for undergraduate students. The psychology building was primarily for research and faculty offices and did not provide space for most students to just "hang out." In addition, unlike students of other disciplines, who had designated learning spaces that students identified as theirs, undergraduate psychology students were required to "borrow" other disciplines' space. An interviewee put it this way:

> One thing that's amazing with the [psychology] building ... there's no lecture rooms. You know, like, psychology students have to go [to another building] to have their lectures. Whereas, like, if you're a physiology student, if you're a chemistry student, each building has their own lecture hall.

Membership Status
Transition processes, competency development, and research tasks were key elements in positioning students to be more active participants in the disciplinary community. Students reported a different kind of experience with professors compared with previous years, and an altered personal orientation toward their academic work. Not only were students showing a greater capacity for and interest in the academic aspects of their education, they also perceived that faculty were "letting them in" to participate in the disciplinary community in ways they had not done previously. The literature on the development of an identity as a member of a specific community suggests that individuals define and redefine themselves over time – identity is constructed through social interaction, and an identity assumed by an individual and accepted by others locates an individual within a particular social space. The redefinition of oneself as a "more serious student," as one interviewee said, corresponded with the perception that faculty were treating them as more valued members of the disciplinary community.

For example, students commented on the nature of advanced-level courses compared with lower-level courses. One student noted that "second-year courses are still really basic courses. And you have to take them. They're really, really basic and really boring." Similarly, speaking specifically of psychology courses, another noted that "first year was more general because they're trying to give ... a general introduction to Psych ... trying to give a bit of history ... to touch on a lot of different ... schools within psychology." Only once the foundation had been laid were courses "a lot more interesting" and "in-depth."

These changes in the nature of students' academic abilities and interests were key prerequisites to feelings of belonging to the disciplinary community and were a sign of growth toward "competent membership" (Tinto 1993, 121) within it. Research within the classroom was similarly an indicator that drew attention to the shifting relationship between faculty and students. Upper-level psychology courses had a strong research focus compared with other courses within and outside of psychology. In addition to enabling students to participate in research projects, faculty typically incorporated results from this research into their course lectures. Faculty tended to integrate current research into their lectures so that "the lectures were all on the newest, up-to-date papers with the most interesting things that had to do with the subject. So, it was fascinating." This approach was something that was less likely to happen in "first and second year [where] it was more ... strictly based on the ... textbook" because "it just doesn't work" with lower-level students. Students discussed the use of research examples as part of a different kind of connection with faculty. Rather than being lectured "at" from a textbook, students felt that faculty were acknowledging undergraduates as competent members of the disciplinary community by offering insights into faculty research projects and sharing with them work in progress. According to one student, one result of integrating current research with upper-level lectures was that

> you sort of get the impression that the ideas you come up with now, because you're on top of the field, are questions that maybe could be further research; you're sort of that close to it being in third and fourth year.

Interviewees talked about enjoying the classroom experience more than they had in previous years and attributed this in large part to a more meaningful relationship with their psychology professors. Even though students would identify professors they considered to be poor teachers, on the whole students were positive about the instruction in their upper-level courses. This was also linked to interviewees' first-year experiences. One described his first year as a "learning experience" that included surmounting the "hurdle" of "incompetent professors," by which he meant professors who "just didn't seem to realize that they're not teaching" or who were dismissive of students' queries and requests for help. Another student suggested that first year was a "filtering out" process. Faculty were seen as reluctant to invest energy in students who would not be long-term members of the academic community. Such students would also be ineligible candidates for future membership in a particular disciplinary community.

> It seems like profs know first and second year; they're not trying to excite you they're just sort of "Okay, I've done this for twenty years, here it is. Here's another batch of first years, half of you aren't going to be here next year." So, they don't really care.

By comparison, once students reached third year they reported having experiences with a greater proportion of "better," "more interesting," "nicer," and "responsive" professors. According to one student, once in third year, "it definitely seems like the quality of the professors ... has been night and day. I've run into a lot more quality professors ... I'm sure it's not just me. I'm sure it's them."

Students also perceived their relationships with professors as qualitatively different from what they had been in previous years:

> The profs lecture more as if they respect you for knowing stuff. Whereas before, they were just kind of, they're on this automatic pilot where they spiel off their first-year science lecture number ten. And then they go.

> This is what's really nice about moving up. I think through the years you get your better professors who are interested in the topics they're teaching and interested in you as a person learning what they have to say.

> You've been exposed to enough knowledge now that your ideas aren't just sort of stupid questions that the prof is going to answer, because half of the time the prof can't answer them because you're asking questions that maybe have never been asked before.

> I think all the profs I have ... are the top ... As you get higher up, I think they really know their stuff, like, you know, you think you stumped them, but you know, but here they are coming up with [the answers].

Once again, the link with the important phase of competency development is emphasized. The knowledge base that students have developed in the first two years of their program facilitates the establishment of a relationship between faculty and students "on a different level." As evident among survey respondents, there was support for interviewees' perceptions: 61 percent of survey respondents agreed that psychology professors had greater respect for their ideas now that they were in third year.

Discussion

The processes of building a knowledge base and learning the values, languages, and knowledge assumptions associated with psychology were key competencies that required more time and engagement with the discipline. Coursework and involvement with research were integral aspects of this competency. Students underwent a transition from a greater interest in and preoccupation with social pursuits and activities to a greater interest in and engagement with academic aspects of their university experience. Respondents were more focused on academic goals, were more engaged academically, and found academic work more interesting.

These changes corresponded with a perception among interviewees that coursework and professors were qualitatively better now that they were in third year. Interviewees suggested that professors treated students differently in first and second year because of the high expected attrition rate, but once students were in the upper-year levels, professors treated them with more "respect" and with interest and concern about what they were learning. Students also suggested that this difference was related to their ability to ask "intelligent" questions and to challenge professors in their fields of expertise. The data reveal the longitudinal process of establishing oneself as an actively participating member of the disciplinary community and demonstrate that members of a community are "situated" insofar as "the subject positions they inhabit are constituted by the particular community" (Howard 1997, 130). Competency development and a growing interest in academic aspects of their undergraduate experience helped to reposition students from peripheral to core community members.

The competency development and transition processes enabled greater participation in the disciplinary community at the same time that they defined the parameters of that participation. As students interested in psychology, and as interested psychology students, a new kind of relationship with faculty emerged. As suggested by their discussions of feelings of greater competence and comfort within the classroom that enabled students to more freely address their teachers, contribute more to classroom discussions, and intellectually challenge faculty with questions that had not yet been asked or that they might not be able to answer, students "spoke" with a stronger voice that was more easily "heard" by faculty. The data reveal the evolution of an identity, highlighting the social repositioning of students that eventually resulted from it.

A key power relationship affecting the lives of undergraduate students is that which exists between students and faculty. Romer and Whipple (1991) identify undergraduate students as existing at the lowest levels of a "power line" compared with faculty, who reside at the top. Despite the power imbalance, students were able to develop a stronger subject position within the disciplinary community, which resulted in the acquisition of power resources. In this study, it was evident that over time students acquired greater resources, such as information about the values and culture of the disciplinary community, relevant theories and research procedures, greater understanding of the effort and time needed to meet academic requirements, and confidence in their academic abilities. The mechanisms that facilitate the acquisition of resources are highlighted. Developing competence and the process of transition contribute to the repositioning of students as more powerful actors within the disciplinary community insofar as these actions serve to endow students with greater resource capacity. For example, the accumulation of a knowledge base in psychology provided students with additional resources with which to engage with other community members, and especially with faculty. The transition from social to academic interests helped to redefine students as "more serious" participants in the disciplinary community and thus enhanced their status as academically competent participants within the community.

Evident in this study was the role faculty played in "letting students in" to the disciplinary community. Students prior to third year often felt as if they were "just a number" and that faculty were not interested in them as community members. By third year students were beginning to perceive a positive difference in the way that faculty treated them. Students readily recognized their own maturation and development as they progressed through their courses, but they also recognized that faculty were "gatekeepers" who to a certain extent controlled access to involvement in the disciplinary community, whether through the presentation of stimulating and interesting lectures or access to laboratories as research assistants and researchers. The power of faculty to control students' involvement in the disciplinary community extended from the laboratory to the classroom, and the manner in which students participated in the disciplinary community was a reflection of the interest and expectations of faculty. This aspect of student-faculty interaction was particularly evident in the way in which students assessed their relationship with faculty before third year. Interviewees identified first-year students in particular as generally not ready to engage with the community in terms of its academic content. A period of knowledge development was required to position them as competent community members.

As noted, the literature indicates that at the upper levels, academic integration is of greater importance to student success and retention than is social integration, which plays a more important role in the transition to university for first-year students (e.g., Ferguson 1990; Terenzini, Theophilides, and Lorang 1984; Tinto 1993). The dominant models of retention and attrition in Canada have been adapted from the work of researchers in the United

States, in particular from the work of Tinto (1975, 1993). One of the key concepts informing the retention model put forth by Tinto involves the successful integration of students into the social and intellectual communities of the university. Tinto suggests that early voluntary withdrawal from university is the result of not becoming a competent member of at least one community in the university. Researchers (e.g., Bean 1982; Pascarella and Terenzini 1991) have shown that as students progress through their degree, the importance of integration into the disciplinary community gains in significance. This study has shown that "competent membership" in the disciplinary community is a longitudinal process that involves a number of steps. Students undergo a process of socialization and integration that involves a phase of competency development followed by the two parallel phases of developing a knowledge base and undergoing a transition from a focus on social integration to one on academic integration. Once students become "repositioned" as "more serious students" within the disciplinary community, they are "invited in" to the community in a variety of ways. "Invitations" take the form of acknowledgment from faculty that they are knowledgeable and important members of the community.

Specific mechanisms are utilized as means of incorporating students into the community. In the context of the discipline of psychology in this study, this took the form of greater involvement with research, more meaningful interaction with faculty, a feeling that faculty were "better," and confidence that students had important contributions to make to class discussions. The results of this study suggest that understanding the meaning of competent membership in the context of Tinto's (1993) model of retention and attrition entails determining the mechanisms that enhance and inhibit membership within a particular community.

The results of this study also suggest that other concepts that inform Tinto's (1993) model may be clarified. Student-focused higher education literature has shown that often the concept of academic integration means little more than grade average or number of contacts with faculty outside of the classroom (Anderson 1988; Stoecker, Pascarella, and Wolfle 1988). This study has shown that academic integration into the disciplinary community is a multidimensional phenomenon that involves a complicated process of negotiation and acceptance by other members of the community, most importantly by faculty. This study may inform the operationalization of the concept of academic integration by recognizing that it encompasses a wide variety of student activities and relationships with faculty. Further, Tinto's (1993) persistence model proposes the importance of integration into at least one community of the university, but it does not operationalize the meaning of integration into a specific community and does not identify the mechanisms that facilitate that integration. The disciplinary focus of this study identifies an important community for third-year undergraduate students and highlights the mechanisms specific to integration into it.

Promoting community membership and involvement implies obligation and responsibility on the part of both the student and the university. If students are to become full members of the academic and disciplinary communities, an institution must provide equal access and opportunity for that participation. The results of this study suggest that one way to meet this obligation from an institutional point of view is to restrict enrolment in psychology programs. Although initial access would be restricted, once enrolled, students would have greater access to resources within the program. In order to provide the possibility for active participation of all members without expanding teaching and research infrastructure (e.g., number of faculty, laboratory space, and equipment), universities may have to limit enrolment or resort to similar restrictions.

Discussions of the importance of integrating undergraduate students more fully into the research functions of the research-intensive university are increasingly common. If an institution such as RIU is to take seriously the value of integrating undergraduate students more fully into the research functions of the university, in the case of psychology at RIU, it is imperative that the provision for students to participate as researchers on a research project with a faculty member should be greatly expanded. This type of interaction between students and faculty has proven to greatly enhance community involvement and belonging among students. Faculty reward structures should reflect the value of faculty interaction with undergraduate students, inside and outside of the classroom.

Increasing student involvement with faculty research has a number of implications for federal funding initiatives. For example, Social Sciences and Humanities Research Council of Canada grants programs are evaluated on criteria intended to reflect the objectives of a specific program. If one such objective were the enhancement of research and teaching through the involvement of undergraduate students in the research project, faculty would begin to think of creative ways to include undergraduates. The Natural Sciences and Engineering Research Council of Canada has implemented an Undergraduate Students Research Awards program designed for students in the natural sciences and engineering. This is a model that could be instituted for students in other program areas.

Consistent with literature on the undergraduate student experience (Pawluch et al. 1994), evidence from this study suggests that physical place and designated space promote a sense of identity and belonging. In this study, the absence of space for psychology students was an issue that should be addressed. Students identified space that "belonged" to other departments or programs but noted an absence of psychology lecture halls or undergraduate psychology student lounges. The provision of useful space for student interaction is imperative and should be embarked upon to promote community involvement. Further, the importance of student-faculty interaction to overall student development (Astin 1993; Bean and Kuh 1984; Pascarella and Terenzini 1991; Tinto 1993) has been well documented. To promote informal student-faculty interaction, a lounge area where interaction is possible and encouraged should be provided. Assigning a large lecture hall or classroom to a specific discipline for student and faculty use outside of class time could temporarily alleviate space shortages.

Given the powerful influence of research and student-faculty interaction on the promotion of community involvement, the intersection of the two may usefully be enhanced. Student involvement in faculty research could take the form of participation in research colloquia or seminars in which faculty and student researchers present research ideas or works in progress to other members of the disciplinary community. Kuh asserts that higher education institutions are characterized by a distinct ethos that "carries messages about the relative importance of various educational functions" (1993, 22) and influences student behaviour, attitudes, values, and learning. Not unlike other large research-intensive institutions, RIU, as its policy documents indicate, exhibits a strong commitment to research and academic excellence, and, as students in this study noted, is characterized by a culture of competition and isolation. For the research colloquia as suggested here to be successful in promoting student and faculty involvement and a willingness to publicly present innovative or nascent ideas, it may be necessary to cultivate a culture of collaboration and support rather than a culture of critique and competition.

An RIU policy document on research and teaching suggests the need for a "reassessment of our course credit and curricular requirements to ensure that undergraduates have opportunities to take research intensive, integrative capstone courses where there is increased credit for their increased effort." This idea of "increased credit for increased effort" may easily be extended to an overall community involvement credit system whereby students are allotted credits for participating in various ways in the academic and disciplinary communities of their university. The greater the level of physical and psychological involvement (Astin 1984), the greater the reward may be in terms of points that may be accumulated and translated into academic credits. Not only may this type of activity, supported and encouraged by the institution, promote greater community ties, it may also enhance extracurricular learning that has been shown to contribute to overall student development (Chickering and Reisser 1993; Pascarella and Terenzini 1991; Roberts and Clifton 1991, 1992).

Some literature on teaching and learning argues that class size is an important factor contributing to or inhibiting student motivation and development (McKeachie 1980). Recent research suggests that other factors such as course content, instructor ability and knowledge, and year of study (Feigenbaum and Friend 1992; Gilbert 1995) may be more important than class size. The data in this study showed that, as Gilbert suggests, "learning is not a spectator sport, and active, personal inquiry can and does occur in large classes" (1995, 4). However, this study also showed that highly competent teachers who love their subjects and respect their students contribute to an experience of "mattering" (Schlossberg 1989; Schlossberg, Lynch, and Chickering 1989). Students are often marginalized within the classroom "by virtue of their youth, their lack of a productive role, [and] their dependency on the academy for legitimation" (Palmer 1990, 15). The notion of "hearing students into speech," establishing a setting in which student voices are not marginalized but are valued as contributors to the disciplinary discourse (Palmer 1990), may be achieved by allocating some portion of lecture time to small group discussions, question and answer sessions, or collaborative problem solving (Gilbert 1995); by drawing students into classroom conversations; and by valuing their contributions (Palmer 1990).

The case study showed strong support for research as a mechanism for enhancing community membership and sense of belonging. A unique aspect of the psychology department at RIU is the strong integration of research into the undergraduate curriculum within the classroom, through the use of "credit studies" and by building research opportunities into the curriculum for specific groups of students. Because this study focused on a single discipline, a question that arises is the extent to which research is a mechanism of inclusion and exclusion in other disciplines. If it is, what form does this research take? In what ways does it exclude and/or include specific groups of students? Are there disciplinary differences in the meaning and conduct of research that influence students' experiences of community? In addition to a specific disciplinary focus on research, what other aspects of disciplinary differences influence community? For example, what role does learning the language, values, and knowledge assumptions specific to a particular discipline or field of study play in boundary definition and identity formation?

This study focused primarily on the time students spent on campus and did not consider to any large extent other "domains" of students' lives, such as family, work, and off-campus volunteer and other activities. Given that the competing demands facing students are many, extending this study to include off-campus domains would be useful. In addition, this study was limited to traditional-age, full-time students. The meaning of community for other groups of students such as returning women, part-time students, or mature students was not explored. Further study of the impact of residence and commuting patterns is also warranted. The significance of commuting should be followed up by focusing on those who commute from locations near campus and those who travel substantial distances to attend university.

Finally, subsequent studies should examine the meaning of community for transfer students. The experiences of those students who transfer from a college would further our understanding of the phenomenon of community for a group that has not had the same opportunity to build relationships with peers and faculty as nontransfer students have had. It would be useful to examine whether transfer students' experiences at a college provide competency development opportunities similar to those of their nontransfer peers. Further, students from a college may articulate the meaning of an ideal and an actual community, based on comparisons between their college and university experiences. This might provide insights into community-building strategies at a university.

Notes

1 Students eligible to participate in this study were those who had chosen psychology as their major, had been at the research site for at least two years, were traditional age (between ages 18 and 24), and enrolled full-time.

2 Approximately 60 percent of all third-year psychology students at the research site satisfied the eligibility criteria. At the time of survey administration it was not possible to eliminate ineligible students from the sample, so questionnaires were sent to all 203 third-year psychology major students. A total of 130 (64 percent) questionnaires were returned. Fifty-five respondents were eliminated because they did not meet the study criteria. Five questionnaires were returned as undeliverable.

3 Students were asked to compare their experiences before third year with experiences now that they were in their third year, using a scale from 1 to 7, where 1 was less engaged/important and 7 was more engaged/important.

References

Anderson, K.L. 1988. The Impact of Colleges and the Involvement of Male and Female Students. *Sociology of Education* 61, 3: 160-77.

Astin, A.W. 1984. Student Involvement: A Developmental Theory for Higher Education. *Journal of College Student Personnel* 25, 4: 197-308.

–. 1993. *What Matters in College? Four Critical Years Revisited*. San Francisco: Jossey-Bass.

Atkinson, R. and S. Cope. 1997. Community Participation and Urban Regeneration in Britain. In *Contested Communities*, edited by P. Hoggett, 210-21. Bristol: Policy Press.

Bean, J.P. 1982. Student Attrition, Intentions, and Confidence: Interaction Effects in a Path Model. *Research in Higher Education* 17, 4: 291-320.

Bean, J.P., and G.D. Kuh. 1984. The Reciprocity between Student-Faculty Informal Contact and Academic Performance of University Undergraduate Students. *Research in Higher Education* 3, 21: 461-77.

Becher, T. 1989. *Academic Tribes and Territories – Intellectual Enquiry and the Culture of Disciplines*. Milton Keynes, UK, and Philadelphia: Open University Press.

Brent, J. 1997. Community without Unity. In *Contested Communities*, edited by P. Hoggett, 68-83. Bristol: Policy Press.

Chickering, A.W., and L. Reisser. 1993. *Education and Identity*, 2nd ed. San Francisco: Jossey-Bass.

Cohen, A.P. 1985. *The Symbolic Construction of Community*. Chichester, UK: Ellis Horwood.

Corlett, W. 1989. *Community without Unity. A Politics of Derridian Extravagance.* Durham: Duke University Press.

Donald, J. 1997. *Improving the Environment for Learning. Academic Leaders Talk about What Works.* San Francisco: Jossey-Bass.

Feigenbaum, E.Y., and R. Friend. 1992. A Comparison of Freshmen and Upper Division Students' Preferences for Small and Large Psychology Classes. *Teaching of Psychology* 19, 1: 12-16.

Ferguson, M. 1990. The Role of Faculty in Increasing Student Retention. *College and University* 65, 2: 127-34.

Gilbert, S. 1995. Quality Education: Does Class Size Matter? *Canadian Society for the Study of Higher Education, Professional File,* no. 14, Winter.

Hativa, N., and M. Marincovich, eds. 1995. *Disciplinary Differences in Teaching and Learning: Implications for Practice.* New Directions for Teaching and Learning, no. 64. San Francisco: Jossey-Bass.

Howard, T.W. 1997. *A Rhetoric of Electronic Communities.* Greenwich, CT: Ablex Publishing.

King, A.R. Jr., and J.A. Brownell. 1966. *The Curriculum and the Disciplines of Knowledge. A Theory of Curriculum Practice.* New York: John Wiley and Sons.

Kolb, D.H. 1981. Learning Styles and Disciplinary Differences. In *The Modern American College,* edited by A. Chickering, 232-55. San Francisco: Jossey-Bass.

Kuh, G.D. 1993. Assessing Campus Environments. In *The Handbook of Student Affairs Administration,* edited by M.J. Barr, 30-48. San Francisco: Jossey-Bass.

Kuh, G.D., and E.J. Whitt. 1988. *The Invisible Tapestry. Culture in American Colleges and Universities.* ASHE-ERIC Higher Education Report no. 1. Washington, DC: Association for the Study of Higher Education.

McKeachie, W.J. 1980. Class Size, Large Classes and Multiple Sections. *Academe* 66, 1: 24-27.

Palmer, P.J. 1990. Good Teaching: A Matter of Living the Mystery. *Change* 22, 1: 11-16.

Pascarella, E.T., and P.T. Terenzini. 1991. *How College Affects Students. Findings and Insights from Twenty Years of Research.* San Francisco: Jossey-Bass.

Pawluch, D., R.W. Hornosty, R.J. Richardson, and W. Shaffir. 1994. Fostering Relations: Student Subculture in an Innovative University Program. In *Doing Everyday Life. Ethnography as a Human Lived Experience,* edited by M.L. Dietz, R. Prus, and W. Shaffir, 340-53. Mississauga, ON: Copp Clark Longman.

Poplin, D. 1979. *Communities: A Survey of Theories and Methods of Research.* New York: Macmillan.

Roberts, L.W., and R.A. Clifton. 1991. *Measuring the Quality of Life of University Students.* Centre for Higher Education Research and Development. Monograph Series, vol. 1. Winnipeg: University of Manitoba Centre for Higher Education Research and Development.

–. 1992. Measuring the Affective Quality of Life of University Students: The Validation of an Instrument. *Social Indicators Research* 27, 1: 113-37.

Romer, K.T., and W.R. Whipple. 1991. Collaboration across the Power Line. *College Teaching* 39, 2: 66-70.

Rosenberg, M., and B.C. McCullough. 1981. Mattering: Inferred Significance to Parents and Mental Health among Adolescents. In *Research in Community and Mental Health,* vol. 2, edited by R. Simmons, 163-82. Greenwich, CT: JAI Press.

Schlossberg, N.K. 1989. Marginality and Mattering: Key Issues in Building Community. In *Designing Campus Activities to Foster a Sense of Community,* edited by D.C. Roberts, 5-15. San Francisco: Jossey-Bass.

Schlossberg, N.K., A.Q. Lynch, and A.W. Chickering. 1989. *Improving Higher Education Environments for Adults: Responsive Programs and Services from Entry to Departure.* San Francisco: Jossey-Bass.

Stoecker, J., E. Pascarella, and L. Wolfle. 1988. Persistence in Higher Education. A Nine Year Test of a Model. *Journal of College Student Development* 29, 3: 196-209.

Terenzini, P.T., C. Theophilides, and W.G. Lorang. 1984. Influences on Students' Perceptions of Their Personal Development during the First Three Years of College. *Research in Higher Education* 21, 2: 178-94.

Tinto, V. 1975. Dropout from Higher Education: A Theoretical Synthesis of Recent Research. *Review of Educational Research* 45, 1: 89-125.

–. 1993. *Leaving College: Rethinking the Causes and Cures of Student Attrition*, 2nd ed. Chicago: University of Chicago Press.

–. 1997. Classrooms as Communities. Exploring the Educational Character of Student Persistence. *Journal of Higher Education* 68, 6: 599-623.

6
Co-op Education: Access to Benefits or Benefits to Access?
Garnet Grosjean

Cooperative (co-op) education is a model of academy-industry cooperation that allows students to acquire a broad-based, general education and discipline-specific work experience at the same time. The combination is popular with students, and the demand for co-op programs continues to grow.

Co-op is a form of *continuous contextualized learning* (Grosjean 1999b) that moves students between the classroom and workplace contexts. Academic learning is operationalized when students undertake relevant, paid employment on a work term. Work experience is theorized when students bring their on-the-job learning back to the classroom for further analysis and reflection. In its most basic form, a co-op program allows students to spend a semester in the classroom to develop theoretical knowledge, followed by a semester in the workplace to implement theory and develop skills in practical application, before returning once again to the classroom to engage in further academic study. This alternating cycle between classroom and workplace continues for the duration of the undergraduate program, and usually extends completion time by one year. Students are paid "market rates" while on work placements with employers and graduate from their disciplines with undergraduate degrees and a "Co-op Designation," signifying a base of discipline-specific experience. Co-op programs may be either voluntary or mandatory.

Attempts to establish a body of knowledge about cooperative education have provided much useful information on practical outcomes (Fletcher 1989; Hilliard et al. 1995; Pratt 1993). Less effort, however, has gone into defining co-op as an educational model, alternative program, or a strategy for learning. Studies report that "something happens" when students enrol in co-op programs (Rowe 1989; Van Gyn 1996) and describe what happens to co-op students upon graduation (Cash 1979; Mueller 1992; Pittenger 1993). However, there have been few attempts to understand what happens in between or to describe what students experience as they participate in co-op programs.

Despite the importance attributed to co-op education in the literature, and the positive views held about the program by researchers, little systematic information has been collected on the co-op process (Grosjean 1999a). The literature asserts that co-op students get better jobs, get them faster, make more money, and are, in general, well-rounded and productive citizens. While these benefits are all attributed to co-op, there is little empirical evidence to describe how these advantages are generated. Also lacking are detailed accounts that could shed light on what happens to students when they participate in a co-op education program and how they come to understand and make meaning out of their experiences. In other words, the voices of students are largely missing from the literature. The study described in this chapter was undertaken to address these knowledge gaps. It situates co-op in the context of current debates on access to, and relevance of, higher education and explores the tension between the two different facets of co-op: human capital investment and pedagogical innovation.

The chapter is divided into five sections: The first section provides a brief history of co-op education to establish its foundation as an alternative educational strategy. The second section briefly outlines the study site, describes study participants, and details methods of data collection. The third section reports findings of the study, including the role of co-op in the development of skills and competencies, financial benefits of co-op, communities of workplace and classroom practice, transfer of learning, and issues of access to co-op. The fourth section provides a discussion of the findings; it also describes certain implications for co-op policy and practice and provides suggestions for further research.

The Co-op Tradition

The concept of cooperative education began to take shape during the summer of 1894, while Herman Schneider, a recently graduated civil engineer, was building bridges for the Shortline Railroad in Oregon (Ryder 1987, 4). Schneider discovered two things about the students who were hired to work on this project. First, many of the students were performing part-time work that bore little direct relationship to their fields of study or future careers. These students required money from summer employment to fund their education. Second, the difficulties students experienced in adapting their classroom skills to real work situations in the field indicated that certain elements of engineering practice could not be adequately conveyed in the classroom.

When Schneider later began teaching at the University of Cincinnati, he set about finding a way to correct these problems. Schneider reasoned that if students could earn money at the same time as they were accumulating relevant practical experience, this "would enable many worthy young men to attend school who otherwise would be excluded [for lack of financial resources]" (Park 1946, 8). Access to higher education was viewed by Schneider as a key to social mobility and also as a way of preparing university-educated engineers for the changing workplace.

In 1906 Schneider initiated co-op education as a six-year program of instruction in mechanical, electrical, and chemical engineering carried on in cooperation with a number of Cincinnati's electrical and machinery companies. During the school year, students alternated weekly between the industrial shops and the university and were required to work full-time during the four-month "summer vacation." In this way, students in the program spent four years at the work site and two years in the college classroom. In order to participate in the program, students were required to sign a contract and were paid at a starting rate of ten cents an hour while in the workplace. The "Cincinnati plan" as it was referred to then, was well received by both the university and participating industries. Following the success of the initial program, Schneider became a leading proponent for co-op, encouraging expanded participation in educational and industrial circles.

Following fifty years of expansion in the United States, co-op arrived in Canada in the latter half of the 1950s, attracting neither fanfare nor much resistance. At that time, the Kitchener-Waterloo area of Ontario contained primarily manufacturing, business, and insurance industries. The only post-secondary degree-granting institution in the area, Waterloo College (a Lutheran seminary founded in 1911 and affiliated with the University of Western Ontario), was located in the city of Waterloo. Spurred on by J.G. (Gerry) Hagey, president of Waterloo College, a group of local businessmen – some of whom had transferred from the United States to head up subsidiary companies in the area – decided in 1955 to establish a technologically oriented university. From their familiarity with the US co-op model, and following an investigative tour of a number of universities offering co-op programs, this group opted for a similar model. In July 1957, seventy-five men "who wanted to be engineers" were admitted to the Waterloo College Associate Faculties, a collection of prefabricated huts (which later would become the University of Waterloo) located adjacent to Waterloo College (Redmond 1992).

Compared with the rate of expansion in the United States, co-op took root slowly in Canada, with only fifteen higher education institutions participating during the 1960s and 1970s. However, as word of the benefits of co-op spread so did the level of interest, and by the late 1980s, sixty Canadian higher education institutions offered co-op programs to approximately 27,000 students. A decade later, 110 higher education institutions and 61,000 undergraduate students were participating in co-op (Waterloo University 1998), indicating a growing interest in this type of programming and attesting to the success of Schneider's original concept. From modest beginnings assisting engineering students to connect theory and practice, co-op has become a North American educational phenomenon and is now being exported worldwide.

Research Design

The study reported in this chapter was conducted in the province of British Columbia (BC), where there has been a dramatic increase in the demand for co-op during the past decade. For example, of the twenty-seven public institutions[1] that make up the BC post-secondary system, only four do not offer co-op programs. Between 1992-93 and 1999-2000, there was a doubling in approved co-op program offerings, from 92 programs in 1992-93 to 187 in 1999-2000. Co-op student work-term weeks[2] increased 72 percent during the same period – from 90,000 work-term weeks in 1992-93, to more than 155,000 in 1999-2000. In BC, the majority of these work-term weeks are spent in the private sector, where placements, at 70 percent, are higher than the national average (The University Presidents' Council [TUPC] 2000). With 11,450 students enrolled, BC has the second-largest number of co-op students in Canada.[3]

Coast University (a pseudonym) is a community of slightly more than 17,000 students, and 1,900 faculty and staff. It is located on approximately 350 acres overlooking the ocean, just fifteen minutes from a major metropolitan centre. Coast University is ranked one of Canada's leading comprehensive universities, with a tradition of excellence in the arts and sciences. One of the university's distinct attractions is its extensive co-op education programs. Co-op permeates the ethos of the university, which boasts one of the largest university cooperative education programs in Canada, with co-op programs in forty-six academic areas across eight faculties.

Using a nested case study design and a detailed set of criteria (see Grosjean 2000 for details), I carefully reviewed the co-op programs and selected four individual co-op programs (business, chemistry, engineering, and geography) for inclusion in the study. In addition to consulting the historical and documentary records, in November and December 1997 I used an in-class survey to collect data on co-op students' experiences of their programs (N = 1,012). From January to June 1998, interviews were conducted with co-op coordinators (N = 7), faculty (N = 27), co-op students (N = 45), and university administrators (N = 7). Student interviews were "in-depth," lasting from one to two hours and exploring methods of recruitment, forms of regulation, effects of learning context, academic implications, and employment outcomes.

Of the total number of co-op students participating in the study,[4] 64 percent[5] were male and 36 percent female. According to self-reports of respondents' backgrounds, more than three-quarters of participants (79 percent) had lived in Canada all their lives or were Canadian citizens. The dominant cultural group was English-Canadian (53 percent). Chinese-Canadians were the next largest group (10 percent), with the balance representing Canada's multicultural diversity. One-quarter of the students (26 percent) were between 18 and 20 years of age; a further 36 percent were 21 to 22, and 24 percent were 23 to 24 years of age. A smaller number of students (14 percent) were 25 years or older. There was no marked difference between the age of male and female students or in the distribution of age, or cultural background, across programs. Of the students selected for interview, twenty-three were female and twenty-two were male, and represented the various cultural backgrounds of students participating in co-op.

The next section of this chapter presents findings of the study using information drawn from the student survey and quotes from the individual interviews that relate to students' reasons for enrolling in co-op, the role of co-op in the development of skills and competencies, the financial benefits of co-op, the purpose of communities of practice in co-op, transfer of learning, and issues of access to co-op.

Findings

Findings derived from more than one method of investigation and multiple sources of evidence allow for the development of converging lines of inquiry resulting in triangulation of data sources and perspectives (Yin 1994, 92). With triangulation, potential problems of credibility are addressed, because multiple sources of evidence essentially provide multiple measures of the same phenomenon. Thus, a more complete picture of the phenomenon of co-op is obtained that is likely to be viewed with greater confidence.

Why Do Students Enrol in Co-op?

Co-op students indicated that they attend university for intellectual development and to improve their chances of employment on graduation. Aggregate survey results indicate that students enrolled to improve their chances of deriving a good income from employment when they graduate (95 percent), to gain knowledge of a field of study (93 percent), for general self-improvement (92 percent), and to acquire specific job skills (91 percent). Fewer students enrolled to find out what they enjoy doing (77 percent) or to gain a broad liberal education (71 percent). More geography students than students in other co-op programs indicated that gaining a broad liberal education is an important reason for attending university, while engineering students appear more closely focused on a future professional career.

Students pursued co-op for a variety of individual reasons. Each student approached his or her studies with a "learning orientation," which may include academic, personal, vocational, or social reasons for seeking higher education. These reasons were not made explicit in the survey data but became apparent through student interviews.

For example, when asked why they enrolled in co-op, some students suggested that it was an aid to deciding what they might want to do in the future:

> I felt that if I did something where I had the opportunity to ... try out different jobs and see what it was like, then I would come out with something a little closer to what I wanted to do.

Some students enrolled in co-op both for the experience and to assist in making decisions about future career directions:

> I wanted some actual work experience. And, I just thought that co-op would be a good way to go because if I was working in the field that I was studying, then I would get a better idea if that was what I wanted to do.

Others enrolled as a result of peer pressure, and the financial incentives offered by co-op:

> I had friends that were in co-op programs at other schools. Basically, they had nothing but good things to say about it, and since I was paying for school on my own, I thought it would be a good chance to try and make some money to offset the costs, and also gain some experience.

Once admitted to the co-op program, students must ensure that they successfully complete the required discipline-related coursework, maintaining a sufficiently high grade point average (GPA) to remain in the program, and complete a prescribed number of co-op work terms in order to graduate with the co-op designation. It was during the time spent on the work term that co-op students maintained that skill development and learning were most profound.

Skill Development and Learning

It is now well recognized that learning and skill development are context-dependent.[6] When students discuss their experience of the co-op work term, learning and skill development almost inevitably enter the conversation. By operationalizing classroom learning in the workplace, some students began to see the relation between theory and application and the practical relevance of what they were studying. During an interview, an engineering student eloquently described how, on her second work term, she was able to apply what she learned in class to the professional workplace and not only see the relevance of the classroom learning but also begin to understand her future role as a civil engineer:

> I really like bridges, and this was a civil engineering co-op, and I was building bridges. I was designing bridges. I was right in there making the calculations, deciding what thickness I wanted. It was just using what I had studied in class, and it's really brought my coursework into context. Studying it in the course, and just plugging away at problems that you think are useless and totally made up, and you don't see why anybody would want to do that. And then in real life you're actually applying it to make a bridge. It made me realize that this is what I'm going to be doing as an engineer when I graduate, which is awesome!

While approximately one-quarter of students interviewed spoke of the importance of being able to practise in the workplace what they had previously learned in class, more than one-half spoke of the impact that learning in the workplace had on their academic performance. A third-year female engineering student described learning skills in one work term that "actually helped [me] in a subsequent work term." Her academic courses did not help her on the job, but "skills learned on the job helped me once I returned to the classroom." This emphasis puts learning flows in reverse, with workplace learning providing students with a better understanding of their academic coursework:

> You learn a lot more on the job because you can see how it ties in so many different ways to what you are learning. And that is better. In class we might learn a particular concept A, whereas in the workplace we learned B, C, and D. But they tie into A. But we never knew that they tied in until we did it. So, yeah, I think you learn more in the workplace. And, you come back with skills that you wouldn't have learned otherwise.

For other students it was not simply a case of transferring what they had learned in the workplace back to the academic classroom. The experience and skills acquired in the workplace also contributed to increased self-confidence. Self-confidence was what made a second-year female engineering student "very excited about learning how to weld, drive a forklift, and work with piping and pumps" on her work term. She felt that the skills she developed "would benefit me in the future" but more importantly she proclaimed, "it allows me to just feel totally competent!"

Once students understood how things were related to each other, it gave them a feeling of "being in control" of their learning. Not only did they see the world in a different way and "make sense" of it from various perspectives, they also had the confidence to select knowledge appropriate to particular situations. By drawing on what they needed when they needed it, they began to recombine their knowledge in different ways, thereby developing enhanced critical-thinking skills to meet new and more challenging situations.

A majority of students contended that learning skills in the milieu of workplace practice led to a deeper understanding than could be provided in the classroom:

> When you do it from an application standpoint, you're curious as to "Hey, what happened here?" Because you don't know what's happening, you have to basically think about what was going on, and you learn a lot more when you're doing the problem solving than when someone in the classroom just tells you what's going to happen.

The learning that happens in the workplace seemed to possess a durable quality. The activity involved in practical application affected how students remember, and subsequently recall, the procedure when required:

> When I learn something in the workplace I remember it. Once I have a chance to use it, it just makes sense. I could go back to the same job I did four years ago and still remember how to do all the basics. I may be a bit rusty, but I will remember it, whereas if I was to go back and try to recite a formula I learned in first year – no way!

The co-op program allows students to develop a repertoire of professional skills and accumulate a body of industry-specific work experience. Through their forays into the world of work, they began to form opinions of the value of that experience to employers making hiring decisions:

> I think when an employer sees, "oh well, she's worked in a big plant, she has worked out in the oil fields, she has done this, she has done that," I think that will give me a way better chance for the job over someone who has just been in school for four or five years.

A small number of students perceived discipline-specific experience to be of such importance that they extended the duration of their undergraduate program to undertake more than the required number of work terms and gain specific types of experience. They believed that the additional work experience would assist them in landing the "perfect job" or furthering their career ambitions.

Without exception, students perceived that the co-op designation acts as a signal to potential employers that they possess workplace-relevant skills and experience. "What it's saying to an employer is that I am confident, I am capable. I may not have the specific skills, but I have these general skills that I can mould and adapt to your situation." Students viewed the designation as a guarantee of future employment: "Even if I never graduate with honours, at least I'll have co-op, and that will count for something to employers."

Networks and Social Capital

Another important element of the co-op work-term experience is the ability to establish a network of workplace contacts. Just as human capital (Becker 1975; Mincer 1989) is defined as the knowledge and skills that an individual accumulates over time, social capital can be regarded as the network of relationships that an individual accumulates over time (Bourdieu 1973, 1986; Coleman 1988). Coleman stresses that as an asset,

> Social capital is defined by its function. It is not a single entity, but a variety of different entities having two characteristics in common: they all consist of some aspect of a social structure, and they facilitate certain actions of individuals who are within the structure. (1990, 302)

The value of these aspects of social structure is that co-op students can use them to achieve their goals. For Bourdieu (1997), too, social capital is relational; it is directly tied to membership in a group. The amount of social capital possessed by individuals depends on the size of the network of connections they can effectively mobilize, and the amount of capital (economic, cultural, or symbolic) each member of that network possesses. The network, in effect, exerts a multiplier effect on the capital possessed by the individual.

Consequently, networks formed during co-op work placements can extend beyond the work terms to shape students' perceptions of the labour market and assist with employment opportunities upon graduation. Through repeated work terms students began to understand how they could increase their access to information and opportunities by establishing networks of contacts. It is then incumbent on students to maintain and enhance their networks through contributing to them, as well as drawing on them, to assist their transition from the university to the world of work upon graduation.

> It's all relationships and networks. It's getting to know your colleagues, and them getting to know what skills and abilities you can add to their project. And also having contacts in other companies, being able to find out what is going on by consulting contacts inside a company so you can prepare yourself properly.

As one student suggested, "If you know people in a company, when they need to hire someone they can say, 'Gee, I know him, I have worked with him.' Or, 'we trained him, so we should give him a job.' That sort of thing." Students soon came to understand that they could increase their access to opportunities by increasing the number of networks in which they participated:

> You do build connections. Lots of third and fourth work-term people got the jobs they are in now, because of where they worked before. They met someone that works at a private company or even in the government, stayed in communication with them, and were able to get their next work term where they wanted. So, when you do graduate, you have built some connections, and you are able to turn that into a full-time job.

The development and maintenance of networks was viewed by students as instrumental in providing employment opportunities upon graduation. Knowledge of employers' expectations and information derived from networks of contacts developed on work terms shaped co-op students' perceptions of the labour market and impacted their future career decisions.

Financial Benefits

Students who received market-rate wages on work terms had the financial resources to delay graduation to accumulate additional work experience. Waged work also allowed co-op students to complete an undergraduate degree relatively debt free. While financial resources are an important consideration for all university students, they are of special significance for those planning to proceed to graduate school. Co-op students could continue their education with a clean financial slate:

> Thanks to co-op I will graduate debt free, which was a requirement of mine when I enrolled. I am not going to be beholden to student loans after I graduate, because I want to go to graduate school and that will cost plenty.

For many students in the study, co-op was seen as an investment in human capital. For example, a female engineering student was certain that a co-op designation, combined with "relevant experience gained on work terms," would launch her career. A female business student switched from science to business because of her perception that a large number of science graduates were unemployed, and the belief that a co-op business degree "would provide greater opportunities for stable employment." A male engineering student felt certain that graduating from the co-op program would enhance his degree and "provide him with skills and experience that would make him more attractive to future employers." These and other comments indicate co-op students' perceptions of the value of human and social capital accumulation for immediate employment and future career – a value not readily available to non-co-op students, raising questions of how access to the benefits of co-op is regulated.

We know from the research literature that certain economic benefits accrue to participants in co-op education – co-op students get better jobs (Petryszak and Toby 1989; Wessels and Pumphrey 1995), get them faster (Gardner and Koslowski 1993), and make more money (Somers 1995) than their non-co-op counterparts. In British Columbia, graduates from university co-op programs also have lower amounts of student loans, command higher starting salaries, are more likely to be in jobs related to their education, and are more likely to find jobs that provide additional training than conventional students (Grosjean 2000; TUPC 2000).

Furthermore, relevant skills developed in co-op are portable. These are important considerations for university graduates seeking employment at a time when the workforce is highly mobile and the organization of capital and production is being fundamentally restructured.

Communities of Practice
Wenger (1998) describes communities of practice as groups that form and function as a unit to work on a particular project, after which they dissipate, with members becoming part of new groups and projects. In co-op, students participate in communities of practice in both the workplace and the classroom.

Communities of Workplace Practice
One of the benefits provided by the co-op work term is an opportunity for students to develop discipline-related skills in a workplace community of practice (Lave and Wenger 1991; Wenger 1998). When co-op students arrive at a workplace to begin a work term, they enter a community of practice. Adaptability to changing work environments, requirements, and participants in both current and adjacent communities of practice is thus an increasingly important attribute of workplace success. Lave and Wenger (1991) interpret learning in communities of practice as a gradual and social process in which initial observation is followed by carefully orchestrated processes of co-participation – or *legitimate peripheral participation*. The responsibility for learning is mutual between novice and expert. Reciprocal teaching and learning occur at individual rates. Novices assume responsibility for learning by interacting with peers and by participating fully in the learning experience.

Supervisors and co-workers were good sources of knowledge about specific areas of practice:

> I was placed in with a team of workers and we got really good training. They provided small training courses with hands-on experience both from our supervisors, and other team-members.

With assistance from professionals in the workplace, co-op students increased their proficiency and skill level. And as they increased their skill level they were given additional responsibilities:

> My last work term did get my foot in the door in engineering. And I mean I got to learn a lot. And they did make a point of showing me, you know, this is how you do this, "OK. And, today you are going to learn this and this." And I certainly knew how to do a lot more when I came out.

The value of professional experience came to the fore as students developed confidence in their workplace skills:

> Experience is the key to that confidence that takes you there. Experience ... You have the concepts, but you have anxiety about how they work in the real world. Whether you know it or not, all those unknowns are causing you little dents in your confidence. When you get out there, and you really try it, you start to see that it's do-able, this stuff is do-able. And you realize that you can pretty much work in any situation and make things happen, and make it work. I think experience is the absolute key!

Through experience in the professional workplace, students saw firsthand how hiring decisions were made. This reinforced their perception of the importance that employers place on relevant skills and experience. At this stage, students began to adopt the characteristics of the members in the professional workplace and started to develop a "professional persona":

> It comes down to the way you carry yourself more than anything. And that is something that I learned on the work terms. In a professional type job, you interact with a lot of people and a lot of different personalities, and you have to learn how to deal with those personalities and how to get around that. It is something that you don't really get much of in school.

An important part of learning to be a professional was learning the language and norms of the professional workplace (see Chapter 5, this volume). While co-op students were on a work term they were immersed in the culture of their profession and had an opportunity to engage in practice the way professionals do, situated in a community of practice. They began to think "like a professional" and to see their role as one of becoming a "junior professional" rather than a co-op student. One student explained:

> It was incredible learning and professional development, just working with them as a co-op student. We took part in everything. We participated in the group meetings and it made us feel like real engineers.

Students contend that their workplace experience helped them once they returned to university:

> You learn how to conduct yourself in a business environment, which defi-
> nitely helps when you're dealing with professors back here [at university]
> or even lab TAs. The work term gives you a chance to show the world what
> you can give to it. And that's been the biggest growing experience for me.
> I've learned a lot about the world, but more about myself and how I interact
> with other people.

After experiencing a number of co-op work terms, some students formed specific ideas of the direction they wanted their careers to take. They then began to actively position themselves for entry into that field or area of practice and demanded more challenging work placements:

> Clearly what you are willing to take as a first-year student is quite different
> from what you're willing to take as a third- or fourth-year student. Because
> you are expecting, you are wanting, to learn more. You have more knowl-
> edge. You have more experience. You have more expertise. You want more
> and different challenges.

Some were even willing to take lower-paying work terms in exchange for enriched work experience, which they believed would benefit them after graduation:

> In the next work term I am not interested in the pay or anything like that,
> I am interested in getting some good-quality experience that is going to
> help me once I graduate. That's really what I'm looking for.

On their return to the classroom, therefore, many students sought to ac-
cumulate as much job-specific coursework as possible to ensure a smooth transition to a job of their choice on graduation.

Communities of Classroom Practice
Communities of practice are not restricted to the workplace. While the lit-
erature reported above focuses on the workplace, the classroom can also be considered a community of practice. Unlike their associations with supervisors and co-workers, co-op students' participation in the classroom takes place in a context framed by relationships among faculty, students, and coursework.

Once students had confirmed their courses for an upcoming academic term, they sought out friends and classmates in their co-op cohort to exchange information about experiences on the work terms. Students considered this a valuable opportunity to "find out" about employers and discuss future plans:

> When you come back to class from a co-op term it's just really good to sit down and talk with friends and other co-op people about your experience. These are the same people that we are in class with and we all do co-op at the same time. So it's good to get together and talk about what we learned, and who had a good co-op, and what the job was like, and what we want to do for the next one, and what the company was like to work for and what the people were like, and all that. I mean it's good for co-op students to get together because that's how word of employers gets around and how we plan our life.

Most students saw only benefits in networking with members of their cohort to exchange information and ideas about coursework and classes, but there was a possible downside. Some students felt that the structure of the co-op program restricted their ability to develop networks with students outside their particular program or cohort:

> The only people that we usually see are people in our rotation, the people who are on the four-months-on-four-months-off rotation, who you're always at school with and always at work with. So it is harder to keep the same friends actually who aren't in the co-op program:

> The bad point of co-op is that all of my friends are engineers. I only know engineers. And every time I desperately try and escape and meet some other people, you know, I always get sucked back.

Some students perceived difficulty in returning to the routine of the academic term after spending time in the workplace, and particularly about being able to "pick up where they left off" in their studies:

> When other students [non-co-ops] go straight through they have eight months at a time, and you obviously don't forget things between one semester and the very next semester. Whereas with us, you go on a four-month work term and if it's not related to the courses you just took you forget everything. And then when you come back to class you have to go and relearn it all from the textbook.

This student made the point, however, that by constantly revisiting the material – "What was that? How do I do that again?" – they were actually reflecting on previous learning and "finding ways to make it useful" without having to relearn it "a year or two after you graduate."

Those who were confident of doing well in their courses, and who knew the importance of grades in the academic context, welcomed the opportunity to return to familiar ground:

I am known to be pretty anal about my courses in school. I know how important grades are. And, when I get off a work term it's just like I can relax a bit more back in school. Because I know that I have the knowledge and I have the skills and I can do this. And I don't have to worry as much about it as I do with a job.

The co-op rotation suited the learning style of some students – to such an extent that they found it difficult to follow a traditional academic pattern of semestered coursework:

I find co-op is good for giving you a break from school. I have a real problem going to school for eight months at a time. It is really hard. And I like going out on the work term, because it gives me a break. But I'm still using my brain. I am still using the stuff that I am learning in school. But it gives me a break from the academic setting.

The emphasis on grades, and the way the academic portion of co-op is structured, bothered some students. There was a perceived trade-off between high grades and "real" knowledge. A learning style structured around short-term memorization produces high marks, but at the expense of understanding. One student argued that "the whole [idea] of going through university is to learn how to learn. Not to learn how to do a particular thing or job." If the university is doing its job, it won't matter which discipline students are in; they "will still learn how to learn." The difficulty comes, she argued, when students are asked to learn something without an opportunity to develop understanding through application. "If I haven't used it I don't remember it," she explained. "Although I get really good marks, [and] I'm told I am strong in this field, I can't remember the coursework." The immediate course demands were such that previous learning was displaced by current material. This waste made her feel "really sad" that she had spent so much time and "so much effort learning how to learn" when, without opportunities to practise what she had learned, she "won't remember anything from her courses."

Transfer of Learning
In each co-op program the disciplinary courses provided basic knowledge of the field, and the workplace provided opportunities to develop knowledge through application. During interviews some students discussed trans-

ferring recently acquired skills from one arena to another. For example, one student described how knowledge and skills acquired in the classroom benefited subsequent learning in the workplace:

> Basically it's the problem-solving skills and the stuff you learned how to do in class, in a different way that helped me in the workplace. It's not like stuff you actually learned that you could apply. It was the way you thought about the stuff you learned.

The student demonstrated an understanding of the importance of reflection and praxis when transferring skills learned in the classroom to the workplace. Another student suggested that it was not just the possession of skills that was important but rather an understanding of how they could be applied in different situations that made them transferable:

> They say that transferable skills are really the key these days, and I think I have some of those, also the ability to learn and to adapt. I have got transferable skills out of my co-op jobs that can be applied to other jobs. So, it's not exactly what you have learned in class, it's understanding how your job skills and personal skills apply to other things.

In addition to revealing the potential for transfer of knowledge between the dual contexts of co-op, the results indicate that the co-op rotation suited the particular learning style of some students. They found that the work term's practical experience provided a foundation that later allowed conversion of theoretical knowledge into understanding, rather than the other way around. For others, the alternation between the classroom and workplace helped to structure the learning required for a profession:

> If you learn it in school first, and then do it on the job, you don't learn it as well. For me it's better the other way around. I'd rather see my hand learn it first and then my head. So, learning the application is more important first and then I can understand the theoretical part when I come back into the classroom.

Some students contend that academic coursework prepared them only to a certain level. To "do a job professionally," they argued "requires that employers provide some training, to increase levels of proficiency," and "enable individuals to either stay with the employer or move across to another company at the same level, or even move up." Another student summed up the role of co-op as follows:

The role of co-op is one of interlacing the two. Co-op really is that link between the two kinds of learning ... and it provides something that eventually
leads to a career not just a job.

For many co-op students, learning the course material in their program
was hard work. As one student put it, "in the workplace students learn to
work, and in the classroom they work to learn." Both contexts demand
different types of thinking skills:

With co-op it's a different way of thinking and working. At work it's a lot
more mechanical, a lot more applied thinking, whereas at school it's a lot
more theoretical, a lot more sort of tugging on your brain. Whereas at work
it's, well, if you don't know something, you just go ask somebody.

To develop an understanding of the course material, and to be motivated to learn it, some students needed to relate learning to future workplace use. Subsequent application on the work term then reinforced
understanding:

If you have the course before [the work term], then you know what you can
do with it. It makes it a lot more interesting, and if it's a lot more interesting
to me, I tend to work harder at it, so I understand it a lot more. Rather than
just this thing on the blackboard – section X, that you have to know by mid-
term or memorize by the exam, and that you scuffle out of your brain right
after it – co-op reinforces it, so it sort of gives you a greater appreciation and
understanding of the course material. It sort of links the two together.

Although some students were enthusiastic about linking the classroom
with the workplace, others expressed reservations. Some students described
their dissatisfaction with the academic component when course instructors
failed to acknowledge what had been learned on the work term. Enthusi-
asm for classroom learning was quickly dampened when students were not
given the opportunity to integrate workplace and academic learning on
their return to the classroom:

I came back and I think I'd really done some growing over the time I was
doing co-op – I really had a great time on co-op. It was disappointing that
there was so little follow-up. I just felt that here I was back in the classroom
again, and I was doing the same old-same old. Everything that I'd learned
on co-op had sort of been forgotten. I just felt that, "Yeah, they've forgotten
about what I've just done." They weren't interested in my experiences – I
was back in school, and I was just another student expected to do the same
old things in class again.

Rather than having his co-op experience reinforced, this student felt that he was being socialized back into a subordinate status in an academic classroom, where he was *taught* about a discipline rather than learning and enhancing disciplinary skills, and understanding.

Students complained that learning workplace procedures in the classroom did not seem to be "real" and therefore the procedures were not taken seriously. There was a feeling of artificiality attached to learning something out of context:

> In class you do cases and stuff and apply concepts to live situations in the classroom, but it's still just in a book. Like it's still not really taken seriously. It's not really real.

> Sometimes I really have trouble trying to just concentrate on learning something in class. Like, it just isn't real. And I try as much as possible to do all the regular assignments, to try and keep up on top of things. But when they stand there and tell us how important this is, and try to make us learn something in class, I just keep thinking, it's school, it isn't real.

One student described the difference between learning in the classroom and learning in the workplace as the difference between "the textbook world and the real world." For many, classroom learning did not take on meaning until there was an opportunity for practical application. This indicated that co-op students attributed much of their learning and skill development to the work term. The "co-op effect" is the perception that learning takes place as a result of the activities of practical application in the workplace, not through the activities of the classroom. What goes on in the classroom, students suggest, is not learning but "study" or the "learning about" a discipline.

Who Has Access to Co-op?

Students also suggest that access to co-op is less than equitable. Access to co-op programs is becoming increasingly restrictive. Only "the best" students are admitted. Screening – or "creaming" – by academic grades (GPA) controls entry. The concept of screening was a recurring theme in student interviews:

> What they are doing is they are screening people coming into the co-op program and they are only taking those who have a high academic average, which may in one sense be interpreted as those people who would be successful anyway.

In some co-op programs, high-achieving students are actively recruited. Shortly after results of first-semester exams are known, those with a high GPA receive a letter of invitation from a co-op coordinator.

If our GPA was over a certain number we got sent a letter saying "we think students of your calibre would benefit from the co-op program. Why don't you come to an interview or an introductory session?" So that's how I found out about it – I was drafted into it!

Because of the recruitment of top achievers, access to co-op programs is limited to those with sufficient levels of academic capital. After enrolment, ongoing access to the "best" work terms is restricted to the "best" students (those with the highest GPA), thereby reinforcing the creaming process. One student – himself a beneficiary of creaming – summed it up like this: "good work terms go to those students who have good grades. It's as simple as that." Another student echoed this response:

I know of students who wanted to get into co-op and [because of their GPA] they couldn't. And a lot of people just barely squeaked in and basically, they didn't get very good work terms. They were kind of given the left-overs.

Student accounts of screening by GPA are supported by institutional research conducted on undergraduate students at BC universities. For example, a study conducted at one university indicated that one-half of co-op students at that university entered with academic averages of more than 85 percent, compared with one-third for non-co-op students in the general undergraduate population. This difference became more pronounced at the highest academic level, with more than 21 percent of that university's co-op students entering with an academic average above 90 percent, compared with fewer than 10 percent for the general undergraduate population.

Interestingly, there was a certain level of support by co-op students for this type of screening. Some even suggested that, due to a perceived shortage of "good" co-op jobs, there should be more vigorous screening to reduce the number of co-op admissions:

I think they should screen people a bit more carefully and then stick with the ones they select and make sure they are able to get jobs.

Faculty members also echoed this sentiment during interviews, when commenting on which students in their programs they thought might benefit from co-op. As one faculty member stated,

I think it's a mistake to argue that co-op is equally beneficial for all students. I think there's pretty convincing evidence that students [with a higher GPA] who can adapt to the rotational schedule will benefit far more from [participation in] co-op programs than others do.

GPA is one of the most powerful screening and selection tools co-op coordinators use, but how much does a high GPA tell us about a student's ability to successfully complete a co-op program? Clearly, students with high GPAs are capable of meeting the demands of academic coursework, but there is little evidence that these same skills will benefit them in the workplace. As a screening device, therefore, academic GPA has certain limitations. However, to answer the question of how it became the tool of choice for screening and what it actually does tell us, we must look beyond individual issues of access.

Discussion

The results of this study indicate that co-op students are highly aware of the benefits accruing to appropriate work experience. Because of the time spent in the workplace, co-op students have a substantially greater opportunity to obtain current information on jobs in the field, and to meet potential employers than do non-co-ops (Grosjean 1999b). For many co-op students the networks developed during these work terms (social capital) prove beneficial during the transition from university to the labour market.

Co-op students also derive financial benefits from their program. They are paid "market rates" while on their work terms. Thus they develop an understanding of the exchange rates (labour for money) of particular jobs and skill categories while they are accumulating industry-specific experience (experiential capital). Then, by selecting subsequent courses of study, co-op students can develop expertise in areas of high or "rare" skill demand, situating themselves to command an enhanced income upon graduation.

To understand how students make meaning of their co-op experience, we must understand how they perceive learning, and the contexts – both academic and workplace – where learning takes place. Interestingly, when asked the question, "in your program, what does learning mean to you?" the first reaction of a large majority of students was to begin describing learning on their work terms. The co-op work term appeared to them to be synonymous with learning, and they had to make an effort to focus on the concept of learning in relation to the classroom. One student explained that "what we do in the classroom is study"; learning, in contrast, "takes place on the work term when we get to see how something actually works." In discussions with other students, it became clear that this was a commonly held perception of learning among co-op students.

The work term appeared to have a strong enough impact on students' perceptions of learning that the pedagogical activities of the co-op classroom were diminished, and those of the workplace enhanced. In the workplace, one "learns by doing" and by emulation. As one student described it, "If you want to learn you have to find somebody that knows and does what you eventually want to do and find out what you need to do to be able to do the same thing."

It is not surprising, then, that with repeated forays into the discipline-specific workplace, co-op students have access to – and benefit from knowledge of – changes in the labour market. The alternating structure of the co-op program enables them to closely monitor changes in labour market trends. Current and constant contact with the labour market provides co-op students with a decided advantage over their non-co-op counterparts in the competition for good jobs.

While on a work term, co-op students developed knowledge through guided participation in goal-directed activities of the practice. Learning occurred during engagement with routine and nonroutine problem-solving activities under the influence of a particular community of practice. Through repeated activity in work situations with similar sociocultural practices, a student could, over time, develop a repertoire of skills that would become associated with expert practice. According to Billett (1999), knowledge acquired in this way is more likely to later transfer across settings that share similar sociocultural practices.

It appears that what co-op students learn through the everyday activities of the workplace is different from what they learn in the routine activities of the classroom. Different workplace settings present opportunities for a variety of activities, experiences, and guidance. This being the case, appropriate placement becomes a critical factor in the quality of workplace learning. Through direct (from supervisor) and indirect ("the way we do it here") guidance, co-op students on work terms gain experience, which reinforces and extends their knowledge. In some cases the workplace might also offer opportunities for students to develop certain specialized skills in areas that are not offered by the university. This was evidenced by those students who chose to extend their number of work placements to acquire specific experience. For example, to enhance their applications to medical school, some chemistry students exceeded the required number of work terms to gain experience at a large drug manufacturer or at a cancer agency. Engineering students often sought extra work terms in a specific area to enhance their chances of employment in a specialized field.

In the workplace, as students learned disciplinary skills, they also learned how to be members of a situated community. In this way, co-op students learned not only content knowledge but also disciplinary norms, expectations, and standards in a particular area. Learning generally occurred through the experience of the activities and cultural norms of the discipline. Co-op students moved from novice to expert through co-participation with members of the disciplinary community. Thus, co-participation allowed for learning through performance and engagement within a community of practice rather than solely through cognitive acquisition of knowledge – the dominant mode in the academic context.

The co-op workplace, then, was seen as a situated community of professional practice where students learned on the job. Classrooms were sites where students learned *standards* of disciplinary practice. That is not to say that disciplinary *skills* were not learned in the academic context. But despite attempts to simulate the professional context in the classroom, disciplinary practices and discourse learned there were not those of the workplace. As student comments above make evident, learning workplace procedures in the classroom did not seem real and, therefore, the procedures "weren't taken seriously." The academic context within which the students were taught certain disciplinary procedures was perceived to be distinctly different from the professional context to which co-op students aspired. The social roles and communicative practices were also perceived as distinctly different in academic and workplace settings.

Thus, co-op students were able to develop skills and abilities beyond what could be developed by non-co-op students. For example, co-op students developed teamwork skills by participating in project teams during their work terms. Decision-making skills were enhanced in the co-op workplace when students were given increasing responsibility for a project while on their work term. That co-op students were able to develop specific job skills is understandable when one considers that they had an opportunity to "try out" their skills on successive work terms as they progressed through their program. Learning that takes place in the dual contexts of co-op programs, therefore, both influences the development of critical-thinking skills and assists students to form a deeper understanding of their field of study. The ability to develop discipline-specific skills and abilities was a benefit that accrued to students who were able to gain access to co-op education programs. However, access to co-op may not always be equitable.

Access to co-op programs and the subsequent ability to accumulate a variety of capital is restricted to those who already possess high levels of academic capital. As well, a type of collectively owned social capital – embedded in the co-op credential – enhances the pre-existing cultural capital commanded by university students. This combination of effects permits those students who already possess capital to accumulate more. Restrictive access policies, combined with the fact that co-op programs require considerable financial subsidization, continue to privilege an already relatively privileged group of students (Grosjean 1999c).

The study points to the importance of context in skill development and learning. Evidence shows that co-op students have opportunities to develop teamwork, communication, and decision-making skills. In learning the procedures of a particular workplace, co-op students gained knowledge of what types of activities were expected of employees in that particular setting. In learning how things were done, students were also introduced to the power

relationships and division of labour within the workplace. Through participation in teams, individual workers came to know their fellow employees
better and also learned more of the role each played in the workplace. Fewer
and fewer workplace functions today are performed by individuals; therefore employees are required to come equipped with the skills and competencies that will allow them to function as contributing members of a team
(Carnevale, Gainer, and Meltzer 1990; Evers, Rush, and Berdrow 1998).
Embedded in the concept of teamwork skills are individual characteristics
and interpersonal skills that enable individuals to "get along" with others
(Hamilton and Hamilton 1997). Therefore, effort should be made to provide opportunities for students to develop teamwork skills in the classroom through interaction with other students in group projects or group
assignments.

The study reinforces the importance of integrating learning that happens
in the workplace with that of the classroom; co-op students perceive their
professional development as dependent on learning in both contexts. Students returning from work terms are not reinforced for the appropriateness
of the skills they have learned in the workplace. Nor are they encouraged to
discuss the benefits or drawbacks of the skills-learning process they experienced. Reinforcement of this kind is needed to strengthen students' resolve
and motivate them to learn more. Faculty must find ways to enable co-op
students returning from work terms to reflect on skills and knowledge gained
in the discipline-specific workplace, thereby assisting students to reflect on
their experience and share this information with their classmates. Solicit-
ing comments and questions about workplace practice from students who
have recently returned from work terms could benefit all students in class.
The sharing of current information regarding professional practice
among students in the classroom would provide an alternative source
of knowledge for students in class and allow the professional practice
regarding a discipline to take on a more real-life perspective than that
presented in textbooks.

The findings of this study also indicate that once students are admitted to
a co-op program, support networks are important to the way they perceive
their experience. Developing networks of contacts in the workplace (social
capital) was shown to lead to direct opportunities for employment when
students complete their program. There is also a need to develop support
networks in the classroom to socialize students into the culture of co-op
and assist them to develop academic self-confidence and motivation to learn
(and ultimately increase GPA). Students who experience similar assignments,
deadlines, work-term competition, and classroom dynamics share a common experience that can usefully be explored. Co-op seminars or study
groups, organized by faculty members interested in co-op, could provide
additional support and encourage student-faculty interactions.

With restrictive access to co-op and privileged opportunities for "good" jobs becoming the norm, co-op is showing signs of becoming an elite program. The traditional image of co-op was a bootstrap – a way for students from lower socioeconomic levels to access the benefits of higher education. Now the image is a silver spoon – a program that increases opportunities for those already privileged.

A trend affecting access to co-op is the rise in supplementary program fees being instituted by some programs. All students pay a "co-op fee" while on a work term in order to assure continuous registration in their university program and help cover administrative costs. The co-op fee has traditionally been equivalent to the cost of a three-credit academic course. In 1996-97 two BC institutions began charging a $50 application fee for students wishing to enrol in co-op. By 1999-2000, in addition to charging the regular co-op fees, seven BC institutions were adding between $50 and $500 for processing fees, semester fees, program fees, or workshop fees. Charging additional fees beyond the standard tuition further restricts access to those with adequate financial resources. To improve equality of access to co-op education, alternative funding strategies must be explored. Institutions should investigate ways to provide financial assistance to students from lower socioeconomic levels to enable them to benefit from access to the experiential, social, and economic capital derived from co-op participation.

A recommendation for improvement to co-op programs that can be implemented with little effort or financial cost is the establishment of a listserv for each program to house a database of "tips" or "solutions to problems" encountered in the co-op workplace. Such an undertaking could be based on the successful program created by Xerox France and the Xerox Palo Alto Research Center (PARC) in California (Durance 1998). This would be a way for co-op students to share their "tricks of the trade." In its most basic form, it would require a small group of students, coordinators, and faculty to set up the program and act as a review board to screen submissions for authenticity and uniqueness before they are posted to the list archives.

Once the review board accepts a tip from a co-op student, the student's name would be attached to the tip and it would be posted on the listserv and added to the database. In this way students would gain recognition for finding creative solutions to novel problems each time a new tip was accepted for the listserv. The database would become a resource for both current and future co-op students to access in times of need. The establishment of the listserv would be a way for students to share their workplace experiences when they return to campus. The database would reinforce both workplace and classroom learning and help make the new knowledge explicit through the listserv and reinforce it tacitly for students.

Longitudinal research is required to investigate the "co-op effect." For example, is it possible to investigate the cumulative effect of co-op work-term experience to determine if the strength of the co-op effect is related to the length of time students are enrolled in a co-op program? This would assist in identifying the optimum number of work terms required for students to derive maximum benefit from co-op. In other words, longitudinal research could answer the question, What is the minimum number of work terms that are required to maximize the positive aspects of workplace experience on the professionalization of co-op students?

Further research is needed to explore the connection between the profession or discipline in which students are enrolled and their varying experiences of co-op, as identified in this study. Why, for example, do students in one program over-invest in discipline-specific work experience while students in other programs indicate no interest in going beyond what is necessary to obtain the co-op qualification? Is this a localized phenomenon or does it extend to programs beyond those studied? What are the implications of this practice for the structure and function of future co-op programs?

The results of this study indicate that through the use of selective admission criteria and regulation of access to discipline-specific work experience, co-op is becoming an elite program. Further research is needed to investigate whether students accepted into the program are provided with considerably more opportunities than regular students. Because co-op programs consume more resources than regular programs, and because certain benefits accrue to students in these programs, there is a need to investigate if co-op is creating vocational elites (Grosjean 1999c) at the expense of other undergraduate students in the university.

In summary, the results of this study indicate that knowledge about knowledge helps co-op students become aware of the norms, values, and assumptions that underpin professional work. Learning in the dual contexts of co-op can help students reflect on how expertise is linked to professional identity. Co-op's practice-oriented programs can enable students not only to transfer "theory *to* practice" but also to combine "theory *in* practice." Practice-oriented education allows co-op students to tackle the complexity of "real" phenomena intellectually rather than being limited by the extent or shortcomings of theoretical approaches. Relevant education can be accomplished through a curriculum that combines a dynamic approach to teaching and learning in the university, with the involvement of practitioners in teaching and other activities in the workplace.

Notes

1 The BC post-secondary system consists of four traditional universities and one specialized university, five university colleges, eleven community colleges, three provincial institutes, two Aboriginal institutes, and the Open Learning Agency.
2 Work-term week is a measure of the total number of weeks students are employed while on a co-op work term.

3 The province of Ontario leads Canada, with 35,121 students enrolled in post-secondary co-op education programs.
4 A total of 1,012 undergraduate students completed the student survey. Of these, 73 percent (N = 737) were co-op students. It is the co-op students in the sample that are the focus of this study, and therefore, unless otherwise stated, the following results relate only to data drawn from co-op students.
5 Because of rounding of percentages in this section, totals may not always equal one hundred.
6 For example, see Billett 1996; Brown, Collins, and Duguid 1989; Engeström 1994; Entwistle 1984; Hamilton and Hamilton 1997; Lave and Wenger 1991; Marsick and Watkins 1990; Scribner 1984.

References
Becker, G. 1975. *Human Capital*, 2nd ed. New York: NBER.
Billett, S. 1996. Towards a Model of Workplace Learning: The Learning Curriculum. *Studies in Continuing Education* 18, 1: 43-58.
–. 1999. Guided Learning at Work. In *Understanding Learning at Work*, edited by D. Boud and J. Garrick, 151-64. London: Routledge.
Bourdieu, P. 1973. Cultural Reproduction and Social Reproduction. In *Knowledge, Education and Social Change*, edited by R. Brown, 56-69. London: Tavistock.
–. 1986. The Forms of Capital. In *Handbook of Theory and Research for the Sociology of Education*, edited by J.G. Richardson, 241-58. New York: Greenwood.
–. 1997. The Forms of Capital. In *Education: Culture, Economy, and Society*, edited by H. Lauder, A.H. Halsey, P. Brown, and A.S. Wells, 46-58. Oxford: Oxford University Press.
Brown, J.S., A. Collins, and P. Duguid. 1989. Situated Cognition and the Culture of Learning. *Educational Researcher* 18, 1: 32-42.
Carnevale, P.C., L.J. Gainer, and A.S. Meltzer. 1990. *Workplace Basics: The Essential Skills Employers Want*. San Francisco: Jossey-Bass.
Cash, S.H. 1979. *Employability and Job Satisfaction of Co-op versus Non-Co-op Business Graduates*. Boca Raton, FL: Florida Atlantic University.
Coleman, J.S. 1988. Social Capital in the Creation of Human Capital. *American Journal of Sociology* 94 (Supplement): S95-S120.
–. 1990. *Foundations of Social Theory*. Cambridge, MA: Belknap Press of Harvard University Press.
Durance, B. 1998. Some Explicit Thoughts on Tacit Learning. *Training and Development* 52, 12: 24-32.
Engeström, Y. 1994. *Training for Change: New Approach to Instruction and Learning in Working Life*. Geneva: International Labour Office.
Entwistle, N. 1984. Contrasting Perspectives on Learning. In *The Experience of Learning*, edited by F. Marton, D. Hounsell, and N. Entwistle, 1-18. Edinburgh: Scottish Academic Press.
Evers, F.T., J.C. Rush, and I. Berdrow. 1998. *The Bases of Competence: Skills for Lifelong Learning and Employability*. San Francisco: Jossey-Bass.
Fletcher, J.K. 1989. Student Outcomes: What Do We Know and How Do We Know It? *Journal of Cooperative Education* 26, 1: 26-38.
Gardner, P., and S. Koslowski. 1993. Learning the Ropes: Co-ops Do It Faster. *Journal of Cooperative Education* 28, 3: 30-41.
Grosjean, G. 1999a. *Cooperative Education and Internships: Systems of Articulation between Higher Education and the Economy*. Invited paper for the "International Conference on the Dialogue between Higher Education (New Universities, Fachochshulen) and the Economy: Experiences and Outlook," Vienna, Austria.
–. 1999b. *Higher Education and the Economy: Enhancing Articulation through Co-op Education*. Paper presented at the "What Skills Matter in the Economy?" conference, Vancouver, BC.
–. 1999c. *Vocational Elites in the Academy: The Trojan Horse of Co-op?* Paper presented at the "And the Walls Come Tumbling Down: Non-Traditional Learners in the Academy" Conference, Vancouver, BC.

–. 2000. *"Doing Co-op": Student Perceptions of Learning and Work*. Unpublished doctoral dissertation. Vancouver, University of British Columbia.

Hamilton, S.F., and M.A. Hamilton. 1997. When Is Learning Work-Based? *Phi Delta Kappan* 78, 9: 676-81.

Hilliard, G., S. Pearson, B. King, and J. Young. 1995. Undergraduate Cooperative Education in Maritime Canada: Placements, Placement Sectors and Placement Locations. *Journal of Cooperative Education* 30, 3: 56-64.

Lave, J., and E. Wenger. 1991. *Situated Learning: Legitimate Peripheral Participation*. Cambridge: Cambridge University Press.

Marsick, V.J., and K.E. Watkins. 1990. *Informal and Incidental Learning in the Workplace*. New York: Routledge.

Mincer, J. 1989. Human Capital and the Labour Market: A Review of Current Research. *Educational Researcher* 18: 27-34.

Mueller, S. 1992. The Effect of a Cooperative Work Experience on Autonomy, Sense of Purpose, and Mature Interpersonal Relationships. *Journal of Cooperative Education* 27, 3: 27-35.

Park, C.W. 1946. Origin and Development of Cooperative Courses at the University of Cincinnati. *Journal of Engineering Education* 36: 420-23.

Petryszak, N., and A. Toby. 1989. *A Comparative Analysis of Cooperative Education and Non Cooperative Education Graduates of Simon Fraser University*. Vancouver: Simon Fraser University.

Pittenger, K. 1993. The Role of Cooperative Education in the Career Growth of Engineering Students. *Journal of Cooperative Education* 28, 3: 21-29.

Pratt, C. 1993. *Procedures and Outcomes for Students in Cooperative Education*. Unpublished doctoral dissertation, Seton Hall University, South Orange, NJ.

Redmond, C. 1992. *University of Waterloo: A Brief History, Images of Waterloo*. Waterloo: Office of Information and Public Affairs, University of Waterloo.

Rowe, P. 1989. Entry Differences between Students in Cooperative Education and Regular Programs. *Journal of Cooperative Education* 26, 1: 16-25.

Ryder, K.G. 1987. *Social and Educational Roots. Cooperative Education in a New Era: Understanding and Strengthening the Links between College and the Workplace*. San Francisco: Jossey-Bass.

Scribner, S. 1984. Studying Working Intelligence. In *Everyday Cognition: Its Development in Social Context*, edited by B. Rogoff and J. Lave, 9-40. Cambridge: Harvard University Press.

Somers, G. 1995. The Post-Graduate Pecuniary Benefits of Co-op Participation: A Review of the Literature. *The Journal of Cooperative Education* 31, 1: 25-41.

TUPC. 2000. *2000 BC University Baccalaureate Graduate Survey: Report of Findings*. Victoria: The University Presidents' Council.

Van Gyn, G.H. 1996. Reflective Practice: The Needs of Professions and the Promise of Cooperative Education. *Journal of Cooperative Education* 31, 2: 103-31.

Waterloo University. 1998. *University of Waterloo Factsheet*. Available at: <http://www.adm.uwaterloo.ca/>.

Wenger, E. 1998. *Communities of Practice: Learning, Meaning, and Identity*. Cambridge: Cambridge University Press.

Wessels, W., and G. Pumphrey. 1995. The Effects of Cooperative Education on Job Search Time, Quality of Job Placement and Advancement. *Journal of Cooperative Education* 31, 1: 42-52.

Yin, R.K. 1994. *Case Study Research: Design and Methods*. Thousand Oaks, CA: Sage.

7
The Four Rs Revisited: Some Reflections on First Nations and Higher Education
Michael Marker

It is not enough for universities to focus their attention on "attrition" and "retention" as an excuse to intensify efforts at cultural assimilation. Such approaches in themselves have not made a significant difference, and often have resulted in further alienation. (Kirkness and Barnhardt 1991, 14)

Over ten years ago Verna Kirkness and Ray Barnhardt wrote an article that has since become one of the most frequently cited works on First Nations[1] participation in higher education. The four principles of "respect, relevance, reciprocity, and responsibility" (the four Rs) that they outlined have become reference points for graduate student papers and journal articles discussing a wide range of cross-cultural education contexts. A recently published research paper on American Indian students' cultural strategies at universities cites Kirkness and Barnhardt for recommendations "to celebrate American Indian ethnicity on campus" as a way to avoid attrition and alienation (Huffman 2001, 19).

Kirkness and Barnhardt's article continues to draw attention a decade after its publication because it frames the discussion around what the academy can do to transform itself rather than how Aboriginal people should adapt and assimilate to the needs of the university culture. In many ways their work was a forecast of the growing self-determination movements of Aboriginal people throughout North America that would find expression in the challenges to Eurocentric canons of knowledge in the universities. Indigenous ways of knowing and community values have, so far, been disruptive to the conventions of academic disciplines and to the ways that social science research methodologies have consolidated themselves. But the question remains: has the academy simply been disrupted? Or have things actually been transformed as a result of Indigenous scholarship and presence? Has the university simply provided surface accommodation for Indigenous knowledge, or have the deeper structures of knowledge production become questioned and examined for a fundamental ethnocentricity? The challenge of the four Rs was to transform the university into a place where Aboriginal people would feel more welcomed into the broad intellectual enterprise and encouraged to express themselves from their own cultural and thoughtworld perspective. Has there been a genuine change in the academy? Or do the recommendations of a decade ago remain unheeded today? How much has changed, and how much has stayed the same in the decade since this article was published?

In many ways there has been a general and significant advancement in the level of cultural responsiveness to the Indigenous perspective, but there are notable differences among regions and institutions in North America. The cross-cultural context of each university is created both by an institutional culture tending to perpetuate the norms, values, and interests of administrators and alumni and by outside economic and cultural pressures. And while, on the one hand, there has been an opening of opportunities and alternative approaches to university-based knowledge in the last decade, on the other hand, successful programs for Indigenous students have often been overwhelmed by evolving post-industrial and technocratic trends that have negated many of the gains made in equity and access. An emphasis on preparing students for careers in a globalized marketplace has frequently rendered the place-based knowledge and identity of Indigenous people to be an antiquated and contentious voice, listened to only in the most nonchalant fashion. The Indigenous voice is contentious in that, as Bowers, Vasquez, and Roaf observe, "science is being used as the basis of a new ideology that justifies the 'extinction' of cultures that do not 'adapt' to the expanding network of computer-mediated intelligence required by the global economy" (2000, 192). Indigenous place-based knowledge requires an understanding of the moral proportions of oral traditions and long-sustained relationships with the land. It implies and prescribes particular forms of restraint and responsibilities from communities and individuals who have a sense of belonging to the land. Industrial and post-industrial society replaces traditional cultures that are oriented around this sacred sense of place with an individualized identity that is malleable and transportable throughout a global marketplace. Such dominant perspectives on identity and economics rush past and push aside Indigenous patterns of knowledge. First Nations are confronted with a spectrum of economic trade-offs in collaborations and compromises with higher education. Many Indigenous communities, in evaluating the assortment of difficult choices and dilemmas, now take the view that "over the long term the loss of local knowledge and patterns of moral reciprocity essential to traditional communities will become more significant to the world's ecological well-being" (Bowers, Vasquez, and Roaf 2000, 193). While it is difficult to make broad generalizations about the problems Indigenous people face in higher education, the themes of "respect, relevance, reciprocity, and responsibility" from the Kirkness and Barnhardt article remain a potent template to evaluate the terrain.

In this chapter, I examine some contexts of Indigenous participation in higher education, critically focusing, in part, on the development of Native studies, now called First Nations studies in Canada. These programs have occupied a kind of in-between space at the universities where Indigenous students have acquired undergraduate and graduate degrees. They are tenuous spaces located between disciplines and departments, and often between the university and the Aboriginal communities. For my part, rather than subject these programs and the general context of Aboriginal higher education to a point-by-point consideration of how they stack up to the decade-old challenge of the four Rs, I prefer to keep the Kirkness and Barnhardt article in the background of my discussion and refer to it as a challenge that remains mostly unanswered. I will discuss four considerations that I think are structural and conceptual challenges for academic collaborations with Indigenous people. Aboriginal people experience a culture clash around the themes of (1) research, (2) methodology, (3) theory, and (4) community. And while it can be said that many ethnic minority students experience cross-cultural tensions trying to adjust to the environment of a university campus, for Indigenous students, the conflicts are more than just getting used to schedules, transportation, and food differences; the clash often occurs at the deepest levels of assumptions about reality and epistemology (Barnhardt 2002). In the last section of this chapter, I describe some aspects of the Ts`kel First Nations Graduate Studies Program at the University of British Columbia and point to ways that Aboriginal programs can avoid marginalization in the academy.

Anthropology and the Development of Native Studies Programs

In the introduction to their edited volume *Native American Studies in Higher Education: Models for Collaboration between Universities and Indigenous Nations*, Duane Champagne and Jay Stauss (2002) chart the cross-currents and rip tides that Aboriginal people and their allies have navigated to create programs at universities. In the stories of successes and setbacks at colleges and universities, there is a common theme – or rather, a common complaint: the programs lacked solid ground from which to build an academic sense of purpose that could be understood by discipline-based faculty and administrators. Holistic Native approaches to knowledge and social organization were not compatible with the compartmentalized, expertized knowledge of the academy. Another theme that emerges is the question of where to locate Indigenous studies within the administrative structure of the university. Many, if not most, of the Native studies programs developed in both

Canada and the United States began as components of anthropology departments. Anthropology, as a discipline, has had an ambivalent relationship to the development of Native studies. This is a very long and complex story, intertwined with the emergence of ethnohistory as a discipline, but the short version is that many anthropologists had a monopoly on the discursive space about tribal peoples until about three decades ago, when actual Indians showed up in the academy to challenge anthropology's "expert" voice with their own voices of experience and cultural authority. Anthropology departments have perennially argued that the academic content of Native studies would best be taught through the discipline of anthropology. In the meantime, while anthropology might have a respectable reputation in the academy, it has a rather dubious reputation in Indigenous communities. It is important to note that some anthropologists have established excellent, respectful relationships with Indigenous communities; these are exceptional cases though and not the general way things have gone. Biolsi and Zimmerman make the point that it is not simply a matter of always doing harm either (though plenty of harm has been done); it is more a matter of anthropologists' neglect of important ways of framing ideologies, leading them to "conduct studies on issues completely and utterly irrelevant to Indian welfare" (1997, 15). Moreover, although anthropologists have been keen to publish volumes on the most exotic and irrelevant aspects of Indigenous cultures, they show scant interest in undertaking studies that highlight the cultures of universities. For an understanding of higher education from an Indigenous perspective, there is a need for a series of cross-cultural case studies that bring forth the voices of Aboriginal students and Native and non-Native faculty, administrators, and community members. Such studies are exceedingly rare. An excellent example of this kind of in-depth, case-study approach to higher education settings is Gilmore, Smith, and Kairaiuak's "Resisting Diversity: An Alaskan Case of Institutional Struggle," which locates the setting and then brings forth the dialogue on "clashes of epistemology" (1997, 94).

The Four Rs and the Classroom

Placing issues of respect, relevance, reciprocity, and responsibility in the foreground of discussions about First Nations participation in higher education means that many mainstream students and faculty will have to change the way they relate to Indigenous students. Aboriginal students frequently face a hostile environment in classes since, for them, social and political issues merge with their own identity struggles. Present discussions about First Nations are often contentious because of unresolved treaties, land claims, and a neoconservative attack on Aboriginal sovereignty. As Ken Coates points out, conservative political parties "will use this academic critique to support their opposition to expanding First Nations' rights" (2000,

194). However, while Canadian First Nations students frequently face antagonism in classrooms, American universities are much more culturally impenetrable places for Indigenous students due to the kaleidoscope of Indian stereotypes embedded in the American psyche and because of the colossal inertia of American ethnocentrism. A more detailed, comparative look at Indigenous experience in Canadian and American universities is beyond the scope of this chapter; nevertheless, it should be noted that there are important differences here that call for considerable analysis in the writing on First Nations in higher education. It should also be noted that such comparative writing is missing from the literature up to now. Henry Srebrnik has concluded that "these are indeed very distinct types of educational environments, and each is to some extent reflective of the differing cultural and pedagogical philosophies that have emerged in Canada and the United States" (1993, 381).

According to Kirkness and Barnhardt, seeing the university from the viewpoint of Indigenous people is one of the best ways to probe the culture of the academy, thereby making the familiar strange. They cited the work of William Tierney, a major scholar of American higher education and academic culture, who called for a broader assessment of the challenges to a transformative Indigenous presence in the academy. Rather than promote separate Native studies programs, Kirkness and Barnhardt advocated a larger cultural change for the entire university as a result of engaging with the perspective of Indigenous people. The goal was to make the norms of the academy visible as culturally specific practices while fostering a respectful cross-cultural dialogue with Aboriginal people. Anthropology has an ostensible commitment to making the familiar strange as a central part of the ethnographic enterprise. Unfortunately, research has focused mostly on describing Indigenous and third world communities rather than the "exotic" cultural practices of universities and other dominant institutions (Wisniewski 2000). There is considerable evidence that universities continue to be places that are less than respectful toward Indigenous people. Indeed, Ray Barnhardt has noted that "Native students trying to survive in the university environment (an institution that is a virtual embodiment of modern consciousness) must acquire and accept a new form of consciousness, an orientation which not only displaces, but often devalues the world views they bring with them" (2002, 240).

The Academy from an Indigenous Viewpoint: Research, Methodology, Theory, and Community

The four Rs provide an important template for discussing the general themes of what universities can do to become more culturally responsive to First Nations. However, there is a need to examine the tensions around the ways universities have used categories and terminology that often collide with

Aboriginal ways of approaching knowledge. In this sense, the conditions of respect, relevance, reciprocity, and responsibility must confront the ways in which academic culture has controlled the meaning of terms such as research, methodology, theory, and community. In 2003, I attended a meeting of directors of Native studies programs from the United States. The meeting was hosted by Evergreen State College in Olympia, Washington. Toward the end of the two days of conversations, Donald Fixico, director of the Native studies program at the University of Kansas, proposed that we focus our collective and individual efforts on four realms: research, methodology, theory, and community. We all agreed that these four focal points needed much development in clarifying an Indigenous perspective on academic work. One of the central problems is that these words are presently owned by an academic culture that has some consensus on the legitimate definition of these terms and activities. Indigenous scholars must either invent new words and then struggle against the current to wedge them into the academic lexicon, or expand the meaning of conventional terms to include Indigenous perspectives. This means, essentially, seizing a word and saying, "this is what we mean when we say science, or epistemology, or respectful methodology." Some Indigenous scholars like Vine Deloria, A. Oscar Kawagley, and Greg Cajete have taken this approach of seizing powerful words like science and using them to describe Indigenous knowledge. Prior to the arrival of these Indigenous intellectuals, the shibboleth of "progress" consigned tribal understandings to a primitive past, long since superseded by modern science. Indigenous thinkers have pointed to the limits of conventional terminology as they explained how their own Aboriginal languages referenced time, place, and sacred reality in ways that expand the possibilities for understanding nature, consciousness, and moral conduct.

For both Aboriginal and non-Aboriginal students, the university is a journey through a particular kind of knowledge (see the chapters by Colleen Hawkey and Garnet Grosjean in this volume). In the course of their academic progress and preparation to conduct research, they encounter themes that challenge their values and worldviews; they develop cognitive and communication skills that ask them to critique the home and community culture from which they came. Academic life is, at its best and worst, a transformative experience. Aboriginal students perceive education as a good journey when they feel themselves gaining a deeper understanding of their own experience within the framework of a genuinely respectful comparative cross-cultural encounter that carefully considers advanced tribal knowledge alongside traditional academic knowledge. Too often though, the academic language that is used to describe reality has a built-in ethno-bias toward individualism and against traditional forms of knowledge. The historic and ethnohistoric past is too often dismissed as irrelevant for understanding the substantive nature of the contemporary world. There is a prevailing notion, both in the academy and in the larger society, that the past is dead, that grandma and grandpa's life was hard, full of drudgery and boredom, and that ancestors' ways of living were inferior to present forms of social structuring: that things are getting better and that they will continue to improve. The zeitgeist is focused on the present and the future, not on the past. For Indigenous people though, as Okanagan author Jeanette Armstrong has said, it is difficult to see in the contemporary world how to make sense of things "without stepping back into history and living in the old way" (Thorpe 2001, 250). Meanwhile, Aboriginal students are confronted by a continuous barrage of messages from professors, politicians, and the media, all saying versions of the same thing: "You can't live in the past!" For Aboriginal people, the past is tied into their relationship with land and their sense of the sacred. It is an affront to them to say "You can't live in the past." Navajo scholar Rena Martin explains some fundamental differences: "I am not arguing that non-Natives are not connected with their environment – there is just a difference in how words like 'connection' or 'ties' are used. Relationships defined are ancient and tied to community knowledge and religion" (2001, 36). Thus, while non-Native students might experience the challenge to their worldview as an iconoclastic pressure and a sometimes painful widening of their horizons, Native students regard the pressure to abandon their traditional values as assimilation and nullification of their own identity. Under these conditions of culture clash, the "transformation" of attending university is not an expanding of intellectual possibilities; rather, the university becomes a space of alienation that lures Aboriginal students away from community and sense of place to a kind of nowhere metropolis, where they wander as strangers through a maze of careers and "choices."

Research and the Self

Research is a slippery term in this cross-cultural context. The conventional academic use of this word refers to a systematic approach to gaining knowledge; the "researcher" relentlessly searches for facts or data. Unrelated or irrelevant data are disregarded and emphasis is usually placed on a very narrow kind of questioning, compartmentalizing, and specializing knowledge. While Indigenous modes of gaining knowledge can also be systematic, they usually involve connecting diverse points of reference that defy disciplinary or methodological boundaries and draw on an individual's relationship to people, animals, the landscape, and an oral tradition that frames a time-space arrangement. Dreams and meditative states can factor in to knowledge acquisition. This is not to say that Indigenous research is not empirical, but only that it is not narrowly empirical toward ends that are isolated from the concerns of community, a community made real by the stories from ancestors who established a sustainable presence on the land.

Commonplace approaches to research usually push the inquirer to relentlessly get the information and bring it back to the academy, where it becomes processed and made acceptable. This approach resembles an industrial model of resource extraction. In an Indigenous approach, by contrast, the knowledge seeker spends time in preparation and rituals that produce a state of humility, sensitivity, and openness. In this method, the knowledge seeks the student rather than the other way round. This results in a more holistic and integrated understanding of phenomena that resists constrictive and contrived taxonomies. It also produces a state of consciousness in the Aboriginal intellectual that makes no separation between scientific and moral understandings.

The moral sense of performing research is often ignored in graduate schools. While feminists, post-structuralists, and critical theorists have pointed out how methodologies are biased in terms of both epistemology and moral values, their discussions often neglect to consider the deeper levels of moral development and transformation that are implicated in performing research. Qualitative researchers frequently consider themes of collaboration, community, and power differentials in relationships with informants, but an Indigenous methodology must go beyond this and connect the inquirer to an ancient sense of the journey for knowledge. From an Indigenous perspective, the knowledge seeker must go through a period of training that foregrounds her or his own self-reflection as a way of preparing to become receptive to wisdom. Once the proper preparations and ceremonies have been observed, the individual can receive knowledge without harming herself or himself or the community. Knowledge is powerful and potentially dangerous if one is not ready to receive it properly; a deep and sublime sense of relationships is required. Keith Basso has written about how, for the Cibecue Apache, the pursuit of knowledge is inextricable from the moral relationship to the land: "Knowledge of places is therefore closely linked to knowledge of self, to grasping one's position in the larger scheme of things, including one's own community and to securing a confident sense of who one is as a person" (1996, 34). It is difficult to imagine an Indigenous student successfully bringing this kind of a conversation into a mainstream graduate seminar on research. In most research methodology courses, matters of the development of self are pushed aside, segmented away from the more central focus on validity, reliability, or the controlling for variables in data acquisition. While qualitative methodologists have sometimes promoted a more self-reflective and autoethnographic style, this continues to be a less than dominant research paradigm that lacks broad acceptance, even in the social sciences. The emphasis on specialization in the academy means that questions about community and respectful conduct are seen as belonging to philosophy or some category of humanities; methodology –

actually inextricable from epistemology and considerations of power – in this circumstance becomes abbreviated to mean only technical information and training. The underlying epistemological assumptions in methodological training are given scant attention. The culturally specific values and goals of such militant efficacy are seldom examined or dismantled.

Methodology: "Clean the Shed First"

Aboriginal students often experience a great deal of tension when trying to construct a methodology that respects traditional knowledge protocols but still responds to the institutional expectations about how research must be conducted. For example, elders who have traditional knowledge are often unwilling to sign a document that gives consent to the researcher and the university. Such formality can be viewed as an insult and as a sign that the Native student has been assimilated by the colonizing university. Elders usually prefer a more traditional gesture that respects both the sense of sacredness and the sense of intimacy between the speaker and the listener. University protocols, on the other hand, tend to emphasize the need to remain detached and objective when conducting research. The researcher is expected to extract information from people under conditions that maximize distance and anonymity. Informants are frequently expected to tell stories and provide knowledge for free, without any compensation. Moreover, delicate cultural negotiations often occur that can be contradictory to the ways in which universities validate the research exchange relationship. As an example, a First Nations graduate student at a British Columbia university proposed a methodology in which he would give an elder a small gift of tobacco for his storytelling and knowledge transmission. The proposal was rejected by the ethics review of research office after the anthropology department studied the matter and concluded that the student's and elder's assessment of traditional research protocols was not correct. Giving gifts in exchange for the gift of knowledge is an unacceptable methodology to the university except when the participants are paid in a fashion that is consistent with the university's administrative and cultural standards. Tobacco is particularly problematic in this cross-cultural dialogue.

Elders are often quite generous with their knowledge, but they may wish to see some reciprocal spirit of consideration from the researcher. My grandfather was of this type. Wanting to learn how to make something or understand something, I would ask him to show me. He would say something like, "I'm busy right now grandson, but if you want to learn that, it won't be easy. You find me tomorrow morning and I'll take you out and show you how to do that. For right now though, why don't you clean out my shed. It's a bad mess and I can't find some tools that I need in there. Yep, you go clean the shed, and then I'll show you what you want to know." I was not always happy about this exchange; cleaning the shed was a big, unpleasant job and could take all day. But, it was a test of my sincerity about wanting to learn something. In the end, a context was created where I learned not only what I wanted to know, but I also learned how to clean a shed. The research methodology provided my grandfather with both a clean shed and an attentive student.

Theory and Story

It is exceedingly difficult to make Indigenous knowledge, which is based on place and experience, relevant in an academy that exalts the most abstract and placeless theories about reality. Aboriginal ways of knowing elude more universal theorizing because they are usually conveyed through oral tradition, which frames reality around the storied features of the landscape. The university, on the other hand, is oriented toward the transportability of both knowledge and credentials; its gaze focuses on a vast ocean horizon but misses its own reflection. Academics often know a great deal more about the work of their international colleagues than they know about the history and ecology of the land that the university is sitting on. From an Indigenous perspective, it is as though the academy has no actual roots and simply floats above the ground. One thinks of Jonathan Swift's floating island of Laputa, from *Gulliver's Travels*, where the professors indulge in trivial but ferocious arguments. Intellectual work often proceeds in a fashion that is cut off from the natural ecology and without regard for human or environmental consequences. Contrast this disconnected theorizing with Greg Cajete's description of Indigenous knowledge: "Traditional education is a vehicle for the ecological sense and the spiritual ecology of the people" (1994, 165). An Indigenous sense of theory is concerned with the interconnected relationships in a specific place. A focus on the smallest aspect of a place that invokes the spiritual relationship that binds reality together creates a more genuine sense of the universal and global, while attempts to form abstract theories fail in that they must always be conditional and confined to a disciplinary discourse. In a sense, theory might be the most difficult word to "seize" in the academy. Indigenous people have always explained the most intricate aspects of relationships through their oral traditions. Many aspects of oral traditions emphasize transformation. The stories offer insights into cause and effect relationships that not only explain reality but give particular kinds of moral insights about relationships embedded in the land. This is what Vine Deloria (1994, 122) has referred to as a "sacred geography." An Indigenous theory will inevitably collide with the academy's insistence on separating the sacred from the secular since the story has a power to affect not only the consciousness of the individual but also the spirit of the person. The transformation going on in the story often reproduces itself in the transformation of the individual who hears the story.

The Community of Real People

Indigenous scholars are often caught up in the tension of wishing to sustain an engaging presence in the academy and, at the same time, wanting to be involved in and helpful for their own communities. The university and the First Nations communities are two separate worlds that tend to contradict each other with regard to goals and values. There are significant questions with regard to who benefits from research conducted with Aboriginal communities. The university often has different expectations about what kinds of research questions should be explored and how the research should be conducted in these communities. Competitive grant evaluations tend to favour researchers who have a substantive publication record, not necessarily a long-standing reputation of commitment and integrity within a First Nations community. Work with the community is neither acknowledged nor rewarded at the university. Moreover, researchers are encouraged to get something published quickly and spend only a minimum of time in a community. This has led to a number of studies that provide incomplete or inaccurate descriptions of Aboriginal communities. If scholars are engaged in research that is of no direct benefit to the community, the community may want, as my grandfather did, some compensation and show of commitment to the community's self-determined development. Too many non-Native researchers have gone into communities without finding out what research these communities might need. They have conducted themselves in ways that are not respectful and have published works on topics that are sensitive, private, and personal, too often neglecting an analysis of larger political and economic issues. The one-sided power relations between researchers and First Nations communities has, of late, changed radically since many tribal councils and cultural committees have imposed strict guidelines regarding community access and subsequent publication of research (Piquemal 2001; Lomawaima 2000).

It is essential that connections be made from both directions. Indigenous community members should be invited to the university and encouraged to share their experiences, insights, and desires, while researchers should travel to First Nations communities learning to listen carefully to elders and community leaders. University researchers can become too attached to the artificially created academic "community" and too alienated from the community of real people who, in Aboriginal communities, are the recipients of the legacy of colonialism. University faculty and graduate students have much to gain by spending time in an Aboriginal community listening to elders and traditional knowledge specialists. Elsewhere (Marker 1998) I have discussed the paradigm shift that often occurs for professors who leave the physical space of the university and spend time teaching or doing other work in Indigenous communities. This practice is consistent with both the "respect" and "reciprocity" components of the four Rs, especially if researchers are also willing to learn from rather than simply about Aboriginal people. An excellent example of how these themes are practised is Ray Barnhardt's description of university professors trying to "teach" a 50-year-old Native leader: "With our limited experience, we were not in a position to teach him much that he did not already know, but as university professors who had descended from the ivory tower to participate, however briefly, in his world, we were in a position to help him validate his grounded knowledge by putting it in the context of our book knowledge. Through this process, we greatly expanded our own store of useful knowledge" (2002, 242). An Indigenous perspective asserts – insists – that knowledge from the community is as valuable as the knowledge contained in the academy. If universities are sincere in their efforts to create a space for Aboriginal students, then they must also create a space that welcomes the participation of Aboriginal communities in the knowledge-exchange relationship. At the University of British Columbia, the Ts`´kel graduate studies program has been making these connections between the university and the First Nations communities.

Ts`´kel and the Vision of Eagles

Ts`´kel is a program for graduate studies located in the Faculty of Education at the University of British Columbia. Ts`´kel is a Halq'emelem word that means golden eagles. The name was chosen in counsel with Sto:lo elders and highlights the vision and transcendence of the eagle spirit in the students who attend from throughout Turtle Island (North America) and abroad. It is important to note that while all Indigenous cultures are celebrated and potentially represented in the Ts`´kel program, the traditional sense of place and the local Coastal Salish culture are honoured through the name, and the university's physical location on the land of the Musqueam people is acknowledged. The structure of Ts`´kel represents one way to deal with a number of the problems encountered in Native Studies programs. Ts`´kel began in the mid-1980s following the success of the Native Indian Teacher Education program at UBC. Aboriginal teachers, returning to the university for advanced training and administrative credentials, desired a program of study that emphasized knowledge related to the unique circumstances of First Nations communities and band schools. Over one hundred individuals have earned graduate degrees through Ts`´kel, which has evolved to include a substantial PhD contingent. In many ways, Ts`´kel now serves as both a professional program in educational leadership and an academic program of interdisciplinary Indigenous perspectives on social and educational topics. While Ts`´kel was originally conceived as a professional program of graduate studies for First Nations students in education, the courses are now attended by students from many disciplines. The point to emphasize here is that it is not enough for universities to simply increase the number of First Nations graduates by providing programs out of an equity goal.

Ts`´kel functions to provide both a culturally grounded education for First Nations students and an Aboriginal perspective on – and critique of – mainstream educational content and goals. In other words, First Nations knowledge and perspectives are not just for Aboriginal students; they are both a tonic *and* a polemic that need to be engaged with throughout the university. Vine Deloria has maintained that "viewing the way the old people educated themselves and their young gives a person a sense that education is more than the process of imparting and receiving information, that it is the very purpose of human society and that human societies cannot really flower until they understand the parameters of possibilities that the human personality contains" (1991, 21).

Native studies programs have too often been pushed to the margins of university discourse or immobilized by being encapsulated within anthropology departments. Ts`´kel has evolved out of the broad field of education concerned with both practical and theoretical issues within a faculty of education. This has provided a home base for Native studies research and discussion that is neither cut off from academic disciplinary traditions nor absorbed by rigid disciplinary boundaries. Anthropology's ongoing internal debate about its classic "four fields" orientation is an example of this kind of knowledge boundary maintenance that confounds the growth and development of interdisciplinary Indigenous knowledge in the academy. While education, as an academic discipline, has had a difficult time defining a credible knowledge base and is too often seen as a weak field of intellectual endeavour, it provides the right combination of academic resilience and emphasis on praxis that appeals to Indigenous goals that link political and cultural work to the life of the community. In many respects, it has been the emergent work of Indigenous scholars like Linda Smith, Marie Battiste, A. Oscar Kawagley, and Jo-ann Archibald, coming from schools of education, that has revitalized a languishing educational discourse in both post-colonial studies and the established disciplines. Much of Vine Deloria's writing has focused on conceptual themes in Indian education. However, establishing a vibrant Indigenous academic presence by way of an educational studies approach requires constant clarification to a university population that tends to equate education with narrow concerns of pedagogy and classroom proficiency. This is particularly a problem in the United States as both neoconservatives and discipline-ingrained academics have asserted that "there is no knowledge base for pedagogical practice that is even remotely comparable to those of other professions" (Cochran-Smith and Fries 2001, 6). Neoconservative critics of teacher training have viewed education departments as contributing little in the way of either knowledge production or pedagogical skill development. The political right has viewed university education courses as so much ideological proselytizing for an agenda of political correctness. Teacher education is also considered to be a series of intellectually fuzzy "hoops and hurdles." It remains "a highly contested premise that there is a knowledge base in teaching and teacher education based on rigorous research and professional consensus" (Cochran-Smith and Fries 2001, 9). Academics coming from social science disciplines have often viewed colleagues in education departments as lacking scholarly rigour and as endlessly mired in the vicissitudes of schooling debates. This disciplinary vagueness of education as a field has worked to the advantage of Indigenous mobilization at UBC and elsewhere. Since education is a study that can permeate the discussions of all other disciplines – education is concerned with the transmission of knowledge – it can focus attention on all aspects of university culture and process. This parallels the ways in which Indigenous knowledge is not confined to one department or one discipline but is rather an orientation that can engage with, and problematize, the taken-for-granted assumptions of the academy. In this approach, Indigenous knowledge and methodology cross all disciplines – similar to the way in which educational studies is interdisciplinary.

Ts`kel has emphasized an Indigenous perspective on subjects rather than a withdrawal from conventional disciplinary fields into a Native studies academic isolation. In many respects, this is consistent with Kirkness and Barnhardt's challenge to bring an Aboriginal perspective into mainstream disciplines and discourses rather than promote a separate Native studies field. This has produced a wide range of intersecting alliances with professors who not only work with First Nations graduate students but learn to critique the conventions of their own disciplines by engaging with the knowledge base and perspective of the student. This provides a broader institutional transformation based on the presence of Indigenous students and the reordering effects of Indigenous knowledge. In this sense, education becomes not simply a discipline but a foundation for unifying both knowledge and action: a form of praxis. The success of this approach relies on the respectful relationship between faculty and students – an acknowledgment that this is a cross-cultural moment of engagement. The success of this arrangement also relies heavily on the leadership of First Nations faculty, who supervise research committees and provide a challenging exchange with colleagues across the departments. Students in Ts`kel have written theses and dissertations on a diversity of topics related to law, medicine, sciences, history, literature, philosophy, linguistics, and many others. In almost all cases the studies have a direct link and a practical applicability to the concerns of the Indigenous communities the students come from. Ts`kel students and alumni have won national awards and have published groundbreaking works both in Canada and internationally.

It must be said, however, that employing an interdisciplinary educational studies model for a graduate program in Indigenous studies is not a panacea for the entrenched problems of academics' need to protect their disciplinary turf. In 2003 I designed a new course on Indigeneity and technology that was reviewed by a faculty senate committee. The course syllabus was sent out for review to the anthropology department, which decided that the course was simply a feeble version of an anthropology course. By adding some advanced "anthropological" readings and renovating the outline, I satisfied the anthropology department and the course has now been approved. This did not actually improve the course; it only added readings that were more relevant to anthropologists and less relevant to Indigenous concerns. One begins to suspect that a number of problems encountered by the Native studies programs described above are related to their earlier "nurturing" by departments of anthropology.

Both Equity and Content

While the directorship of Ts`'kel remains in the Faculty of Education, the graduate students come from departments throughout UBC. The centrepiece of the program consists of two Indigenous research methodology courses that are taken by all students in the program. These courses provide students of First Nations ancestry from all disciplines a place to discuss common concerns and approaches to research in an advanced seminar setting. These two courses are open only to Ts`'kel students, but other graduate students who have had experience in Aboriginal communities and who demonstrate sufficient discernment related to cross-cultural content may be admitted as Ts`'kel associates. These seminars are protected spaces for Indigenous discourse. They provide an equity access for First Nations students who, in years past, have not been welcomed into the educational system. They also provide an opportunity to relate cultural and academic knowledge in a secure environment.

In some respects, Ts`'kel has been evolving into an Indigenous university integrated within a mainstream university. Ts`'kel functions like a clearinghouse for courses, ideas, and methodologies that work toward the purposes of Indigenous scholarship. And while the students engage in an interdisciplinary study across the university, they also appreciate the home-away-from-home qualities of the First Nations House of Learning as they gather with other graduate students to celebrate an Indigenous academic community. The Longhouse, as it is called, provides informal spaces for meetings, computer access, a student lounge, an elders' lounge, and an extraordinary great hall that has been used for conferences and graduation ceremonies. Traditional houseposts, carved by Indigenous artists, and an architectural design based on large westcoast cedar plank houses, give a strong sense of the presence of Aboriginal people and culture in the university community. Ts`'kel PhD students defend their theses at the First Nations House of Learning.

There is much work still to be done, but much has been accomplished that will be sustained for many years to come. There is an ongoing need to expand academic training at the high school and undergraduate level to prepare students for the demands of graduate school. We need to look carefully at the issues of gender distribution among First Nations post-secondary students. In British Columbia in 1999, 63 percent of Aboriginal students were female, compared with 55 percent for the non-Aboriginal population. Moreover, the age distribution of Aboriginal students placed them as older than the non-Aboriginal population (Ministry of Advanced Education 2000, 7). There is a pressing need to bring young adult Aboriginal males into higher education; the group with the highest suicide rate in Canada is that of Aboriginal male youth. There is also a need to increase the numbers of First Nations faculty and provide mentoring and publishing opportunities for Aboriginal academics who are just beginning their careers.

If universities wish to recruit and retain First Nations undergraduate and graduate students, they must work with Aboriginal faculty and staff, who provide the direct link to the First Nations communities. They must provide resources to encourage and support the academic achievement of Aboriginal secondary student and adult learners to help introduce them to university work and participation in academic culture on the basis of a respectful, cross-cultural dialogue. This ongoing conversation between universities and First Nations communities should utilize the four Rs as a template that not only benefits the Aboriginal community but transforms the educational relationships within the academy as well. If university and government officials really examine the principles of the four Rs, changes in the educational climate and modes of knowledge exchange will follow. This then becomes not simply an equity issue but rather an issue of healthy institutional change and evolution related to respecting the valuable contributions of Indigenous knowledge and perspectives.

We should continue to revisit the four Rs and raise questions about the relevance, reciprocity, respect, and responsibility of the academy in establishing relationships with Indigenous people. At the University of British Columbia there has been significant growth in First Nations mobilization. Our goal is to sustain this growth and increase Indigenous engagement. That being said, it is imperative to foster an international context of comparative Indigenous studies that will bring other sites into focus. For example, while understanding American contexts is important, it is equally vital to study Maori, Pacific Islander, Australian, and Latin American contexts as potent reference points. Rather than being seen as disruptive to Western knowledge customs, Indigenous knowledge, predicated on relationships and a spiritual connection to the land, may provide a means to connect the disparate elements of separate disciplines into a whole. Marie

Battiste has expressed this need to avoid the marginalization of First Nations knowledge:

> The real justification for including Aboriginal knowledge in the modern curriculum is not so that Aboriginal students can compete with non-Aboriginal students in an imagined world. It is, rather, that immigrant society is sorely in need of what Aboriginal knowledge has to offer. We are witnessing throughout the world the weaknesses in knowledge based on science and technology. It is costing us our air, our water, our earth; our very lives are at stake. (2000, 201)

There is a shortage of writing about Indigenous reality in the literature on higher education. The issues for First Nations are complex and embedded in cross-cultural questions that, up to now, have evaded many scholars of higher education. In this chapter, I introduce emergent themes that are moving from the margins to the centre, that are frequently disruptive, but increasingly integrated into the whole.

The Kirkness and Barnhardt article from over a decade ago told of a monkey who is so obsessive with its habitual way of getting food that it is caught and sold to a zoo. In this metaphor, we were warned that the comfortable patterns of university life and knowledge production not only alienate Indigenous people but impede healthy institutional change. Interrupting the lemming-like journey of Western technocratic knowledge could become the most powerful and enduring legacy yet of First Nations education.

Acknowledgment
A version of this chapter appeared in the *Canadian Journal of Native Education* in 2004.

Note
1 In this chapter I use the terms Indigenous, Aboriginal, First Nations, Indian, and American Indian somewhat interchangeably. Each one, however, is selected for different emphasis. An explanation of linguistic usage for each term defies the space of a footnote. All of these terms are used by tribal people to refer to themselves in broad contexts. Suffice it to say that Native people prefer to refer to themselves and each other by specific traditional names in their own languages. The terms used here are broad categories with exceedingly complex histories of usage.

References
Barnhardt, R. 2002. Domestication of the Ivory Tower: Institutional Adaptation to Cultural Distance. *Anthropology and Education Quarterly* 33, 2: 238-49.
Basso, K. 1996. *Wisdom Sits in Places: Landscape and Language among the Western Apache.* Albuquerque: University of New Mexico Press.
Battiste, M. 2000. Maintaining Aboriginal Identity, Language, and Culture in Modern Society. In *Reclaiming Indigenous Voice and Vision*, edited by M. Battiste, 192-208. Vancouver: UBC Press.
Biolsi, T., and L. Zimmerman. 1997. *Indians and Anthropologists: Vine Deloria Jr. and the Critique of Anthropology.* Tucson: University of Arizona Press.

Bowers, C.A., M. Vasquez, and M. Roaf. 2000. Native People and the Challenge of Computers: Reservation Schools, Individualism, and Consumerism. *American Indian Quarterly* 24, 2: 182-99.

Cajete, G. 1994. *Look to the Mountain: An Ecology of Indigenous Education*. Durango, CO: Kivaki Press.

Champagne, D., and J. Stauss, eds. 2002. *Native American Studies in Higher Education: Models for Collaboration between Universities and Indigenous Nations*. Walnut Creek, CA: AltaMira Press.

Coates, K. 2000. *The Marshall Decision and Native Rights*. Montreal and Kingston: McGill-Queen's University Press.

Cochran-Smith, M., and M.K. Fries. 2001. Sticks, Stones, and Ideology: The Discourse of Reform in Teacher Education. *Educational Researcher* 30, 8: 3-15.

Deloria, V. 1991. *Indian Education in America*. Boulder, CO: American Indian Science and Engineering Society.

–. 1994. *God Is Red: A Native View of Religion*. Golden, CO: Fulcrum Publishers.

Huffman, T. 2001. Resistance Theory and the Transculturation Hypothesis as Explanations of College Attrition and Persistence among Culturally Traditional American Indian Students. *Journal of American Indian Education* 40, 3: 1-23.

Gilmore, P., D. Smith, and A. Kairaiuak. 1997. Resisting Diversity: An Alaskan Case of Institutional Struggle. In *Off White: Readings on Race, Power, and Society*, edited by M. Fine; L. Weis, L. Powell, and M. Wong, 90-99. New York: Routledge.

Kirkness, V., and R. Barnhardt. 1991. First Nations and Higher Education: The Four Rs – Respect, Relevance, Reciprocity, Responsibility. *Journal of American Indian Education* 30, 3: 9-16.

Lomawaima, K.T. 2000. Tribal Sovereigns: Reframing Research in American Indian Education. *Harvard Educational Review* 70, 1: 1-21.

Marker, M. 1998. Going Native in the Academy: Choosing the Exotic over the Critical. *Anthropology and Education Quarterly* 29, 4: 473-80.

Martin, R. 2001. Native Connection to Place: Policies and Play. *American Indian Quarterly* 25, 1: 35-40.

Ministry of Advanced Education Training and Technology. 2000. *1999 BC College and Institute Aboriginal Former Student Outcomes*. Victoria, BC: Queen's Printer.

Piquemal, N. 2001. Free and Informed Consent in Research Involving Native American Communities. *American Indian Culture and Research Journal* 25, 1: 65-75.

Srebrnik, H. 1993. Football, Frats, and Fun vs. Commuters, Cold, and Carping: Social and Psychological Context of Higher Education in Canada and the United States. In *Canada and the United States: Differences That Count*, edited by D. Thomas, 380-406. Peterborough, ON: Broadview Press.

Thorpe, D. 2001. The Spirit of the People Has Awakened and Is Enjoying Creation through Us: An Interview with Jeanette Armstrong. In *Native American Voices: A Reader*, edited by S. Lobo and S. Talbot, 249-53. Upper Saddle River, NJ: Prentice Hall.

Wisniewski, R. 2000. The Averted Gaze. *Anthropology and Education Quarterly* 31, 1: 5-23.

8
Welcome to Canada? The Experiences of International Graduate Students at University
Regina Lyakhovetska

Since the Middle Ages, universities have attracted students and scholars from many different countries. Today, this tradition continues (Huxur et al. 1996). In the mid-1990s an estimated 1.5 million students worldwide attended universities outside their home countries (Canadian Bureau for International Education [CBIE] 1997). In 1999, approximately 42,400 international students were enrolled in Canadian universities, about 14,600 of whom were graduate students.

International students have often been considered a convenient population for examining academic, social, and psychological problems of adaptation and attitudinal changes; however, the international student experience itself has been peripheral to the concerns of researchers (Altbach 1991). The benefits that international students bring are not well documented. The contributions they make to the teaching, learning, and research functions of institutions are often not recognized. The needs and aspirations of the students themselves are not well understood. Lack of sensitivity on institutional and community levels to what international students are experiencing is considered to be one of the main barriers to their integration (Cunningham 1991). Indeed, it has been charged that international students are "generally held in low esteem by host institutions" (Lulat 1996, 6).

As international students are increasingly becoming a public policy issue and a focus of internationalization in Canada, studies providing valuable background and insights on their issues and experiences are needed. The purpose of this chapter is to present the results of a study that examines experiences of international graduate students with respect to their academic and social life, finances and employment, as well as their experiences with student services and perceptions of inclusion in campus community. International students' views about university internationalization were also examined. Data were gathered through individual in-depth interviews and a focus group.

International students are defined as students who are neither Canadian citizens nor permanent residents of Canada. International students require student authorizations to study in Canada. A small number will have special ministerial or diplomatic permits (CBIE 2001). International students must demonstrate that they are able to pay the fees for their course or program of studies. They must financially support themselves and accompanying family members, and pass an Immigration Canada medical examination. In addition, they must satisfy authorities that they are not inadmissible to Canada and they will leave Canada at the end of the period they are allowed to stay (Citizenship and Immigration Canada [CIC] 2002).

This chapter consists of four sections. The first section gives an overview of international student issues in Canada as identified by CBIE surveys of international students in Canada, studies by Association of Universities and Colleges of Canada (AUCC), and individual researchers across North America. The second section describes the research design. The third section presents the findings from the interview sessions and the focus group. The last section presents discussion, recommendations, and suggestions for further research.

International Student Issues
Over the past two and a half decades, a number of trends in the development of international student issues in Canada have emerged. The growing numbers of international students were a concern in the late 1970s. The number of international students increased steadily, peaking at 36,068 in 1983. Increases in students from Asia and the United States created the impression of significant growth. Since then, differential tuition fees have been implemented, and work restrictions and immigration restrictions put in place. As a result, in the mid-1980s the numbers of international students in Canada at the post-secondary level started to decrease. Between 1988 and 1991 the number increased to 37,034 before dropping steadily over the next four years. By the beginning of the 1990s, the problem had become reversed: it became necessary to increase the numbers of international students. The absence of any specific measures to encourage international students to come to Canada meant engaging in active recruitment. Today, institutions are increasingly involved in recruitment of high-fee-paying international students under the banner of internationalization. Despite the promotion of the academic value of internationalization for the teaching, learning, research, and service aspects of higher educational institutions (OECD 1989; AUCC 1995), it is the economic dimension, with emphasis on marketing Canadian education abroad and on the short-term benefits of income generation, that raises significant pedagogical concerns, ethical issues, and policy implications.

CBIE's *National Reports on International Students in Canada* (1987-2001) show that, increasingly, Canada is becoming the provider of education to the students from the richest countries in the world. In 1999, approximately 40 percent of international university students in Canada came from Asia and 10 percent came from the United States. In 1999-2000, less than 2 percent of international university students were supported to some extent with funds from the Canadian International Development Agency (CBIE 2001). International students are believed to play an important role in terms of bringing international perspectives to the classroom, bringing significant economic benefits to universities and local communities, and providing connections for Canada's long-term trade and diplomatic interests (AUCC 2001). Other rationales for hosting international students include "increasing institutional profile in target countries" and "increasing enrolment in specific programs" (Knight 2000, 53). Nonetheless, responding to the needs of international students for higher education opportunities currently ranks very low with host institutions. Nationally, there is a notable absence of policy on international students in Canada and on international education in general.

Although international students report high levels of satisfaction with their overall experiences of studying in a foreign country (Song 1995; Walker 1999), many encounter academic, social, and financial difficulties. International students bemoan their lack of success in making friends with domestic students (CBIE 1989; Ishii 1997; Nebedum-Ezeh 1997). The majority of their friends are co-nationals and other international students. They report a lack of participation in campus activities. Many international students experience difficulties in adjusting and integrating into the local academic culture (Huxur et al. 1996; Thornstensson 2001). While domestic students also face problems when entering a new academic setting, for international students these "normal" problems are compounded by new academic challenges, new customs, different living arrangements and styles, new forms and codes of social life and behaviour, unfamiliar food, a foreign language, and in many cases, the absence of family and friends (Perrucci and Hu 1995). International students are in serious need of supportive academic and social relationships in the university and local communities. Unfortunately, studies show consistently poor use of student services by this group (Cunningham 1991; Nebedum-Ezeh 1997; Walker 1999). They are either uninformed about or unaccustomed to seeking institutional support. The sources of support are limited to an orientation program, ongoing counselling, and nonacademic support. No specific attention is paid to the sources of academic support that international students may need. Despite the findings from many studies that international student services have an impact on recruitment efforts, improvement of international student experiences, and successful integration into the campus community, these services continue to be understaffed and underfinanced. Research also suggests that international students are experiencing considerable financial hardships (Walker 1999). Government and institutional policy (e.g., differential tuition fees, right-to-work restrictions) is partially responsible for these hardships. These findings from the literature are particularly true for students who speak English as a foreign language and who come from developing or the least-developed countries. Although several studies highlight the benefits that international students bring to host campuses, striking evidence in many studies demonstrates a lack of effort by institutions to meet the needs of international students.

Research Design

I chose Pacific University (a pseudonym) as the site for the study. Pacific University is a major research institution in western Canada with a total enrolment of 39,184 students for the 2002-2003 winter session. More than 3,100 international students from 127 countries study there. International undergraduate students make up 4 percent of the total undergraduate population and international graduate students constitute 17 percent of the graduate population. Fifty-seven percent of international graduate students are male; 52 percent study at the doctoral level. Pacific University has a long tradition and commitment to international cooperation, with partnership agreements with more than 200 institutions in 48 countries. The university's Internationalization Strategy (2003) called internationalization a key component in reaching the goal of being Canada's best university. The key rationales behind internationalization are to ensure international competitiveness of the province and its people, to provide graduates with marketable skills, and to respond to the changes that have occurred in the research agenda, curriculum, and composition of professional staff and students.

I used a purposeful sampling strategy to recruit participants. The participants had to meet the following criteria: they had to hold the status of international students at the time of the study and had to have spent at least one term in a department at the Faculty of Education. My assumption was that international graduate students in education could offer rich insights into international graduate students' experiences in general as they are engaged in the field concerned with the issues of respecting cultural diversity and providing supportive environments for all learners. In October 2001, letters of invitation to participate in a study were sent to all international graduate students in one department at this faculty.

Ten students agreed to participate by returning the consent forms. Each student was contacted by e-mail to arrange a face-to-face interview. They were interviewed over the course of five weeks in November and December 2001. Interviews lasted from one to two hours. At the end of all interview sessions, eight students participated in the two-hour focus group. Interviews and focus group were audiotaped and transcribed. The transcribed interviews were given to the participants for validation. The data were then sorted and analyzed to establish the emerging themes. A helpful step in this analysis was creating tables with participants' quotes for each of the themes identified. This allowed me to look for consensus and contradiction among responses. It also allowed me to collapse a number of categories in cases where two or more had overlapped responses.

Findings

I begin this section by describing the demographic characteristics of the participants, their educational and employment backgrounds before coming to Canada, and their motivations behind decisions to study abroad. The interview and focus group data are presented around the following themes: academic experiences, social experiences, community, student services, finances, employment, satisfaction, and views about internationalization at Pacific University.

Eight participants were 28 to 35 years of age; two participants were 35 to 40 years old. They came from nine different countries. Four students came from three countries in Southeast Asia. Two were from Latin American

Table 8.1

Participants' characteristics

Number	Name[a]	Gender	Country	Degree program	Residence	Marital status
1	Chien	Male	China	Master's	On-campus	Married
2	Meng	Female	China	Master's	On-campus	Married[b]
3	Kenichi	Male	Japan	Master's	Off-campus	Married
4	In-su	Female	South Korea	Master's	On-campus	Single
5	Paola	Female	Brazil	PhD	Off-campus	Married
6	Sofia	Female	Mexico	Master's	Off-campus	Single
7	Tshepo	Male	Swaziland	PhD	On-campus	Married[c]
8	Sarah	Female	United Arab Emirates	Master's	On-campus	Single
9	Rikki	Female	English-speaking country[d]	PhD	Off-campus	Single
10	Steve	Male	United States	Master's	Off-campus	Single

a All names have been changed to protect the participants' anonymity.
b Meng's spouse stayed in their home country. Meng lived with her son and was expecting another child.
c Tshepo's spouse stayed in their home country.
d This student asked me not to identify her country of origin.

countries. One was from the Middle East. Another student was from a country in Africa and two students were from English-speaking countries. (See Table 8.1 for the summary of participants' characteristics.)

Interviewees studied in five different programs in this department. Eight students were at the end of their programs and were working on either graduating papers or theses. All participants had strong educational and employment backgrounds to prepare them for academic success at Pacific University. Six participants had either completed master's degrees or experienced studying in graduate-level programs. All had extensive experience working in a variety of educational settings from the school to the state level. Many thought they had good English skills upon arrival. Steve and Rikki were native English speakers. Sarah, Paola, Sofia, Rikki, and Tshepo had studied in English-speaking countries. Meng was an English teacher in her home country. However, Chien, In-su, and Kenichi had never lived in an English-language environment. Also, both Chien and Steve had no experience of travel outside their home countries.

The participants were guided by complex reasons in their motivations to study abroad. They included better employment opportunities with North American degrees, limited access to specific graduate programs in their home countries, the desire to learn about the West, the wish to expand knowledge in their subjects, and concern about the growing North American influence on educational systems in their home countries.

In-su: I see that people from Korea who study in North America impact our education a lot and force us to adopt certain strategies, philosophies. I wanted to understand more what these strategies are about and how they are going to change the lives of teachers and students at home.

The student from the United States had unique reasons for studying outside of the States:

Steve: In the US there is only one perspective – the US perspective. I wanted to get something different than all Americans get.

The majority of participants had a choice to study in a number of different countries, but they chose Canada. The most commonly cited reason was the image of Canada as a safe country with a well-developed economy, good education, free health care, social services, and friendly people.

Chien: Chinese media shows a lot of violence happening in the US Canada is safer than the US It's one of the major industrial countries in the world.

Another reason was that Canada was becoming a more popular destination for international students:

In-su: Many Korean students now choose Canada. Before they would just go to the US. I wanted to be different from those who studied in the US.

A few students mentioned that lack of knowledge about Canada in their home countries made them choose it over other countries:

Chien: Canada is sort of a mystery for me.

All participants came to Pacific University because of its strong academic reputation. They learned about it from conversations with faculty members in their home countries or from postings and promotional brochures at libraries and educational fairs:

Sarah: Universities from 150 countries come to this fair and Pacific University is one of them. I went to look at their stand and they had this beautiful picture of mountains in the water and I fell in love with that. I looked it up on the Web later and thought it would be a good place to go.

Some liked the information on the university's website and others met university representatives at international conferences. They also mentioned western Canada's proximity to Asia and the fact that increasing numbers of co-nationals were immigrating to Canada:

In-su: Vancouver is very famous in Asia. I think it's because there are a lot of Korean people here; they go back to Korea and sometimes they wear the university's T-shirts in the streets and I saw that: Pacific University in the streets in Korea. So it became familiar to me.

They chose the Faculty of Education because they wanted to learn from Canadian educators, to share their backgrounds, and to bring positive changes to the educational settings in their home countries. Six students mentioned that their goals remained unchanged throughout their studies or changed only slightly. Others indicated major changes in their plans. For some students changes were disappointing:

In-su: Before coming here I did not know exactly what my program was about. I thought I could become a senior administrator in Korea. But I don't feel my learning here can be useful in Korea.

However, several students said their programs opened new horizons for them:

Paola: I never planned to do a PhD program. But I developed a wonderful relationship with a professor from one of my classes. So I became really passionate about the subject. Two years ago in Brazil working ten hours a day, six days a week at a school system, I could have never dreamed that I would have an opportunity to do what I am doing now.

Their goal in the beginning was simple: "get a degree"; but later they started thinking, "Oh, I like to study. I want to continue to learn more."

Academic Experiences

Most students described the academic climate at Pacific University as very different from that of their home universities. For the majority, these differences were positive. Participants from non-English-speaking countries were fascinated with informal relationships between students and professors, freedom to discuss ideas in class, and opportunities to learn from doing research:

Chien: There is more academic freedom here than in a Chinese higher education institution. You don't have to stick to one idea or ideology. It's now changing in China but still not that much as in North America.

These students appreciated the various opportunities such as workshops and conferences offered for student professional development. All said that their home universities offered fewer extracurricular academic activities. They also mentioned the richness of material resources they had discovered:

Paola: I think the academic climate here is very nurturing, very supportive. What amazes me most is the realm of material resources. When I go to the library, the amount of books I am able to access about Brazil written in English and Portuguese just blows my mind.

However, one student was very disappointed by the negative differences she had encountered:

Rikki: There were ten of us in my master's program [when I was a foreign student] in the US. We struggled with different theories, figured them out: we worked together. It's more challenging to create an environment here. You have to make yourself involved; otherwise it is very easy to get lost. Nobody is going to track you down, that's for sure.

I asked a separate set of questions to encourage participants to talk personally about their academic activities at Pacific University. In particular, I asked them about their connections with faculty members. The students who had studied for graduate degrees in English-speaking countries managed to connect with several faculty members:

Rikki: My supervisor and me started to do some really neat things together. I am assisting her with some research and we are writing a paper together.

For others these contacts were rare but very memorable:

In-su: During the first reading break my supervisor invited me to go to her home. She asked me what I needed, if I had any difficulties and she showed me an elementary school. I was really curious what Canadian schools looked like so I was very happy to go there. I think I can never forget that.

Some students explained their difficulties by referring to certain language and cultural barriers:

Meng: In China you are not supposed to be chatting with your teachers, administrators, and staff; all of them are so high above, you have to respect that because you are a student and they are the people who work in the office. You never call teachers by their first name.

One participant said she watched Canadian students who "talk with professors very easily" and "joke with each other" and "understand each other easily." But she did not know "how to make a joke with a professor ... what kind of things I can say."

I asked the participants about their connections with Canadian classmates. The majority of international students in the study turned out to be unsuccessful in establishing meaningful relationships with more than one or two classmates. Differences in language ability, cultural behaviour, and work experiences made it a challenging and disappointing task. However, they had good relationships with other international students:

Meng: I have a few Canadian friends but I cannot meet them. When you meet them, they are always busy. They will say: "OK, if you need my help, call me or e-mail." But I just feel it's not good to disturb them. In one class we had a lot of international students and we all talked to each other.

One student said she had many friends at home but here she felt isolated. Canadian classmates preferred to interact with each other: "I say hello and smile, but they say hello and turn their faces away. I have to find another person. Who? Who?" Even the student from the United States found it challenging to have relationships with Canadian classmates but he took proactive steps to change that:

> Steve: In my first two or three classes I did not know anyone and nobody was rushing up to meet me so I had to take the initiative. I would just go up and stick myself in their conversation.

Several other students referred to their classmates as friendly and outgoing. One particular student called her relationships with classmates "absolutely wonderful." She was establishing "much more meaningful connections with people than in [her] undergraduate years" and "not just on a personal level but in terms of scholarship exchange."

Although all participants were amazed by the amount of extracurricular academic activities the university offered, few took advantage of them. Some were uncomfortable to attend alone; others were unclear regarding what was expected of them in terms of participation:

> Kenichi: I just attend [seminars] and listen to what other people are talking about. I don't know how I can participate positively.

However, PhD students took full advantage of the opportunities to attend and even present at seminars and colloquia. These students presented on topics related to their home countries when they were asked to do so by their professors.

Among master's students from non-English-speaking countries, only one attended conferences while studying at Pacific University. They believed these conferences would be great learning opportunities for them but they needed help in developing their proposals and explaining what was involved in the process:

> In-su: I never participated in conferences abroad. I don't know what will happen. I went to a conference in my country but I went with my professor and other classmates. I knew what to expect.

Other reasons for nonparticipation were lack of time and heavy workloads.

Academic Work

The majority of participants described their academic work as challenging and demanding. Students whose first language was not English reported difficulties in all aspects of academic work such as reading, writing, and speaking. Improving English was the major challenge these students faced:

> Chien: English is a barrier for my studies. I read more carefully and listen more than talk.

Many of them were also out of school for a number of years, so they had to get used to being students again. They also had to get used to the vocabulary specific to the field of education:

> Paola: It's been extremely demanding. It's been a new field for me. I feel like my whole life is on hold. Sometimes my classmates say, "Oh, it took me three hours to read the article last night." And I am thinking, "Oh, my god, it took me three days."

Learning academic writing was a priority for many of these students. Even the student from the United States discovered that he also had a lot to learn in terms of writing in English:

> Steve: I thought I spoke English before I took that class ... The professor sent me to get an "English fluency" textbook ... No matter how hard I tried to improve my writing, it was still not good enough for him.

Few students had no problems with any aspects of their work; if anything it was a challenge that helped them grow.

Class Participation
Most students were satisfied with the majority of their classes and found them interesting and useful. They appreciated learning about Canadian education. However, they had difficulties understanding abbreviations and culturally specific phenomena. These students often assumed the role of listeners and rarely had chances to contribute. In addition, professors did not try to engage international students in some of these classes:

> Meng: In my first term when I joined group discussions, I felt like I had nothing to say. Some classmates would say, "Ok, what's the case in your country?" Then I would get a chance to talk. You don't know anything about education here in the beginning, so how can you talk about it?

The other problem that students from non-English-speaking countries encountered was the spontaneous nature of these discussions. They had difficulties catching up with the fast-changing topics and needed more time to shape their thoughts and phrases in English:

> Kenichi: It's very difficult for me as a non-English speaker to break in a fast-paced conversation based on the knowledge that only Canadian students have. Sometimes I can't follow the discussion.

Many of them did not take any steps to let the faculty or other students in class know they had problems. These international students were afraid to look "stupid" and they did not want to disturb other people with their questions:

> In-su: In my first term I could not raise my hand and ask, "Hey, what is collective agreement or what is CAPP?"[1] So I kept quiet and thought, "OK, maybe CAPP is a 'cap.' If I asked, they would say: "Oh, my god, don't you know what is CAPP???" I did not want to make myself look stupid.

However, a few others tried to get help from classmates sitting next to them:

> Tshepo: I think I have a duty to interrupt and say, "Hang on, what do you mean by this?" I believe it should not be the other people who think for me.

Two PhD students did not have any problems participating in their classes; they had problems keeping quieter. The student from Brazil noted that it was a part of Brazilian culture to be very outspoken:

> Paola: Sometimes I monopolize the discussion almost by myself. I have to tell myself, "Wait a minute, you know, other people need some room here."

All students in the study said that their level of comfort in classes depended largely on whether the professors invited their opinions and asked questions about their backgrounds. Half of the participants said they were encouraged to share their cultural experiences in class and some of them did not hesitate to step into the discussions themselves:

> Paola: I think there is a lot of space to draw from your own background. And what I have found is that people are actually interested in what I am telling about Brazil. Some professors asked me to draw one comparison or another. But I don't sit back and wait for someone to ask me.

A couple of students, however, said their professors and classmates did not encourage them, but they tried to encourage themselves or found encouragement when other international students spoke up:

In-su: If there is another international student in class and he or she starts telling her or his experience outside of Canada, I add my experience.

Rikki said she had not been asked specifically to talk about her country but to her "it's not much of a big deal." A number of participants felt more at ease speaking up in the classes that enrolled many international students:

Kenichi: Classes with more international students where professors invited our opinions were more comfortable for me: nobody was dominant.

Other students pointed out that they would be more comfortable if they heard the professors bring in examples and articles from different cultural contexts, not just English-speaking countries. They would have appreciated more opportunities to compare different educational systems. They wished the instructors maintained more control over class discussions to ensure that they had space to contribute:

In-su: If a professor tells the class that we will talk about education in BC and in Korea, it means he gives me some room to participate; so I feel like a member of that class. Also, some professors just focus on the speaker or talk to a few persons, but I am like, "OK, I am an outsider. I don't know why I am staying here."

All participants benefited from the courses that involved international issues:

Kenichi: In one course someone talked about Japanese higher education and all of us asked this person questions or expressed our opinions about it. I liked that course very much.

These findings are similar to those of Ruth Warick (this volume), whose interviewees felt more like "visitors" than full participants in the classroom. A few international students in this research reported feeling like outsiders and strangers. Opportunities to share their cultural and educational backgrounds increased their feelings of being included.

Social Experiences
Most students spoke negatively about the social climate at Pacific University. They described it as a "lonely place." However, they used their undergraduate experiences as the basis for comparison. One student found the social climate "conducive for one to learn and live happily." But it still could not compare to home, where he belonged:

Tshepo: At home I am a different person because I am not a foreigner. I have more control over culture, language, and general atmosphere. I am familiar with places. I have more contacts to fall back on. I don't have to rely so much on other people.

I asked interviewees if they participated in any events on campus, and what they thought about these events. Most students participated in no more than one or two department gatherings. They managed to participate in just a few trips or welcoming parties on campus. Some thought these events were mostly for undergraduate students; others hesitated to go alone. Several tried to participate whenever they could and enjoyed the events very much:

Kenichi: I was once invited to a home of one PhD student for Christmas dinner through a program at the department. It was a good chance to get acquainted with Canadian people and see how they lived.

Two students did not find the time to participate in events either inside or outside the department. Although few had active social lives according to their accounts, all of them appreciated the opportunities they had. They said that these events allowed them to learn more about different cultures on campus and made their lives more enjoyable, but, most important, they provided opportunities to build connections with other people:

In-su: I liked meeting other graduate students. It's fun. International students are all separated; they need some connection with each other.

The students who received information from e-mail messages, bulletin boards, and campus newspapers participated in few or none of the events. The interviewees who reported the highest participation in social events said that much of their information came from friends, who either invited them personally or forwarded them e-mails:

Chien: If I had more friends who I know very well, I would have probably participated in more social events. They would say, "Oh, you want to go there?" I would say, "OK, let's go together."

I asked the participants who their friends were. All participants in the study came to Canada not knowing any people:

Steve: Many international students that I know did not come here with a group of friends, you know, they came here by themselves. You just don't sit around and say, "Hey, let's all go to Pacific University."

Unfortunately, none reported having made many friends during their studies. The students from non-English-speaking countries said that the majority of their friends were other international students. They needed Canadian
friends but they could meet them only in the classroom. It was easier for
them to socialize with people from their home countries because they shared
a common language:

> Kenichi: I can't explain well my problems in English so I will talk to Japa-
> nese people.

Other international students were also a preferred group because they
could better relate to each other's problems:

> In-su: Canadians just share good things. I don't want to share my weak-
> nesses with them so we share very little of our lives. They will say, "Oh, I am
> sorry, poor you." But when I go with my international friends, they will just
> say, "Oh, don't worry, I have the same feeling."

In contrast, the students from English-speaking countries did not attempt
or even failed to make friends with other international students. Their friends
were Canadian students whom they met on or off-campus. Rikki said she
saw several international students in the department but she did not have
any relationships with them. She added: "so far, I had nothing in common
with these people." However, Steve mentioned being careful in communicating to some Canadians:

> Steve: When I was out in the restaurants, people could tell I am from the
> south of the US just by my accent. And they'll be making jokes about Ameri-
> cans. I never knew that existed! When I went to school, I always heard that
> Canada was just like the US; I thought people thought the same way and we
> were all friends and everybody loved each other and everybody loved the
> United States. But it was just such a naive concept that I had.

After this situation he became much more aware of "what to say and how
to say it."

Community
Many students could not describe the environment for international students at Pacific University as they rarely spent time outside their department:

> Sarah: I have not felt anything special except for that one seminar for
> international students at the department. I felt special because I am an

international student and I was there as a member of a group who had special experiences to share.

The students from non-English-speaking countries felt excluded because the curriculum focused mainly on the developed countries, because of their limited ability to communicate in English, and because they could not freely socialize with Canadian students and faculty:

> In-su: My advisor and secretaries are very supportive but I still feel a huge gap between the faculty, the community here, and me. They go home, I go to residence.

The student from the United States pointed out that there was not enough understanding of the changes international students like him had to make to their lives in order to come to Pacific University or why they had to come in the first place:

> Steve: I left the place where I had worked for ten years: I sold my house, sold everything in my house, travelled three thousand miles not knowing a soul here ... I got asked hundreds of times, "Why are you here instead of the US?" It made me feel like I was not supposed to be here.

In contrast, the three doctoral students described the environment at the department as very welcoming. They felt very much included in the department and campus community. One felt she was included because she was a white English-speaking woman with a job, a car, and friends across the border:

> Rikki: I have made my space. I work in different positions. I feel as a member of different communities. It's good. People say "hi" when I walk into rooms. I can fit in OK.

Two others felt that way because they were active in seminars and social events.

Student Services
The interviewees used very few student services. Two of them reported having negative experiences with financial services and with finding on-campus housing. These problems resulted because the students were unfamiliar with certain Canadian practices – for example, what kind of information needed to be entered into the application for residence in graduate student colleges – and because nobody took the time to familiarize them with those practices. Those from non-English-speaking countries said that although they

needed advice on social matters on a number of occasions, they would never have used the help of a counsellor because they were not accustomed to talking to strangers about personal matters:

> Sarah: I don't know anybody here well enough to discuss personal problems. Whatever happens I have to deal with it on my own or try to get help from people who I trust.

Although the particpants agreed that they could use all services on campus, many of them felt they also needed specific services to address their needs as international students:

> Kenichi: If there are courses or workshops specifically for international students, it is easier for me to attend them. I don't have any doubts about going there.

They spoke of International House not just as a service but as a community to which they could belong:

> In-su: When I go there, I meet lots of people like me, who do not speak good English; it makes me feel much better. I think, "Oh, another one here!" Some people who I met there are still my very good friends. They support me like a family. Sometimes we made our own food; sometimes we went to visit places. If I said something – I have a problem – they say, "Yeah, me too, me too."

Several students, including the ones from English-speaking countries, had a very vague idea of the role and functions of International House and did not "step in there even once." The students who were least familiar with the services available at Pacific University were the ones who got their information mostly from e-mails, postings, and brochures around campus. However, those who used more services said that their advisors or other international students recommended them.

Finances and Employment

Four participants received full or partial funding from their home governments or the Canadian government. Six other students were self-supported and relied on family savings for their funding; five occasionally worked on campus. Steve, who had a full-time job in the US, commuted on a daily basis; he also received US student loans. Two students received permission to participate in a work-study program and one received several bursaries from Pacific University, although both forms of support are granted to international students in very rare cases. They reported having difficult family circumstances that made them eligible for these forms of funding:

Chien: At first I was refused from work-study program. So I went to talk with the financial services advisor. I said, "My money is almost used up. My wife is here. She cannot find a job: she has no work experience in Canada; she does not speak English well. Please give me a chance."

Another student was a single mother. Master's students from non-English-speaking countries who did not have scholarships reported financial difficulties. They could not find good stable jobs on campus; they did not have enough savings; and some needed to support their spouses and children. Many interviewees were upset that they had to pay more than domestic students sitting with them in the same classrooms:

Rikki: I don't know why we pay extra money. Why do we cost more? What do I get that is extra that makes me cost more?

Participants with sufficient financial support were not upset that international students paid more than domestic students. On the contrary, they advanced arguments why this was the case:

Tshepo: International students pay the unsubsidized tuition rate in many universities across the world. A Canadian student pays half of what I pay but they will continue to support the university indirectly as taxpayers when you and I are gone.

Those who spoke English as a second language reported difficulties in finding graduate assistantships and ended up working in low-paid jobs. They felt the employers would not hire them because of a lack of English proficiency and absence of work experience in Canada. Most of them looked for jobs on websites and campus postings. If they got any jobs, they described getting them by accident. All worked because they needed to earn the money to live on:

Meng: I just earn enough money for food, around $300-$400 a month. I tried some better-paying jobs like TAs or RAs. I really wanted to have that experience but it was hard to find any.

Only one student from a non-English-speaking country said her job also provided her with a good learning experience. She liked the fact that she could help other international students at her job. A student from an English-speaking country was extremely satisfied with her employment experiences at Pacific University. She had one or two graduate assistantships every term and could cover both her tuition and living expenses from her income. On top of that, she was getting great academic experiences at her jobs:

Rikki: I am a member of a research team. We are in the process of collecting data, analyzing it, and then hopefully presenting it at a conference. I did a book review for my other job. So this is kind of fun.

She received her information directly from professors or administrators willing to hire her. They knew her from before, as she was a student representative on several committees.

Interestingly, the students from non-English-speaking countries, although most of them worked part-time in addition to struggling with academic work and improving their English, took the time to volunteer. They wanted to make new international students feel welcome and spare them some of the troubles they had to experience:

Sofia: I volunteered in International House because I wanted to be contacted by Mexican students. I felt isolated when I came here, so I thought it would be good for them if they meet somebody who welcomes them.

In contrast, English-speaking students and all but one student who relied on external funding did not do any volunteer work throughout their stay.

Satisfaction
Despite some negative experiences, all expressed overall satisfaction with how things turned out for them at Pacific University. They became more critical and receptive to criticism, and more interested in different cultures; students for whom English was a second language spoke of becoming more comfortable in expressing their thoughts in English:

In-su: I think it's a really worthwhile experience. My attitude has changed. I want to try new things. In my culture we are quite good listeners but here everybody speaks, speaks, speaks ... I was really scared to do that, what will other people think of me? I started speaking up here.

Several students gained new understandings of what it meant to be international students:

Sarah: I come from a different culture, from a different world, so I bring something good with me – something to share with people here. I wish people here would try to learn about my culture and give me an opportunity to learn about Canadian culture. It's a two-way thing: we are here to learn but also to teach.

Steve from the United States felt he became a representative for his country following the events of 11 September 2001:

> Steve: After September 11th, there were several people very supportive to me and there were also people who said some nasty things, but I just shrugged them off. They don't know who I am. Yeah, I am from the US, but what does that mean? It's very hard when you are an individual and you have to defend the entire country.

Many participants talked about having learned a lot of survival skills, becoming more independent and proactive than before. Those students whose goal in the beginning was getting a better job believed they were closer than ever to that goal.

Views about Internationalization

Participant responses suggest that learning about internationalization raised certain expectations. They speculated about implications for teaching, learning, research, and services at the university. Most participants said that internationalization was first and foremost about people and recognition of their diverse backgrounds:

> Steve: It's about people regardless where they came from, instead of everything being Canadian or British Columbian or any other. It's a recognition of who we are, what is our significance and what contributions we can make to campus whether through academics or personal engagements.

They expected to see more services available for international students and increased awareness of international student issues among faculty members, staff, and Canadian students. Several students said that internationalization was also about curriculum that will not be "targeted to serve a particular group of people." A few interviewees said that the university's efforts to internationalize meant only expanded recruitment efforts and tuition increases for international students. The "double face" of internationalization, with its promise both to transform the university and to make money, so vividly discussed in Nelles (2000), has not gone unnoticed by international students. The students were skeptical about the role they thought was allocated to them in the process of internationalization. Some students thought that the university just used its international students to attract more students to its programs:

> Rikki: It's just another marketing line for the university: "We have attracted all these wonderful people from different countries and you are going to have such a great experience because you will hear all these different ways of thinking." It does not mean they care about international students.

In spite of that, the majority of participants were confident that international students were bringing a variety of benefits to teaching, learning, and research. They listed Canadian students, faculty members, other international students, and the university as a whole among the main beneficiaries. Several students mentioned that whenever they could, they tried to challenge the ideas they heard in classes and to express their own perspectives, thus contributing to the learning of all students:

> Paola: People from different backgrounds including myself voice their opinions in the classroom. I raise my hand and I say, "Wait a minute. My experience is different. This is not the way things happen where I come from." In that way I think I have some sort of pedagogical role as a student from Brazil.

Others said that even if they were not able to contribute a lot in class, they expressed their views in papers and journals that faculty members and other students could learn from. Such activities could also generate interest in faculty to undertake research related to international students' countries of origin:

> In-su: I am doing research about Korea for my major paper so another student interested in this research may use it after I leave Pacific University.

They were contributing their knowledge and experience through participation in extracurricular social and academic activities:

> Kenichi: Other students I meet outside the classes can benefit from me. I always talk about Japanese culture and society so they can understand more about Japan talking to me.

Some students said that the university would be able to benefit from them in many indirect ways upon their return to their home countries. They might initiate projects involving Canadian faculty and students. They will continue to share their experiences and make this university known in their home communities through alumni clubs or other networks. These students mentioned that they were already spreading the good name of Pacific University in their home countries and attracting other international students to come:

> Sarah: I talk about it in my home country. I know at least three students who want to come here just because I told them.

Study participants were raising awareness among the faculty about the issues facing international students and thus contributing to the welfare of future international students:

Meng: I wrote a paper about international students' issues. The instructor was never aware of the situation and she said it was very helpful for her to know. Perhaps if she has international students in her classes in future, she will do something for them.

Some students were providing support to other international students in every way they could:

Sarah: I personally helped a few people here since I came. I found them in the Student Union building; they were lost; they were international students. So I took them to the place they were looking for and we became friends.

International students called upon the university to take internationalization more seriously and address their greater involvement. They acknowledged the fact that students and researchers come from all over the world to Pacific University but noted that they are not used as resources:

Steve: Canada is international. The people who come here from all over the world make it international. But there is a difference in "saying" that you are an international university and "being" an international university. Right now Pacific University is still saying it's an international university.

As one student summed it up, "just the fact that there are students here from foreign countries does not mean internationalization. We have to be involved."

Discussion

The findings from this study indicate that the experiences and backgrounds of international students vary. However, a few patterns have emerged. Classroom participation presented challenges for students from non-English-speaking countries. They were uncertain of their English skills, lacked background in Canadian issues, and were not used to participating in spontaneous classroom debates. Participants appreciated learning about Canadian education. It was new knowledge for them. However, they had limited opportunities to contribute to the courses focused on provincial matters. They also needed explanation of specific terminology and cultural phenomena. In contrast, they were highly motivated and enjoyed participation in courses involving international issues. Few interviewees took part in social events and extracurricular academic activities. They did not make good use of student services. Several participants reported feeling excluded from the community. They lacked connections with Canadian students and faculty. Master's students who spoke English as a foreign language had difficulties finding on-campus jobs. They were also financially insecure. Supervisors had a large impact on experiences of international students. The students were more successful when their supervisors advised them about campus resources; took interest in their academic, social, and financial needs; encouraged them to participate in seminars and conferences; and connected them with other faculty members. Participants agreed that international students should be more active in sharing their backgrounds and participating in campus activities, but they needed the university to reach out to them as well and make them feel an important part of campus.

Workig from the findings above, I identified areas where the majority of participants felt their needs were not fully met and where improvements would enable them to have better educational and social experiences. These areas included academic programming, social interaction, community sensitivity, support services, institutional policies, and the role of international students in internationalization. The CBIE and AUCC identified the same areas as important to internationalization in their policy documents and reports. I ask in this section whether experiences of international students are consistent with proposals from these key Canadian advocates for international education.

AUCC (1995) recommended that universities should make full use of the expertise of international students in teaching, research, and in the classroom. International students can be an important educational resource if engaged proactively. However, many participants did not enjoy this kind of recognition. Faculty and domestic students rarely expressed interest in them.

The British Columbia Centre for International Education (2003) stated that friendships that develop between Canadian and international students during their stay in BC contribute to global understanding and to building long-term relationships that foster goodwill between Canada and other countries. My findings show that, although international students may contribute to the development of world friendships by making friends with each other, Canadian students are not necessarily part of these friendships. Studies that arrive at similar findings often generalize this as a problem for the whole international student population. However, my study has found that participants from English-speaking countries were largely successful in making friends with domestic students and unsuccessful in making friends or associating themselves with other international students. Another finding unique to this study is that a number of participants from non-English-speaking countries lacked meaningful connections with faculty members. The CBIE studies question how cross-cultural understanding could be achieved without improved opportunities for international students to know Canadians. If one rationale for accepting international students is to enhance Canada's future trade relations, international students must have extensive and positive interactions with the campus as well as the larger community.

Investigations (AUCC 1995; Nelles 2000) suggest that successful internationalization requires reform in service delivery. The uprooting associated with studying in a foreign country goes far beyond the typical separation issues faced by domestic students. International students are more likely to experience more problems and have access to fewer resources. This research indicates that international students are largely unaware of student services and not used to taking advantage of them. In contrast to those recorded in other studies, participant responses indicate that international students need to use services not just in the beginning of their programs, but throughout their programs. The university should enhance efforts to ensure that international students are aware of existing programs and services and are invited to participate.

This study shows that the university's commitment to internationalization has not fully impacted institutional policies affecting international students. High tuition, limited financial aid, absence of priority housing policy, and limited access to employment create unnecessary financial hardships, especially for those whose first language is not English. Pacific University's mission statement emphasizes that the cost of a university education should not be a barrier to access and that the university plans to continue enhancing scholarship and bursary funds. The question arises whether this commitment means increased support for international students.

Studies prior to this one have not paid specific attention to international students' views of their inclusion in the campus community. Participants at the Organization for Economic Co-operation and Development (OECD) Seminar in Hiroshima, Japan (1989), pointed out that institutions should increase efforts to improve community receptivity for international students. Fourteen years later, this research has revealed that master's students whose first language is not English did not for the most part feel included in either the campus or department community. A few of them felt neither excluded nor included. None reported a sustained effort by the department or the campus generally to welcome international students. In contrast, doctoral students felt very much included. Pacific University's internationalization strategy (2003) stresses maintaining connections with international alumni and encouraging their interest and involvement in the university's future plans. Yet, if some students do not feel part of the community when they are here, there is not much hope that they will identify with the university upon graduation.

International students are not a homogeneous group. In a diverse student body, no one group can be singled out as a minority because they are all minorities (Garrod and Davis 1999). Most participants listed numerous connections with other international students. These ties provided major sources of academic and social support. Some studies frame this phenomenon of international students preferring to interact with other international students as a problem. On the contrary, this finding demonstrates the importance of mutual support among international students on campus and the value of increased efforts to create opportunities for international students to interact.

All participants attested to the fact that their experiences studying abroad had changed them. They became more independent, more confident, and more proactive. Although previous investigations of outcomes of "study-abroad" experiences were of undergraduate students in their early twenties going abroad for a term or an academic year, this research shows that older international graduate students completing their entire degrees in a foreign institution may share the same personal outcomes. The challenges reported did not significantly influence participants' satisfaction with overall experiences. Lulat explained satisfaction with studying abroad as a "testimony to the success in 'negotiating' with an alien educational institution, bureaucracy, people, language and culture, and alien landscape and weather" (1996, 5). Studies consistently show that international graduates with the strongest sense of identity and purpose when they leave their host institution are invariably those men and women who have confronted significant challenges during their study-abroad experience.

When international students discussed improvements they wanted to see in their academic and social life, and later when they explored what internationalization should be about, their answers seemed remarkably similar. In both cases, they wished to see more sharing of cultures on campus, more opportunities for participation in class discussions, more efforts to attend to the needs of people from different cultures, and more integration of international materials and perspectives in the curriculum. Internationalization as understood by international students carries a promise of a more supportive environment, enriched educational and social experiences, and visibility for them and their issues. At the same time, the reality of universities' commitment to internationalization leaves them disappointed when they do not see these changes happening.

The recommendations offered address how international students could better achieve their goals and how a host university could assist them. Academic writing courses as well as introductory seminars about Canadian education, history, and culture would be beneficial for these students. International students who need to improve their English skills should have access to advanced-level English courses taught by professionals. International students would particularly benefit from these courses if they could take them in the first months of their stay before taking classes in regular programs. It would ease their process of integration in the mainstream classroom and provide opportunities to make friendships with other international students.

Professors who wish to increase participation of international students in their classes should invite their opinions and encourage them to share their experiences from their home countries. Classes allowing for comparisons among different educational systems and providing opportunities for international students to reflect on what they had learned and how they can apply this knowledge to their home countries would benefit international and ultimately all students. Examples and articles from different cultural contexts would also increase motivation and inclusiveness. When Canadian issues are discussed, professors need to ensure that terms and abbreviations are explained. Assignments in which Canadian students are encouraged to write papers or design oral presentations together with international students would help both groups learn more about each other. This study calls upon Canadian students to be more attentive to their international peers. Domestic students should encourage their international classmates to share experiences from their home countries in class discussions and provide help in explaining culture-specific terms mentioned in class. International students also need more encouragement to participate in extracurricular academic and social activities. They need to be taught to use student services. Department and faculty orientations designed specifically for international students should include information about services available on campus and explain the benefits of using them. Pacific University should raise awareness of the importance of international students, the benefits they bring to campus, and the issues they face. Regular assessments of international students' needs have to be conducted. It is particularly important for international students to be involved in the debates about internationalization and the meaning of an international campus.

Numerous studies conducted by the CBIE and AUCC show that Canada continues to suffer from the absence of coherent policies in regard to international students and international education in general. International student policy is multidimensional in nature. Strong coordination at the federal, provincial, and institutional levels is necessary to establish this policy. It should contribute to a welcoming environment for international students in Canada. It should benefit the students from the developing countries as well as students from developed countries. Like the CBIE studies and surveys on international students in Canada (1976-2000), this study recommends that policy makers on the national, provincial, and institutional levels consider easing of work restrictions for international students, including those related to working and volunteering off-campus. They should also contemplate increasing scholarship support for students from developing countries as well as for those from countries with poor economies. Increased efforts by educational institutions are necessary to expand campus-based employment opportunities for international students.

Additional research would be useful to establish a strengthened database of international student experiences. Research is needed on how various members of the university community view international students and internationalization. The role of international students in furthering internationalization in higher education requires clarification. More research is needed on how institutions internationalize programs and how they deal with international students. By attending to the needs of international students and building on their strengths, institutions will be improving experiences for all students and enhancing the process of internationalization.

Note

1 The British Columbia Career and Personal Planning Program (CAPP) was established in 1995. CAPP is unique in BC in its legislated requirement for work experience and its span across all years from Kindergarten to Grade 12 (Council of Ministers of Education, Canada 1998).

References

Altbach, P. 1991. Impact and Adjustment: Foreign Students in Comparative Perspective. *Higher Education* 21, 3: 305-23.

Association of Universities and Colleges of Canada. 1995. *AUCC Statement on Internationalization and Canadian Universities*. Ottawa: AUCC. <http://www.aucc.ca/publications/statements/1995/intl_04_e.html> (27 February 2001).

–. 2001. *Recognizing the Importance of International Students to Canada in the Immigration and Refugee Protection Act*. Ottawa: AUCC. <http://www.aucc.ca/_pdf/english/reports/2001/c11_03_02_e.pdf> (10 December 2002).

British Columbia Centre for International Education. 2003. *Importance of Internationalization*. Victoria, BC. <http://www.bccie.bc.ca/Public/Importance.asp> (20 April 2003).

Canadian Bureau for International Education. 1989. *The National Report on International Students in Canada 1989*. Ottawa: CBIE.

–. 1997. *The National Report on International Students in Canada 1996/1997*. Ottawa: CBIE.

–. 2001. *The National Report on International Students in Canada 2000/2001*. Ottawa: CBIE.

Citizenship and Immigration Canada. 2002. *Studying in Canada: Overview*. <http://www.cic.gc.ca/english/study/index.html> (20 November 2002).

Cunningham, C. 1991. *The Integration of International Students on Canadian Post-Secondary Campuses*. CBIE Research Series, no. 1. Ottawa: CBIE.

Garrod, A., and J. Davis, eds. 1999. *Crossing Customs: International Students Write on U.S. College Life and Culture*. New York: Falmer Press.

Huxur G., E. Mansfield, R. Nnazor, H. Schuetze, and M. Segawa. 1996. *Learning Needs and Adaptation Problems of Foreign Graduate Students*. CSSHE Professional File no. 15. Ottawa.

Ishii, E. 1997. *The Experience of International Students: Exploration through Drawings and Interviews*. Unpublished master's thesis, University of British Columbia, Vancouver, BC.

Knight, J. 2000. *Progress and Promise: The AUCC Report on Internationalization at Canadian Universities*. Ottawa: AUCC.

Lulat, Y. 1996. What Does It Mean to Be an International Student? A Personal View. In *CBIE's International Educator's Handbook*, edited by J. Humphries and M. Kane, 5-7. Ottawa: CBIE.

Nebedum-Ezeh, G. 1997. An Examination of the Experiences and Coping Strategies of African Students at Predominantly White Institutions of Higher Education in the United States. Doctoral dissertation, University of Massachusetts. Abstract obtained from *UMI ProQuest Digital Dissertations* (Publication no. AAT 9737567). <http://wwwlib.umi.com/dissertations/fullcit/9737567> (5 May 2001).

Nelles, W. 2000. What's New? Understanding Internationalization and International Education in British Columbia. *Learning Quarterly* 4, 1 (Spring): 7-9.

OECD Secretariat. 1989. Foreign Students: A Leading Edge for Change. In *Foreign Students and the Internationalization of Higher Education: Proceedings of OECD/Japan Seminar on Higher Education and the Flow of Foreign Students*, edited by K. Ebuchi, 33-44. Hiroshima, Japan: Research Institute for Higher Education, Hiroshima University.

Perrucci, R., and H. Hu. 1995. Satisfaction with Social and Education Experiences among International Graduate Students. *Research in Higher Education* 36, 4: 491-508.

Song, Z. 1995. A Study of Female International Students at the University of New Brunswick. Master's thesis, University of New Brunswick. Abstract obtained from *UMI ProQuest Digital Dissertations* (Publication no. AAT MM06968). <http://wwwlib.umi.com/dissertations/fullcit/MM06968> (5 May 2001).

Thornstensson, L. 2001. This Business of Internationalization: The Academic Experiences of 6 Asian MBA International Students at the University of Minnesota's Carlson School of Management. *Journal of Studies in International Education* 5, 4 (Winter): 317-40.

Walker, J. 1999. *Canada First: The 1999 Survey of International Students*. Ottawa: CBIE.

9

The Transition from High School to Post-High-School Life: Views of the Class of '88

Gabriel Pillay

> Students who are in high school are not really prepared for
> the entirely different atmosphere of post-secondary institutions.
> High school students receive graded homework assignments and
> are cajoled along by their instructors in order to make them pass,
> whether they want to or not. Students in post-secondary institu-
> tions are basically ignored by their instructors – with no prior
> warning.

> After going straight into university I found that high school does
> not prepare students for abstract and high level of thinking. High
> school seemed totally concerned with right/wrong answers while
> in post-secondary there is ambiguous issues which first year
> students are unprepared for.

As these quotes illustrate, making the transition from high school to post-secondary education is a challenge for many students. High school graduates require certain knowledge sets to best prepare them for the transition from secondary to post-high-school life. Often, however, students have limited experiences to help them make the transition to this new environment.

In today's competitive and highly demanding society, the importance of accurate and relevant information about post-high-school choices is crucial. High school is one location where students should be able to gain access to information and be assisted in interpreting the material in order to make informed decisions. The transition from high school to post-high-school life is a period of significant change and readjustment. Students move from one system (secondary school) into a new and different world for which they may or may not be prepared.

Over the past decade, British Columbia's post-secondary education system has expanded and diversified. As a result, post-secondary education has become more accessible for British Columbians. Due to expansion of the system, a wider variety of post-secondary institutions and offerings, and extensive articulation agreements among post-secondary institutions, the current post-secondary system offers enhanced selection and educational mobility. Choice and selection are now staples in the marketplace of education in which students are offered a variety of degrees, diplomas, and certificates. Armed with relevant, current, and accurate information, students can make informed decisions that will lead them to their desired educational and career aspirations.

In this chapter, I examine the transitional experiences of British Columbia high school students by utilizing data generated from the Paths on Life's Way Project. This longitudinal study of a large sample of 1988 BC high school graduates includes follow-up surveys conducted in 1989, 1993, and 1998. Specifically, responses to open-ended survey questions collected in 1989, 1993, and 1998 will be used to determine the following: (1) their perceptions of high school and its role in preparing them for the transition to post-secondary life, and (2) their experiences of the transition to post-secondary education and life after high school. These written comments provide some insight into the subjective perceptions, meanings, and interpretations that students have about their transitional experiences after high school graduation. The aim is to assess how the transitional experiences of BC graduates surveyed from the class of 1988 can help to inform policy and practice, to ensure that students make a successful transition from high school to post-secondary education and life.

Research Design

The data in this chapter consist of the actual written responses of survey respondents who answered the open-ended questions on the survey. This survey involved three questionnaires sent out at three different points in time: 1989, 1993, and 1998. In addition to posing specific questions on a range of subjects, each questionnaire also included a final open-ended question to give respondents the opportunity to add other comments. The analysis is based on the responses to these open-ended questions.

In 1989, the total number of responses to the questionnaire was 5,345; 2,765 of these respondents provided comments as invited in the final question. In 1993, 2,030 responses were received, and 1,608 respondents made final comments. In 1998, of the 1,055 individuals who responded to the mail-out questionnaire, 800 made general comments in response to the final open-ended question.

Open-ended responses were coded using the ATLAS/ti program. ATLAS/ti, a visual qualitative data analysis program, facilitates the interpretation and categorization of large bodies of research material. Codes were developed inductively after the comments were read to determine the recurring themes.

Radcliffe describes the process: "the same body of codes was used in the code of the responses to all three questionnaires, although not all codes applied to all the questionnaires. In total there were 29 codes ranging from 'applied education,' 'access,' to 'teaching' and 'work.' The names of the codes aim to reflect the main idea/concept of the comments concerned" (1996, 32).

Because one respondent could comment on many different topics, each topic was coded separately. For instance, the following response from the 1989 questionnaire represents two coded categories. The response makes reference to secondary school graduation requirements and preparation which can be coded as COUNSELLING (high school counselling and counsellors) and TEACHING (teaching and teachers).

> I found in my high school that there weren't enough counsellors or teachers with enough time for students. I had a hard time deciding what to become as did other students and there wasn't enough information given to us.

In this chapter, the unit of analysis is the individual comment, not the individual respondent. Hence, there are more comments than the total number of responses recorded. Data (comments) from each separate survey will be presented and discussed according to follow-up survey year (1989, 1993, and 1998).

Findings

One Year Later: 1989 Follow-Up Study of the Class of '88
In 1989, 5,345 individuals from the graduating Class of '88 completed the first follow-up survey. In total 2,765 (52 percent) respondents provided comments as invited in the final question. The final question on the 1989 survey was as follows: "Your comments are invited."

The experiences of the Class of '88, as recorded by their comments regarding open-ended questions in the first follow-up survey, a year after high school graduation, explicitly reflect the following themes, which will be further developed and discussed in this chapter: beliefs about education; views on high school counsellors and their role in preparing for post-secondary education; high school preparation for post-secondary education; perceived secondary education experiences of participant respondents; and nonparticipant respondents' reasons for not attending post-secondary education.

Beliefs about Education
Of the 2,765 responses to the 1989 question, a total of 50 comments addressed individual beliefs about education. In general, many of the comments recorded (48 percent) expressed a positive belief that further education

(beyond high school) was in fact a "necessity" in life to help ensure, enhance, and secure "employment and career opportunities." Certain patterns and issues become increasingly apparent in the comments. For instance, recent graduates assumed that attaining higher education would enhance "future success," "employment opportunities," and "personal satisfaction."

Beliefs about education one year after high school graduation (1989)

50 responses in total	*Percent of cases*
Education in relation to:	
future success (enhanced standard of living)	6
employment and career opportunities	8
Education is important (in general)	48
Limited worth (value) of education	14
No need for further education	14
Other	14

The following responses are indicative of the beliefs students had about education in general. Several respondents provided comments such as this one about future success and enhanced standard of living:

I believe that post-secondary education is essential to anyone wishing to "get ahead" in the workforce or life in general!

Others talked about increased career or employment opportunities:

I believe income after post-secondary education has a major input on why people go in the first place.

The general importance of education was also an issue raised by respondents:

I guess the main point is to try and tell students of how important an education is, and encouraging students to want to learn. A mind is a terrible thing to waste.

I would like to say that, when your survey is printed; encourage future graduates, counsellors, etc. not to look for the easy way out of school. I did and I have regretted that I did so. The importance of a good education cannot be underestimated.

I think everyone should at least graduate. Post-secondary is very beneficial even if you cannot find work. It enhances your personality.

Some responses (14 percent), however, clearly challenged the belief that increased education could enhance employment opportunity and successes. For instance:

I believe that education is high over-rated.

While I am not presently attending college, I have learned many aspects of life, especially where they concern me; I feel post-secondary is important but not absolutely essential.

High School Counsellors and Counselling
Analyses of survey data revealed that "the lack of influence by secondary school personnel is startling. Fifty percent of female and 52% of male non-participants reported that secondary school counsellors had no influence on their educational decisions and secondary teachers fared only slightly better" (Andres 2001, 23). This is worth noting, for by virtue of their roles and responsibilities in preparing students through planning and guidance, it would be assumed that high school counsellors would significantly influence the lives of students.

The survey recorded 178 responses discussing high school counsellors and counselling. Although some comments were simply critical (e.g., "My Grade 12 counsellor was also very dumb and screwed up constantly"), the majority had good reasons for frustration. As such, the comments generally tend to be negative (e.g., "I have yet to meet a good counsellor") and disparaging toward counsellors (e.g., "The competence of some school counsellors are questionable").

Comments on high school counsellors and counselling (1989)

178 responses in total	*Percent of cases*
Specific comments regarding:	
counsellors	24
availability of counsellors and guidance	16
Extent of personal planning	28
Availability of information	55
Information accuracy	6

It should be noted that a number of respondents took the time to write thoughtful paragraphs in which they expressed their concerns and experiences regarding high school counselling services. The following responses exemplify and stress the general sentiment regarding a lack of guidance in high school:

I am very confused about what to take at university – in high school I would have liked to have been introduced to the opportunities and various choices that I obviously should have, but really know nothing about, i.e.: what getting a biology degree can lead to; is it enough etc.

After getting a BA, is it necessary to continue or is there job opportunities? I received very little "counselling" type information. I'm still not aware of my choices after a full year of university.

The quality of the information supplied by high school counsellors is really disgraceful. For me and many people I know, the counsellors' help was of no help or left them utterly confused or enrolled in useless courses.

Comments specifically about the abilities and capabilities of counsellors totalled 24 percent of those associated with high school counselling. The following responses illustrate the general feeling about counsellor capabilities:

Some counsellors in my high school needed to take some courses in dealing with teenagers. This would enable them to help students rather than put them down.

Counsellors are 100 percent useless in high school. They lack knowledge of the issues and tasks they deal with. The present way they carry out their jobs is a waste of tax dollars. Get some real people who understand the students and the present educational system.

The availability of counsellors also caused some frustration among respondents. For instance, some comments suggested that the limited amount of time available for assistance in planning was attributed to the lack of available counsellors within a given school:

The counselling dept. at my high school was inadequate and almost invisible, even though the graduating class was over 400, and demanded more attention.

Counselling dept. at secondary school was over-worked and under-staffed. Bare minimum of help provided.

Respondents noted that some areas of planning and counselling did not receive adequate (and an appropriate amount of) attention. According to the survey responses, 55 percent of the respondents felt that there was an apparent lack of information regarding post-secondary education and the options available to them:

More information is needed on career opportunities and education possibilities outside of BC. Students need to know their options early in their high school years.

My father obtained the information necessary for my university program. I was disappointed with the counselling for post-secondary education at my school.

Having accurate information is essential to the decision-making and planning process. However, even when information regarding post-secondary education and options had been provided, 6 percent of the responses suggested that the information was inaccurate:

Poorly informed about university by the school counsellor and was given very bad advice.

High school counsellor gave misleading information about requirements for a college program.

My high school counsellor did absolutely nothing for me including telling me wrong information. Because of that misinformation I almost didn't make it to college my first year. She almost told me directly she didn't think I should go to college. She hinted a lot and right now I get C+ and Bs.

Only a few responses (five) rated the performance of their counsellor as being adequate or good. A few respondents offered suggestions to deal with poor counselling that were underscored by a slight sense of sympathy and sentiment (voiced quite infrequently) toward counsellors and their role within schools:

I think the schools do a wonderful job in giving students choices for the future. Programs like "CHOICES" was very good. I hope this will stay in the schools.

I was overly impressed with the support I received at my high school. The counsellors and teachers were very apt in helping me with university applications, transcripts, etc.

High school counsellor's workload should be reduced. They do not have the ability or time to service both personal and career counselling. Specialization is needed to ensure expertise in both areas.

A year after high school graduation, many respondents noted that they required more extensive transitional planning and preparation prior to entering post-secondary education. For instance,

Students in school should have more information on the outside world and truthful how well they can do; and what can be achieved. Not to have them isolated in what they call the "school system."

To summarize, there were a limited number of positive comments concerning counsellors; the vast majority were negative. Respondents stressed a need for guidance and planning to help with future goals. Post-secondary life and education were becoming a reality for them and they felt poorly prepared.

High School Preparation for Post-Secondary Education
Continuing in the same predominantly negative tone as in the comments on counsellors, respondents indicated that high school requirements and programs failed to provide adequate and proper preparation for the transition to post-secondary education. The question dealing with the level of satisfaction with secondary school elicited 216 comments.

Comments on high school preparation for post-secondary education (1989)

216 responses in total	*Percent of cases*
High school preparation for post-secondary (in general)	62
Transition planning and awareness	26
Specific high school subject preparation for post-secondary	22

The majority of respondents on this theme expressed a low level of satisfaction with secondary school preparation in relation to the transition to post-secondary education. A number of respondents commented that their high school failed to adequately alert them to the differences between the secondary and post-secondary educational systems. Also, several respondents said that more directly applicable skills should have been taught at the secondary level, that high school teaching staff needed to be more involved in student planning, and that greater accountability was needed for certain high school subjects (courses). The following two comments provide examples:

Students should be more prepared for the change that occurs when going to college. College is much different than secondary school.

University is not like high school. One goes to a university and is shocked: One is not spoon fed, e.g., notes on board, reminder of assignments due, homework check. High school should give better preparation for post-secondary schooling.

Some respondents provided detailed accounts to express their frustration with high school preparation for post-secondary life.

For example, one respondent also commented on the development of post-secondary skills:

More emphasis on high school learning and habits because college isn't what you expect. Be prepared to work in college but in high school it's casual.

Participation in Post-Secondary Education

In 1989, survey respondents "were asked whether they had participated in the post-secondary education system at any time between June 1988 and May 1989 ... in total, less than 25% had not attended a post-secondary institution within one year following high school graduation" (Andres 2001, 9). Thus, a majority of respondents participated in post-secondary education within one year of high school graduation. In total, 165 responses addressed the topic of post-secondary education in general. It was apparent that many respondents held certain expectations and assumptions about post-secondary education that were not realized. Some noted that university and college class size, administration, quality of instruction, and the "feel" of post-secondary education in general raised unanticipated concerns and issues during their transition.

General comments on post-secondary education (1989)

165 responses in total	*Percent of cases*
Availability of courses and PSE institutions	29
Administration	15
Quality of teaching	21
Transition experiences (in general)	25
Other	15

Becoming accustomed to the post-secondary system was a learning experience with a steep learning curve for many respondents. The following responses illustrate the experiences of many respondents in post-secondary education one year after high school graduation:

I find that most college teachers don't teach, they only lecture. One of my teachers said, "My job is to lecture and yours is to understand."

Tuition fees for the quality of teaching were astronomical. Professors cancel classes, refuse to repeat things, and don't care enough to ensure that students understand what they are studying. And they call this "higher learning."

Some respondents felt that university education was being overemphasized, and made suggestions about options other than attending university directly after high school for the "sake of future graduates."

More stress should be placed upon the importance of the smaller campuses of the community colleges. They offer an excellent education at a small cost and should be promoted that way.

Post-secondary education is something one has to be ready for, or they won't succeed. I was told by parents that I had to go to post-secondary school right away or I would never go back. I wasn't mentally prepared and went, so I ended up not doing that well and being disappointed in myself. I'm now taking a year off to decide what I want to do.

As indicated by the responses above, respondents who participated in post-secondary education directly following high school generally felt unaccustomed to the new system, which apparently they were not fully aware of, informed about, or both, during high school. They felt that high school had not prepared them for post-secondary education by making them aware of differences between the high school and post-secondary education systems.

Post-Secondary Nonparticipants
Of those who did not participate in post-secondary education following high school graduation (less than 25 percent of the survey sample), the majority indicated that they wanted to pursue education; however, for various reasons, they did not. The respondents' reasons for not attending a post-secondary institution following high school are categorized:

Reasons for nonparticipation in post-secondary education (1989)

61 responses in total	*Percent of cases*
Program options and availability	18
Still want to pursue except:	
family obligations	11
employment opportunities	28
financial issues	18
need for or a lack of career planning	28

Most nonparticipants expressed a desire to pursue post-secondary education. However, due to a lack of information about "options" and support ("detailed counselling ... individual counselling"), or changes in "plans," for instance due to "becoming a parent" (11 percent of the responses for not pursuing post-secondary education) or "finding 'secure' employment" (18 percent of the responses for not pursuing post-secondary education), they did not continue. One respondent, cited at length, indicated the need to offer individual counselling for the "nonacademic" student:

> I began completing this form and realized that because I have felt inadequate to continue my post-secondary education from the early age of 13-14 years, most of your questions are not relevant to myself. The public education system is not set up for the nonacademic student like myself; it is geared towards the academic. Your present system needs to work closer to the "real world" of the job market and develop apprentice programs for us nonacademic students. We need a greater choice of direction towards trades: technical positions at an earlier age than after high school graduation. My parents paid for me to take a "Bank Tellers" course, which is privately run and was four weeks long. This gave me the confidence to apply for jobs involving handling money. That's practical. I sure never learned that in my twelve years of school. Our government imports tradespeople and does nothing – or very little – to train our own young people. We are trainable even though we are not academic.

The following responses offer further explanations for nonparticipation by respondents. Regarding employment opportunities:

> At the present time I am not interested in going to post-secondary school as I have a secure full-time job. However, if the courses I am interested in were offered through correspondence, I would look into applying.

> Although I feel a post-secondary education is important, the amount of jobs available in the field I may study are not abundant. My current job I have will guarantee a rate of $16.71/hr. with full benefits for myself and family. Within a year a good paying, stable job; although I'm not presently happy.

Financial issues were also a concern:

> The main reason post-secondary was not pursued by myself was the lack of funds and also I had low grades in school.

After leaving Grade 12 with honours I started at UBC in the fall of '88. Although I had been refused a student loan, I still wanted to try to attend. I lasted a month. My point being that decent post-secondary education is financially out of reach to the students coming from the average family.

Nonparticipants commented on the lack of, and need for, post-secondary planning:

I found that after Grade 12, I did not have the desire to go to school. Having that attitude I quit after first semester. I recommended that if students are not sure of what they want to do. Take a year off because one would waste time and money if one did not want to be there.

I had the requirements and the ability to go on to post-secondary education. I didn't know what to do.

My reason for not attending post-secondary school was I felt I needed more self-confidence before I moved onto more difficult things. By getting a job it also gave me time to think out carefully what it was I wanted to study as well as giving me the money I would need to support myself the first few years. In this way I feel this is my accomplishment and my first step into the real world.

A year after high school graduation, the qualitative data from the first of three follow-up surveys identify a few key themes associated with transition from high school. In general, responses provided on the 1989 survey indicated that post-secondary education was valuable and necessary for enhancing employment opportunities and future successes. As well, many respondents reported negative experiences with high school counsellors, guidance programs, and general preparation for post-secondary education. Although comments generally tended to be negative, these responses offer a source of information to further investigate the needs of individuals preparing to depart from secondary school.

Five Years Later: 1993 Follow-Up Study of the Class of '88
In 1993, a second follow-up survey was sent to the 5,345 respondents to the 1989 study, of whom 2,030[1] (38 percent) responded. Survey participants were asked the following question, which drew a total of 1,608 responses:

Do you have any final comments or thoughts regarding education and work that you want to share with us? In particular, you are invited to comment about the following:

- accessibility to post-secondary education
- the cost of post-secondary education
- work, education, and the economy.

The respondents to the second follow-up survey, as in the previous survey, commented on their transitional experiences from high school, five years after graduation. The commentary below focuses on the following themes: beliefs about education; high school counsellors, counselling, and high school (in general); preparation for post-secondary life; post-secondary educational experiences of participant respondents; and the reasons for not attending post-secondary education provided by nonparticipants.

Beliefs about Education
A total of ninety-five comments referred to beliefs about education. Of those, 25 percent noted that attaining more education would enhance future success and employment opportunities. However, unlike in the previous survey (1989), a greater proportion of responses in 1993 (five years after graduation) indicated that education neither affected nor determined future successes and career opportunities. Furthermore, 19 percent of these responses challenged and questioned the worth (value) of attaining a degree.

Beliefs about education – five years later (1993)

95 responses in total	*Percent of cases*
Enhanced education and:	
future success (enhanced standard of living)	25
employment and career opportunities	19
Education is important (in general)	32
Limited worth (value) of education	45
No need for education	8
Other	8

The following responses detail the expressed beliefs about education of the respondents in 1993.

Regarding enhanced education and future success and employment opportunities, respondents made comments such as the following:

Education, especially post-secondary, is crucial. Young people need to go to school. It is very competitive out in the real world. The more education and experience you get the better.

Education is the key to success and one should never stop the quest for knowledge.

Education has not only enhanced my career prospects, but has also enriched my life with experience, new friends, and opportunities that would never have been available to me otherwise.

Others commented on the limited worth or value of education:

It is [my] opinion today that younger people are overeducated and underemployed, conferring on them a sense of frustration.

These days a university/college degree/diploma is like a high school certificate was ten years ago. You need a post-secondary degree for most jobs and if you don't have one, your résumé goes directly into the garbage.

It seems you don't get anywhere without a degree but you don't get anywhere with it either.

Respondents provided alternatives to enhancing success and career opportunities that were not related to education. As the following responses indicate, after five years it became apparent to some individuals that a degree did not necessarily predetermine and ensure enhanced opportunities.

Plus it ain't what you know in the real world, it's who ya know.

Depending on one's chosen career path, post-secondary education may not be necessary. For example, a business person who owns his own business does not need post-secondary education but rather he needs to know people of relevance to his business.

It doesn't really matter how much education you have because in the long run, it's experience that counts. You cannot get a job without experience.

High School Counsellors and Counselling
In total, thirty-one comments in 1993 were about counsellors and high school counselling. When commenting on counsellors, respondents commonly stated that not enough information, inaccurate information, and the lack of availability of counsellors and guidance (in general) contributed to their inadequate preparation for post-secondary education and life.

Comments on high school counsellors and counselling (1993)

31 responses in total	*Percent of cases*
Specific comments regarding:	
counsellors	1
extent of personal planning	58
availability of information	48
information accuracy	10

According to these thirty-one responses, approximately 58 percent indicated that little or no educational and/or career planning was offered through high school guidance programs. For instance, according to one respondent,

There's nothing in my high school senior years, grades 11 and 12, that prepared me for college. The counsellors should get with it. To know what to take in college, ask the faculty chairperson not the counsellor.

Nearly half of the thirty-one comments (48 percent) indicated a lack of adequate information regarding post-secondary options, choices, and institutions from high school counsellors and guidance programs. Respondents expressed sentiments such as these:

School counsellors do not help students in making career choices. I personally had little confidence in my school counsellor.

More effective counselling assessment must be done at the high school level – not everyone is cut out for university; more thought should be given to college and tech. institutes. Contrary to popular belief, college and tech. institutes are no less respectable than university – all p.s.e. is important and valuable and this idea must be instilled early.

Difficulties in making informed decisions about post-secondary educational options and choices were most often attributed to individual counsellor "mistakes" and "inaccurate information." Approximately 10 percent of the comments reflected distinct dissatisfaction with the information received from counsellors. The following responses reveal the difficulties respondents encountered when trying to make the transition to post-secondary education with little and/or inaccurate information from high school counsellors:

During high school it is not explained very well how to register and courses you need for post-secondary. Now it is even harder I find to go back.

In high school I feel I was never given enough information about post-secondary education to make an informed choice about my Grade 10-12 course choices and grades. Because of this, I never had a career goal in school and I just ended up taking courses without a purpose or plan.

High School Preparation for Post-Secondary Education
Respondents' comments about high school preparation are divided into three general themes: (1) transition planning and assistance; (2) specific secondary school subject, and (3) post-secondary skill development. A majority of the thirty-one respondents (55 percent) who commented on high school preparation expressed that high school "did not prepare them for post-secondary." Only a few stated that "the high school education I received in BC really helped me in undergraduate course work; I did not feel too overwhelmed!"

Comments on high school preparation for post-secondary education

31 responses in total	*Percent of cases*
High school preparation for post-secondary (in general)	90
Transition planning and awareness	52
Specific high school subject preparation for post-secondary	16
Need for developing post-secondary skills	32

The following responses highlight issues related to high school preparation for post-secondary education.
Specific high school subjects were mentioned by some respondents:

High school students should be better prepared particularly in mathematics.

I found two interesting things out of my first year at university. (1) my math skills were way below university levels (I finished with an A in grade 11 and C+ in Grade 12), and (2) my English professor said I had a grade 7 level of English (I had a B in grade 12).

I wish I knew how to write an English paper, essay when I got out of high school. I am learning the hard way!

Others commented on post-secondary skills development:

Lack of critical thinking and writing skills (necessary in post-secondary education) in high school.

Secondary schools should prepare students better (study skills).

Most students who do well at high school don't need to study very much (at least I didn't); therefore they have very poor study skills.

In 1993, respondents still talked about the transition to post-secondary education:

High school, in general, did not give a good view of how this world works and what to expect of it. It lacked in the proper preparation of students for a post-secondary education.

I had no difficulty making the transition from high school to university. I found the course work in first-year university was exactly the same as was taught in high school (science program). The only major difference was in high school we were pushed to do assignments whereas in university we were on our own.

Post-Secondary Participants

Five years after high school graduation, according to a report employing the survey data, "90.5% (n = 2004) had attended a post-secondary institution at some time since June 1988. Hence only 9.5% (n = 210) of the sample had never attended any type of post-secondary institution since high school graduation" (Andres 2001, 3). Forty-two post-secondary participants indicated that they faced distinct challenges with the post-secondary system in general. Similar to the 1989 survey responses, many of the comments focused on the quality of teaching and instruction and the available administrative services at the post-secondary level.

General comments on post-secondary education (1993)

42 responses in total	*Percent of cases*
Quality of teaching and education	36
Availability of post-secondary education	10
Administration	14
Childcare options	5
Costs of education	12
PSE was good (in general)	5

The following comments reflect the difficulties experienced by some of the respondents who had participated in post-secondary education five years after high school graduation.

Regarding the quality of teaching and instruction at the post-secondary level:

Tuition and few classes as well as a sense that administration and the government and even instructors "don't care as long as they get their money" is creating a sense of frustration and cynicism amongst post-secondary students. So those students that actually make it out of high school with a semi-positive attitude towards school are discouraged once they get into post-secondary programs.

Also, teachers seemed to be more concerned with political mumbo jumbo than the education of their students. There is way too much red tape the instructors have to worry about than giving their students time and knowledge.

The responses suggest that many of the challenges and experiences of the respondents in post-secondary were indicative of a possible lack of understanding and appreciation for the distinct nature of post-secondary education in general. Furthermore, based on the constant comparisons made by respondents to the secondary school system, there is an apparent discrepancy between expectations about post-secondary education and their actual experiences.

Post-Secondary Nonparticipants

As previously noted, less than 10 percent of the sample had not attended any type of post-secondary institution since high school graduation. In total, twenty-three responses were recorded in 1993 stating reasons for not pursuing post-secondary education. A majority of the comments (69 percent) by these nonparticipants indicated that they wanted to pursue further education; however, due to issues of family obligations, employment opportunities, and/or financial issues, they were not continuing with their education at this time.

Reasons for nonparticipation in post-secondary education (1993)

23 responses in total	*Percent of cases*
Don't want to attend:	
general	13
needed information and planning assistance	13
grades too low or missing requirements	9
Still want to pursue except:	
family obligations	9
employment opportunities	22
financial issues	39

Respondents' reasons for nonparticipation in post-secondary education can be divided into two categories: (1) those who did not want to continue and (2) those who still wanted to pursue post-secondary education but were prevented from doing so by life circumstances. These two categories are broken down into more specific reasons for nonparticipation. The following responses highlight why some respondents chose not to pursue post-secondary education (they reflect the figures in the table above):

I was married right after graduation and I have been busy with the children. I may need to get more education in the future but not for a few years.

I have no real desire to continue to post-secondary education. I have enough education for my line of work.

I would return to school right now if I didn't have to live in poverty for four years.

According to the open-ended responses provided by the Class of '88, five years after graduation, general beliefs about education were becoming more pragmatic than the idealistic views held one year after graduation (1989). Respondents (like those in 1989) noted, with frustration, that high schools, counsellors, and guidance programs should better prepare students for life after high school graduation. Respondents suggested the need for enhanced planning and guidance programs, increased and more accurate information, greater availability of individual counselling, and more emphasis on developing skills required for post-secondary education and life after graduation.

Ten Years Later: 1998 Follow-Up Study of the Class of '88
In April 1998, a third follow-up survey of the sample of 1988 high school graduates ten years after graduation was conducted. "In total, questionnaires were sent to 1841 individuals and 1055 (57%) completed and returned the 1998 questionnaire. The 1055 survey respondents to all three phases represented 5% of the entire graduating cohort and 20% of respondents to the original 1989 survey sample" (Andres 2001, 1). The final question in the 1998 questionnaire yielded 803 responses and read:

Do you have any comments or thoughts regarding education and work that you want to share with us? In particular you are invited to comment about the following:

- access to post-secondary education
- the cost of post-secondary education
- work, education, and the economy
- today's family
- the lives and times of your generation.

Beliefs about Education

Some respondents noted that education in general was becoming far less useful for enhancing employment opportunities and guaranteeing future success, and after ten years had changed their earlier views of education at graduation. Comments generally fell evenly into four categories.

Beliefs about education ten years later (1998)

43 total comments	*Percent of cases*
Education and:	
future success (enhanced standard of living)	19
employment and career opportunities	9
Education is important (in general)	25
Limited worth (value) of education	25
No need for education	21

The responses provided below represent a few of the topics noted in the table.

On a distinctly positive note, about one-fifth of the responses maintained the belief that education was integral to future success in general and to enhanced career opportunities. The following quotes represent the views of some respondents who still maintained their conviction of the value and importance of education.

The main reason for a post-secondary education is to show potential employers that you can commit to something and see it to the end. It proves to them that you have the capability/drive to complete an educational program/degree. It gives you "a foot in the door" but that is about it.

Education (primarily post-secondary) has played a fundamental role in terms of my ability to make choices for my career path. Because of my education choices I expect I will have a satisfying career, which is very important to me and will greatly improve my quality of life.

However, approximately the same proportion of the comments questioned and challenged that view, suggesting a more limited sense of the worth or value of education:

Knowledge is power. Power is money. Money is everything knowledge is. Knowledge doesn't come from a certificate, it comes from work, experience, and maturity.

Any post-secondary will get you a better job, but not necessarily in your chosen field. Too much education seems to be as much of a problem as no education.

Post-secondary education is rarely valued. It's definitely work exp[erience] and who you know.

High School Counsellors and Counselling
In 1998, only four respondents commented on counsellors and high school counselling. Two of the responses indicated that their high school counsellors and guidance programs provided inadequate information about post-secondary education options, choices, and opportunities. For instance, one respondent stated that "it is too difficult to get proper sec. schooling and not enough direction in these matters." The other two responses noted little or poor preparation for the post-secondary transition faced by these members of the Class of '88. One respondent stated, "I wish we were better educated in high school about post-secondary education options"; "more effort needs to be placed in high school in encouraging PS education whether vocational or university."

Comments on high school counsellors and counselling (1998)

4 responses in total	*Percent of cases*
Extent of personal planning	50
Availability of information	50

The following two themes drew a very limited number of responses. Therefore, responses will not be reported in tabular format.

High School Preparation for Post-Secondary Education
Common throughout all three surveys were comments indicating that respondents generally felt that high school did not prepare them for their later endeavours. As a result, respondents felt that they were left to their own resources and abilities. In 1998, of the four responses for this category, one respondent indicated that "High school was near useless for preparing for university – but I had fun." Another respondent stated, "High school was not challenging and was too easy. I was not prepared for university and I think it is tough for students from rural communities to succeed."

Post-Secondary Participants
Those who by 1998 had participated in post-secondary education since

graduation and who provided open-ended comments on the 1998 survey indicated that post-secondary education was either generally good (for them) or limited in value and use. One respondent noted, "My university years were priceless in a number of ways. I am eternally grateful to my parents for planning financially and enabling me to complete a degree with minimal debt. Furthermore – I met my husband-to-be in school and many of the close friends that I continue to correspond with." Other respondents voiced a different perspective on post-secondary education. For instance, one stated, "At this point in my life, I feel quite disillusioned with post-secondary education. I feel that the education in this country is heading in the wrong direction. It definitely needs a major overhaul."

Post-Secondary Nonparticipants
Nonparticipants in 1998 shared reasons about why they had not participated in post-secondary education that were consistent with the two previous surveys. The majority of the thirteen responses regarding nonparticipation indicated that respondents would "like to attend post-secondary but ... " Family obligations and current employment and financial limitations were predominant reasons for not attending post-secondary education.

Reasons for nonparticipation in post-secondary education (1998)

13 total responses	*Percent of cases*
Still want to pursue except:	
family obligations	61
employment opportunities	23
financial issues	31
Other	15

The following responses exemplify the predominant reasons for nonparticipation in post-secondary education:

> I would like to attend post-secondary, but the cost of living is much higher in bigger centres, and without family to take care of my children, I don't think it will be possible until they are older.

> Hard to maintain a stable financial picture and save for retirement. I would like to return to school on a part-time basis but don't want to quit my job and apply for a student loan.

> Feel fortunate to have a full-time job with advancement opportunities. This discourages me from returning to school to train for a career of my choice.

After ten years of navigating their way through post-secondary life, respondents indicated that their sense of the intrinsic value and importance of education had mitigated their earlier beliefs that post-secondary education would guarantee career opportunities and financial success. In 1989, surveyed members of the Class of '88 felt that high school had not adequately prepared them for life after graduation; this generally felt perception persisted through 1993 and 1998. Over the ten years since high school graduation, planning and preparation for post-secondary education remained an issue for both post-secondary participants and nonparticipants.

Discussion

Comments provided by the BC graduating Class of '88 poignantly illuminate the struggles, challenges, and unexpected realities faced by young adults in making the transition from high school to post-high-school life. These comments were grouped by theme to help counsellors understand this transition from the perspectives of the respondents.

Examples of respondents' comments provided in this chapter illustrated the following themes: (1) high school offered inadequate preparation for post-secondary education and life; (2) high school counsellors and counselling programs did not provide enough accurate information and guidance to students; and (3) the success and satisfaction of these young adults with the transition experience were related to their levels of high school planning and preparation. Also, several minor themes emerged from the analysis: although education is important, its value and worth are subject to personal interpretation; and although post-secondary participation was considered desirable, personal circumstances (family, financial matters, and employment obligations) prevented some respondents from participating.

Positive comments about planning and preparation for post-secondary education were clearly outweighed by the negative ones. Many respondents commented that their high schools inadequately prepared them for the transition between the secondary and post-secondary educational systems. Several respondents said that more applicable skills should be taught at the secondary level, that high school teaching staff needed to be more involved in helping students plan for the future, and that students needed to be better prepared for certain post-secondary education subjects, especially English and math. Generally, respondents felt that they needed to be more aware of career options, to have had more opportunities to explore career options, and to have had a better understanding of how the choices they made in school would affect their futures.

Comments on counsellors and counselling services over a period of ten years revealed that students generally attributed their inadequate planning for life after graduation to poor guidance programs in high school. Some respondents stated that counsellors often had no time (often due to inadequate resources in the high school) to offer proper guidance. A number of survey responses clearly stated that counsellors had somehow failed to supply adequate guidance by providing insufficient or inaccurate information.

As the findings of this study reveal, respondents highlighted the need for the following: (1) access to accurate information, which would help promote greater satisfaction in the guidance provided during high school; (2) information on the vast opportunities and options available to them in the post-secondary system; and (3) the active assistance and support of high school counsellors (and teachers) in their pursuit of post-secondary options.

More and more, counsellors are being asked to be "information specialists" regarding the post-secondary system. They are being asked to offer very specific advice and information to students with a wide range of needs and interests. However, given that there is such a diversity of options leading to various educational and career paths, it may be "difficult for teachers and counsellors, many of whom have worked in the same building for most of their career, to imagine let alone prepare students and clients for this new work world" (Jarvis 2000, 5). Boyer asserts, "high school counsellors and teachers need to work more with high school students so that the student [post-secondary] choice process will be more informed" (1987, 20).

Research has revealed that although "guidance counselling appears to be an important conduit toward academic pursuits" (Lee and Ekstrom 1987, 301), counsellors and teachers are perceived by students to have little impact on the post-secondary aspirations of students (Andres 1993; 2001). The introduction of the career education curriculum into schools provides one way of addressing some of the issues raised by the BC Class of '88 and has ostensibly provided schools, counsellors, and educators with a means of ensuring that the knowledge and skills required to help current secondary students prepare for post-high-school life are taught in schools. A career education curriculum provides teachers and counsellors with guidelines and tools for delivering post-secondary planning and career guidance en masse. Although it does not replace the advantages of individual guidance, given the limited number of counsellors available within schools, it does provide some assurance that students will be exposed to information about planning for post-high-school life.

However, delivery of the career education curriculum is at the discretion of individual schools. Each school's administration and counselling staff determines the structure and content, and teachers who have not necessarily received adequate training to deliver this program often teach career education. Implementation of the career education curriculum was – and still is – extremely varied. The eclectic nature of curriculum delivery in schools means that each school is left to promote career education to whatever level it believes best. While local control of the career education curriculum may be advantageous in that the material can be tailored to suit students from different geographic locations and social and economic backgrounds, it can also remain problematic.

Based on the findings in this chapter, there is a need for further policy- and practice-oriented research focusing on the ways in which counsellors and educators do and could assist students with both common and unique transition experiences. The findings presented in this chapter are solely from the perspectives of the students. Further research, from the perspectives of counsellors, teachers, parents, and students is needed. Such research could explore the extent to which the guidance and counselling system in particular, and the secondary and post-secondary system in general, help to foster agency by senior secondary students through the provision of access to information and assistance with academic and career decision making. In addition, further investigation could focus on the extent to which guidance programs achieve the following:

- providing strategic and ongoing career exploration, development, and planning that engage student interests, abilities, and goals;
- providing personal one-to-one guidance with students;
- providing opportunities to explore the whole spectrum of post-high-school options through the effective use of available resources;
- using the career education curriculum to explore the diversity and uniqueness of the post-secondary system and beyond.

The findings reported in this chapter show that secondary students should have access to specialist counsellors who focus primarily on specific areas of counselling (e.g., personal, post-secondary, or career). Furthermore, as some respondents mentioned, counsellors did not play an active or any role in preparing them for post-high-school life. According to the response analysis, it is evident that young people want more direction; educators cannot assume they will seek out the necessary information for themselves. Schools and guidance programs need to take a more proactive role in providing post-graduation planning (e.g., setting up more one-to-one mandatory counselling sessions).

A mechanism to channel the transmission of accurate and reliable information to future post-secondary students is needed. These information channels should be tailored to meet the needs of students from different geographic locations, social backgrounds, and financial situations. A mechanism for the frequent updating of information throughout a provincial system would help ensure that counsellors are offering accurate and reliable information to their students. Currently, the Post Secondary Institutions of BC (PSI BC) provides some relevant, institution-specific information to high school students and counsellors throughout the province.

The findings of this study support the creation and integration of a resource guide (similar to the current "TIPS"[2] guide developed by the BC Council on Admissions and Transfer) that incorporates key components of the post-secondary system. Such a guide should be developed for high school students to help bridge the gap between what students expect (or assume) and what they experience at post-secondary institutions (e.g., the quality and style of teaching, study demands). This gap, identified as problematic by respondents, can be closed by information. Students, counsellors, and teachers should engage in a dialogue about the following questions: What is life after high school like? What is the difference between secondary and post-secondary education? What do students need to do to prepare for post-secondary life (e.g., financial planning, family and personal expectations)?

The goal of career guidance programs is to provide students with the tools to integrate awareness about themselves, potential careers, and post-secondary education into informed decisions about the future (Henderson 1999). In keeping with this goal, career education programs should recognize, identify, and address the gender and cultural stereotypes of some occupations (see Adamuti-Trache, this volume); provide students with the opportunity to explore a variety of career and educational options through guided research and inquiry; offer structured opportunities for students to learn and develop study and organizational skills and habits to better prepare them for success in the post-secondary system; and supply professional education through university courses and workshops to help teachers teach the career education curriculum and information. Also teacher education students should be encouraged to take career-education-related courses as part of their teacher education program. The rationale for a comprehensive policy for counsellors will help ensure that students have efficient, effective, and equal access to high school counselling services.

Notes
1 In 1998, 190 individuals who responded to the 1989 but not to the 1993 questionnaire were located and answered the 1998 survey. Because some questions were asked retrospectively, the 1993 response rate was boosted to 2,220. However, only the original 1993 respondents (N = 2,030) provided written comments on the 1993 survey (see Andres 2001).
2 Transfer Information for Post-Secondary Success, <http://www.bccat.bc.ca/tips/index.html>.

References
Andres, L. 1993. Life Trajectories, Action, and Negotiating the Transition from High School. In *Transitions, Schooling and Employment in Canada*, edited by P. Anisef and P. Axelrod, 137-57. Toronto: Thompson Educational Publishing.
–. 2001. *Paths on Life's Way Project: Transitions of British Columbia Young Adults in a Changing Society. Phase III Follow-Up Survey – 1998, Ten Years Later*. Vancouver: Department of Educational Studies, University of British Columbia.

Boyer, E.L. 1987. *College: The Undergraduate Experience in America*. New York: Harper and Row.

Henderson, P. 1999. Providing Leadership for School Counsellors to Achieve an Effective Guidance Program. *National Association of Secondary School Principals Bulletin* 83, 603: 77-83.

Jarvis, P.S. 2000. *Academic and Technical Skills and Life/Work Skills and Career Information and Guidance = Success in Career Building*. Ottawa: National Life-Work Centre.

Lee, V.E., and R.B. Ekstrom. 1987. Student Access to Guidance Counselling in High School. *American Educational Research Journal* 24, 2: 287-310.

Radcliffe, J. 1996. *"Over Educated but Underskilled." Views on Applied and Liberal Education by Young Adults in British Columbia*. Unpublished graduating paper, Department of Educational Studies, University of British Columbia, Vancouver.

Conclusion:
From Research to Action

Finola Finlay

The most comprehensive understanding in the world will not do students, institutions, or systems much good unless it results in the formulation of an action plan. This is why we as editors have insisted that each author in this volume attend to the matter of recommendations for changes and improvements in policy and practice. To make a difference, any book that purports to speak to how students experience post-secondary education must also devote itself to how that experience can be enhanced. Although several chapters (McGee Thompson, Hawkey, Grosjean) point to the many ways in which our institutions are succeeding in helping their students thrive, all the chapters highlight the significant challenges facing institutions and systems as they strive to engage, encourage, include, advise, and support students.

A striking aspect of this volume is the range of student voices and the diversity of experiences chronicled in its pages. From young mothers on welfare, students with disabilities, high-achieving co-op students, eager novice researchers, boys and girls in secondary school science courses, students from other countries and from marginalized cultures, to women coping with multiple roles, all have one goal in common: the desire to attain a post-secondary education and to become economically contributing members of society. They may or may not fit the mental picture we get when we say the word "student," but this is what students look like now. Whatever they look like, most economists agree that we need them, and many more of them, to help create and support a vibrant economy. We need them to stay in school, to graduate with their preferred credential, and probably to come back, after a few years in the workforce, to enhance their qualifications. It is critical, then, that we understand what they experience as they move into and through post-secondary education.

While it may still be useful to refer to students as "traditional" or "non-traditional," what this volume illustrates is simply that a student is a student, no matter what she or he looks like. Along with the range and diversity of the student body goes a remarkable commonality of concerns that contribute to the themes that emerge from these studies. Students articulate their need for respect, their response to academic challenge, their desire to belong to the campus community, and their requirements for academic advice and for financial and personal support, not as additions to the academic enterprise (nice to have but peripheral to the real business of acquiring an education) but as fundamental to their ability to progress and achieve their aims. Strong themes emerge from the stories they tell and the pictures painted by the research: themes of inclusion, engagement, access, and gender.

Inclusion

Inclusion emerges as a major theme in several of the studies and provides a fascinating microcosm to study instances where reality can fall short of rhetoric. Situated as critics of the social order, and dedicated to a democratic ideal of education, institutions of advanced education have long promoted admirable policies of recruiting and facilitating the integration of students who are less likely to gain access to post-secondary studies. Although the studies in this volume are located in a Canadian context, American readers will recognize the parallels with controversial affirmative action policies in the United States. The underlying goal of increasing minority enrolments is not the source of the controversy; rather, the means to achieve those goals and the effectiveness of the policies themselves have been the subject of intense debate. As educators on both sides of the border recognize, increased recruiting efforts and targeted admission policies do not guarantee that students will feel welcome or included.

Arguably, the inclusion rhetoric-reality gap is recognizable most tellingly in Lyakhovetska's chapter on international students. As she states, international students are actively recruited "under the banner of internationalization." Despite overall satisfaction, students report feelings of isolation, of difficulties connecting with their Canadian peers, and of being "strangers" in the classroom. As Lyakhovetska points out, this is mainly the case for those students for whom English is not a first language. English-speaking international students may struggle with cultural differences, but they do not face the same difficulties in participating in discussions or in making friends as do many overseas students who do not speak English as their first language. Many North American institutions are facing pressure to attract more international students, often as a source of funding. (Ironically, after 11 September 2001, reporting requirements and visa restrictions are making it increasingly difficult to bring overseas students to campuses in the United States, and there is some evidence that students are turning to Canadians institutions instead.) There is no doubt that *real* inclusion holds the promise of great benefit in the enrichment of the academic and cultural environment for students and faculty, in the broadening of curriculum, and in future economic linkages. Moving to real inclusion will require institutions to make greater efforts to provide integrating social occasions for international and domestic students, and to offer greater encouragement, assistance, and opportunities for non-English-speaking students to improve their proficiency.

For these international students, as well as for the hard-of-hearing students who were the focus of Warick's study, inclusion or exclusion typically occurred within the context of human interaction, most particularly in classroom discussion, professorial teaching, and social occasions and gatherings. Students in both Warick's and Lyakhovetska's studies testified to the difference a sympathetic or knowledgeable instructor can make in a classroom setting. Institutions can address the needs of these students by providing for their instructors seminars and workshops on inclusive teaching techniques. Indeed all students can benefit from a classroom environment that accommodates a variety of learning styles, cultural backgrounds, and language proficiency.

Many of the studies in this volume speak to the need for support from and interaction with caring and knowledgeable individuals – advisors in Pillay's study, instructors and practicum supervisors in Liversidge's, Benefits Office workers in McGee Thompson's, and advocates in Warick's. However, these are the very positions that are under pressure in many institutions and educational systems. Students are increasingly encouraged to use the telephone or Internet for admission, course selection, and registration purposes, and institutions are moving toward encouraging even more self-reliance with the use of electronic advising. Efficiencies can be gained through the use of technology, and it is important for students to take charge of their own academic planning, but institutions must be careful to question students frequently about the effectiveness of their use of technology to streamline administrative and advising processes. If the emphasis is on cost saving, increased reliance on technology can be used to justify cutting back the number of advisors employed. Properly implemented, however, technology can shift an advisor's role from disseminating information to providing detailed advice and professional support and assistance to students when they need it.

This book will be valuable in helping institutions recognize the benefits of tuning in to the actual experiences of students who are First Nations, mothers, disabled, financially disadvantaged, or for whom English is not a first language. Policies of inclusion that do not move to the next step of implementing real change in curriculum and teaching, in instructional methodology, and in the provision of supportive, sensitive, and integrative environments will fail to realize the educational benefits of diversifying the student body, and will risk alienating those who are the very focus of those policies.

Engagement

As with inclusion, the chapters that deal with academic engagement are illustrative of the agency-structure nexus emphasized in Andres's Introduction. In particular, because of the contributors' focus on the students' lived experience, we view the students in many of these chapters in their *relative positions* not only within the institutional structure but also within their other roles related to family, work, disability, and position in society. Students, as agents, must adapt to the structure of the post-secondary institution and actively pursue their educational goals while at the same time paying attention to the other fields in which they must survive and prosper. What these chapters illustrate is that individual students arrive in a post-secondary institution with a variety of abilities, orientations, attitudes, and skills that, as Andres points out, "enable or constrain their ability to integrate socially and academically" (this volume, p. 3). Therefore, in assuming the responsibility to adapt and fit the structure of the institution – to *engage* with it – they interact with it in individual ways. The structure itself is not static but reacts in ways that can be supportive or obstructive.

Academic integration, which most often references the ability of students to adapt successfully to the social and scholarly norms of the institutions, has been seen as an important measure of student engagement. However, several of the chapters in this book challenge us to focus on how the institution, discipline, or program (the structure) can facilitate the integration of the student (the agent) rather than placing the onus to integrate on the student. Three studies in particular in this volume speak to how institutions can organize curricula in such a way as to invite students in to the discipline. Hawkey's study includes many recommendations that can be implemented by institutions (although resource-dependent recommendations may be more difficult) for ways in which students can connect with their discipline. Providing a discipline-based meeting place, for instance, no matter how small, can significantly enhance opportunities for students to connect with others – including professors – in the discipline. Liversidge's study of the time challenges faced by student-mothers carries many implications for the structure and organization of the curriculum. For example, minor changes to schedules (such as setting class start time at 9:00 a.m., when a child will have been dropped at school, rather than at 8:30) can make a difference to mothers struggling to juggle their multiple responsibilities. Predictable, advanced scheduling of clinical time would not only allow student mothers to make arrangements for childcare, but would signal a respectful recognition by nursing faculty of the multiple roles in which their adult students are engaged. Finally, for the many institutions involved in co-op programming, Grosjean's research illuminates, among other issues, opportunities lost through the lack of attention paid by the institution to bridging and mediating the learning acquired in the work placement, once students arrive back in the classroom. If students view classroom learning as irrelevant to the "real world" of the workplace, the benefits of co-op are greatly diminished. The findings of this chapter suggest that faculty who teach in co-op programs cannot simply locate themselves in the ivory tower, but must have the knowledge, expertise, and practical skills to relate theory to practice for students.

Within the retention models referenced by Andres and several of the researchers in this book, academic integration as a predictor of retention calls for students to actively seek and participate in a range of activities. However, what may be realistic expectations for students who are young and single, or for those who are economically, socially, and physically advantaged, may be insurmountable challenges to students who do not fit this profile. Several of the studies in this book remind us that, while expecting students to participate in curricular and extracurricular activities, institutions can recognize that many students face considerable disadvantages in coping with this task and can provide assistance and accommodation to encourage participation. McGee Thompson and Liversidge propose strategies that programs and institutions might consider to encourage and allow participation in a wider range of activities for those students who find themselves juggling multiple responsibilities.

The international student voices recorded by Lyakhovetska, as well as Warick's hard-of-hearing students, are forcible reminders that for students with language difficulties even such a normative expectation as participation in classroom discussion requires accommodation. These are particularly interesting examples, because the adjustments required often pose a challenge to individual behaviours in the classroom – those of the instructor and fellow students. In the agency-structure nexus, what, and perhaps more importantly, who, is considered part of the structure? These chapters remind us that the institutions can provide accommodations (such as FM systems and international student offices) but that individuals must also be encouraged to commit to the task of providing an enabling environment. The Lyakhovetska and Warick studies are invaluable resources for any institution seeking to find ways of influencing both institutional and individual behaviours that create barriers to participation in a variety of activities by all students.

Marker, on the other hand, speaks of the need for institutions not to provide assistance but to transform themselves in more fundamental ways and to question at "the deepest levels" all assumptions about knowledge, learning, and culture. His chapter provides the sharpest critique of the assumption that students must do the "fitting in" as well as the boldest argument for the potential benefits of the "challenges to Eurocentric canons of knowledge."

Access

Although institutions may have relative flexibility to consider and implement change, public post-secondary policy is influenced by many factors, not least the economy and the prevailing political philosophy of the day. In Canada, post-secondary funding is a matter of provincial policy and many Canadian provinces have decreased budgetary allocations to post-secondary education over the last ten years (Doherty-Delorme and Shaker 2003). In the United States, "since 1980 ... the share of state funds used for higher education has dropped to 32 percent from 44 percent" (Burd 2003, para. 11).

The most tangible manifestation of reduced funding is a rise in tuition fees. The effect of high tuition on access is a complex issue. Lowering or eliminating tuition, in and of itself, does not guarantee that underrepresented student groups, such as those from lower socioeconomic backgrounds, will enrol in post-secondary institutions. In Ireland, for example, tertiary education has been tuition-free for several years for most full-time students, but there has been little measurable increase in the number of students attending from target "equity groups" (Clancy 2001, 164). Nonetheless, there is mounting evidence that an increase in tuition and greater student debt loads function as significant barriers to many students in North America. Heisler, for example, states that, as of 1998 "young people from high income families were 2.5 times more likely than those from low income families to have participated in university education" (2002, 2). He points out that increased financial assistance is often poorly accessed by low-income students, and that the prospect of a high debt burden is most discouraging to those who are already economically disadvantaged. These findings concur with an international study conducted by de Broucker and Underwood (1998).

According to a 1998 study by the Nellie Mae Corporation, a major student-loan provider in the United States, "a quarter of private-college grads and about 40 percent of newly graduated doctors and lawyers had student-loan obligations that exceeded their current salaries" (Franke-Ruta 2003, para. 9). The author blamed the inability of federal student aid to keep up with the rising cost of tuition and pointed to the "worrisome social consequences" of graduates who cannot afford to take public-sector jobs, and who must postpone marriage and children (para. 4). Another national US study found that "private loans are becoming increasingly important as a mechanism for financing post-secondary education" (Wegmann, Cunningham, and Merisotis 2003, vii). Loans from private lenders are, in fact, the fastest-growing form of student aid, especially for students attending professional schools.

Funding shortfalls and lack of spaces at community colleges disproportionately affect underrepresented students. In the United States, "higher-education leaders say that deep cuts in state appropriations for those institutions – coupled with the failure of federal student aid to keep up with tuition increases – will do more to undermine minority access than will any other factor in recent history" (Evelyn 2003, para. 7). In Canada also, financial constraints and issues of access haunt many community college students. One of the more poignant pieces in this volume is McGee Thompson's "A Tunnel of Hope." We hear the women in this study state repeatedly that the presence of the provincial Benefits Office on campus is the one thing that has made a real difference for them. At the end of the chapter we understand that the office is to be closed. No doubt these are difficult decisions for government, not taken lightly, but it is impossible not to question, as the students will, the wisdom of such a decision, and to wonder how it can ameliorate the situation of these students who are struggling so hard to get off welfare.

Financial issues are also very real for the international students in Lyakhovetska's study, bearing as they do the double problem of very high tuition and difficulty finding work. Grosjean raises important questions about the equity of access to co-op opportunities for all students. Since participation in co-op programs confers substantial benefit, and access is determined largely by grades, co-op can function to further cement inequities based on the acquisition and retention of cultural and social capital.

The first years of the millennium have seen an extraordinary level of agreement among governments of all political persuasions and at national and provincial or state levels about the value and necessity of increasing the number of college and university graduates. We have been bombarded with statistics indicating that the new economy will call increasingly for higher education levels, and that those without post-secondary education will get left behind. At the same time, tuition has been deregulated in many provinces and states, institutions are faced with recouping a greater portion of their operating expenditures from fees, and financial aid has not kept pace with increased costs. Public policy makers at federal, provincial, and state levels must assess the long-term effects of a shift to a market economy for post-secondary education. How can we ensure that the democratizing ideals of higher education are not swallowed by the rhetoric of deregulation and the marketplace?

Gender

Another long-term issue that seems to resist efforts to change is the underrepresentation of women in science. This is not unique to North America. A recent western European study entitled *Key Data on Education in Europe* (2002) provides figures to show that women dominate in the arts and humanities, social sciences, business and law, and health and welfare fields, receiving 76 percent, 69 percent, 59 percent, and 74 percent, respectively, of the degrees awarded in the countries under study. In contrast, 78 percent of degrees in engineering, manufacturing, and construction are awarded to men. The study points out that several eastern European countries (such as Poland, Bulgaria, and Romania) have been successful in attracting women into math and science fields.

Many countries are attempting to address this issue with special programs designed to attract women to science, math, and the technologies. Adamuti-Trache's findings chart how the roots of that issue stretch back into high school and continue into post-secondary education and the workplace. Although such intractable issues do not lend themselves to simple solutions, several of Adamuti-Trache's practical recommendations *are* implementable by individual institutions or by collaborative projects between high school and post-secondary institutions. Perhaps an in-depth examination of the methods used by the eastern European countries cited above to attract or retain women in scientific fields would also be helpful.

The particular difficulties faced by students who are mothers are underscored in the studies by Liversidge and McGee Thompson. The women relate their struggle to balance their multiple responsibilities and to find time for everything they must do. Most of all they plead for post-secondary institutions to recognize that being a student is but one of the many roles they play and to find ways to accommodate their schedules.

Filling in the Gaps

Although this volume adds substantially to our knowledge of how students experience the post-secondary system, there are significant gaps that future studies might address. Several chapters, as noted, link to the literature on student engagement and illustrate the various mechanisms by which students are connected with their programs, with the norms of the discipline, and with each other. However, much of the literature on student engagement presupposes a body of students that is young, often resident on campus, and studying full-time. A recent study entitled *Findings Focus: CCSSE Results in Key Areas* (2002) reveals that community college students in the United States are significantly less engaged in post-secondary life than university students. The majority of students in this large survey (more than 30,000 respondents) attended part-time (64 percent) and reported very low levels of interaction with other students and with professors. Nevertheless, they reported high levels of satisfaction with their college experiences, a rating echoed by British Columbia college students in the annual Outcomes Survey of College Students conducted by the Centre for Education Information, Standards and Services (2002). Do community college students, especially those studying part-time and working many hours per week, value or need "engagement" in the same way as full-time, younger students do? If not, what are the relevant motivating factors that lead to retention and credential completion for these students?

In Canada, the only provinces that have well-developed transfer systems are British Columbia and Alberta. A growing body of research exists on BC transfer students (BCCAT 2004) but only one research project has probed their actual transfer experiences (Andres 1998, 2001; Andres, Qayyum, and Dawson 1997) and revealed the significant difficulties faced by transfer students. The study raised questions that have yet to be answered: how do institutions welcome, orient, and engage students who arrive halfway through their educational programs? How do institutions assist students to prevent or overcome transfer shock and to integrate more fully into campus activities? Grosjean's study illustrates how students are inducted into a profession, through their participation in co-op terms. But do transfer students, arriving as they do part-way through their degree program, have equal access to co-op placements? Hawkey raises similar concerns when considering the dynamics of the university as community. On a similar note, a recent study of baccalaureate graduates' outcomes five years after graduating found that labour market participation, satisfaction ratings, and further education outcomes for transfer students were indistinguishable from those of students who had entered university directly from high school. What *was* different was the amount of student debt that transfer students carried in comparison to their direct-entry counterparts (Dumaresq, Lambert-Maberly, and Sudmant 2003). What difference do these factors make in the quality of experiences and equality of outcomes of transfer students?

Several of the chapters in this book deal with the direct experience of women students (Adamuti-Trache, Liversidge, McGee Thompson), but none deals primarily with that of male students only. Yet, low participation and completion rates among young men, especially young men from minority groups, are starting to raise concern for many educators. In almost every developed country, women now outnumber men in higher education. In western Europe higher education enrolment has doubled in the last twenty-five years. More women than men graduate from tertiary institutions in almost all the countries included in the *Key Data on Education in Europe* (2002) study, and in some countries four women graduate for every three men. In North America, alarm bells have been ringing for some time. *Business Week* devoted its 26 May 2003 issue to a major examination of "The New Gender Gap," declaring that higher education is "a world made for women." The *Chronicle of Higher Education*, in its 28 June 2003 issue, asked "where are the men?" and stated that 133 women received bachelor's degrees in the United States for every 100 men (Evelyn 2003). The tenor of many of these articles is that there is something about the education system, the culture of the classroom, or the social pressures on young men that militates against their aspirations to higher education. Whatever the cause, all agree that this is a trend with major negative implications for society and the economy in the coming years.

We need to understand the experiences of young men in colleges and universities, and the factors that can enhance or inhibit their credential completion. Perhaps more important, we need to examine their experiences in secondary school, to understand what precedes the apparent lack of interest that many of them display for higher education. Such investigations, however, cannot distract us from continuing to seek answers to the challenges faced by women since, as we have seen, despite escalating enrolments, gender differences within disciplines (particularly mathematics and science) remain intransigent.

Private institutions, long a fact of life in the United States, are now the largest-growing sector of higher education in western Canada. Conservative estimates place the number of students attending private post-secondary institutions in BC as at least equal to the number attending public institutions. Although many private institutions participated in the "On Track" Outcomes Survey (now cancelled), there has been no systematic qualitative examination of the experiences of students at Canadian private institutions.[1] In the light of recent legislative and regulatory changes in many Canadian provinces facilitating the integration of private institutions into the broader post-secondary environment, it is startling to note that we have no idea how many students, if any, move from private to public institutions each year (or vice versa) and how their experiences compare. For those who make the move, do they find that the learning they have acquired in the private institutions is acknowledged and credited? What are the strengths of private institutions that succeed in attracting so many eager learners each year or in selling their programs to sponsoring agencies? Do students find that the reality lives up to the promise?

As institutions increase their online offerings and join consortia to develop online programs and courses, it will become increasingly critical to understand the experiences of students in these programs. What does engagement mean when an instructor has never spoken to a student? What is the nature of an online community, and how is it the same as and different from a campus community? Students in online courses frequently express a high level of satisfaction with their experiences (Giguère 2002) – are there aspects of those experiences that can inform on-campus policies?

Conclusion

In the Introduction to this volume, Andres asserts that the British Columbia post-secondary system presents fertile ground for investigating student experiences because of the variety of institutions – from comprehensive to specialized – and the array of programs offered. However, despite the BC-specific location of many of the studies in this book, Andres claims that "we will highlight how results, implications, and recommendations offered in each chapter can be transferable to provinces and states within North

America and beyond that have post-secondary systems that are similar and dissimilar to that of BC." This claim is justified: although some of the recommendations may be specific to their context, most are readily transferable to any North American post-secondary environment.

Each type of institution in BC, most programs, and all students find convincing parallels in Canadian provinces and US states. Academic administrators, program leaders, and change agents in institutions similar to those described here can, therefore, consider and weigh many of the recommendations in this volume. Where differences in policy and practice exist, the studies nevertheless yield important information. For example, while other jurisdictions may not have the same approach to benefits administration as that described in McGee Thompson's chapter, all income assistance managers are concerned with understanding where and by whom additional support is most needed and most effective.

For post-secondary institutions, some recommendations may be more attainable than others – the provision of meeting space, the integration of knowledge gained in the workplace and the classroom, and the scheduling of one-to-one time with counsellors. Others will need commitment to long-term solutions, to advocacy, to new ways of thinking, to the embracing of truly transformative change. For although students increasingly no longer look "traditional," our institutions are still in many ways run along traditional lines. Can professors and instructors modify their teaching styles to encourage classroom dynamics that promote participation by all students? Can departments, in their curricular organization, reflect the challenges faced by students every day in juggling their multiple roles and responsibilities? Can disciplines provide opportunities for undergraduate students to participate in research or similar induction experiences? Can institutions move from policies that function to increase attendance by nontraditional students to practices that honour the contributions they make to a broader cultural and epistemological environment?

For government policy makers as well, the lived experiences of students are instructive. Prevailing views of post-secondary education hold that students, as the prime beneficiaries, must bear some of the costs. They are, after all, investing in their own economic future. Changes to public policy in North America, influenced by this perspective as well as by the need to hold the line on expenditure, have resulted in increased fees at post-secondary institutions and a burgeoning private sector. Many students are denied access to an education increasingly difficult to afford, while others carry worrisome debt loads. But investing in students' education and ensuring equity of access ultimately benefit all of us socially and economically. Striking the right balance between investment and access may be the single greatest challenge facing public policy makers in the coming decades. Getting it right is critical, both for our students and for our future as a nation.

Too many academic studies end with recommendations for more study, and too few end with concrete recommendations for action, for changes to policy and practice. The recommendations in these chapters are grounded solidly on the evidence and findings of each study. If institutions, systems, governments, and agencies take them seriously and move toward implementation, our students and our post-secondary system will only benefit.

Note
1 The "On Track" Outcomes Survey, in place from 1998 to 2001, was a large-scale survey of students who had completed selected programs at private institutions registered with the Private Post-Secondary Education Commission in British Columbia. Six months after they left the institution, it asked participants for their perspectives on the relevance of their training and on their employment outcomes.

References
Andres, L. 1998. *Investigating Transfer Project, Phase II. Community College Students' Perception of Transfer.* Vancouver: BC Council on Admissions and Transfer (BCCAT).
–. 2001. Transfer from Community College to University: Perspectives of British Columbia Students. *Canadian Journal of Higher Education* 31, 3: 35-74.
Andres, L., A. Qayyum, and J. Dawson. 1997. *Investigating Transfer Project. Phase I. The Transfer Experiences of Students from a Community College to a University.* Vancouver: BC Council on Admissions and Transfer.
BC Council on Admissions and Transfer (BCCAT). 2004. *Annotated Bibliography of BCCAT Research.* Vancouver: BCCAT.
B.C. Student Outcomes: Summary of Survey Results. 2002. Victoria: Centre for Education Information, Standards and Services.
Burd, S. 2003. Public Colleges Are at Odds over Raising Limits on Student Loans. *Chronicle of Higher Education* 49, 45. <http://chronicle.com/weekly/v49/i45/45a02201.htm> (18 July 2003).
Clancy, P. 2001. *College Entry in Focus: A Fourth National Survey of Access to Higher Education.* Dublin: Higher Education Authority.
de Broucker, P., and K. Underwood. 1998. Intergenerational Education Mobility: An International Comparison with a Focus on Postsecondary Education. *Education Quarterly Review* 5, 2: 30-51.
Doherty-Delorme, D., and E. Shaker. 2003. *Missing Pieces IV: An Alternative Guide to Canadian Post-Secondary Education.* Vancouver: Canadian Centre for Policy Alternatives.
Dumaresq, C., A. Lambert-Maberly, and W. Sudmant. 2003. *The Class of 1996 Five Years after Graduation: Comparing BC University Outcomes for Direct Entry and Transfer Students.* Vancouver: Planning and Institutional Research, UBC.
Evelyn, J. 2003. The "Silent Killer" of Minority Enrollments. The Chronicle of Higher Education. *Chronicle of Higher Education* 49, 41. <http://chronicle.com/weekly/v49/i41/41a01701.htm> (20 June 2003).
Findings Focus: CCSSE Results in Key Areas. 2002. Austin: Community College Survey of Student Engagement.
Franke-Ruta, G. 2003. The Indentured Generation. *The American Prospect* 14, 5. <http://www.prospect.org/print/V14/5/franke-ruta-g-sr.html> (1 May 2003).
Giguère, L. 2002. *A Profile of B.C. Transfer Students Registered with the B.C. Open University.* Vancouver: BC Council on Admissions and Transfer.
Heisler, P. 2002. *Promoting Access to Postsecondary Education.* Ottawa: Caledon Institute of Social Policy.
Key Data on Education in Europe 2002. 2002. Luxembourg: Office for Official Publications of the European Communities.
Wegmann, C.A., A.F. Cunningham, and J.P. Merisotis. 2003. *Private Loans and Choice in Financing Higher Education.* Washington, DC: Institute for Higher Education Policy.

Contributors

Maria Adamuti-Trache has a PhD in Statistical Physics and a broad experience in teaching and research in physics. Also, she holds an MA in Higher Education in the Department of Educational Studies at the University of British Columbia and is employed at UBC as Statistical Consultant in the Faculty of Education and Data Analyst with Edudata Canada. She is interested in developing longitudinal research related to schools and post-secondary institutions, transition from higher education into the labour market, and the role of cultural and social capital in shaping educational and career pathways. Her current research focuses on equity issues related to the underrepresentation of women in scientific fields with particular emphasis on career choices, persistence in scientific careers, alternative options, and professional success of girls and boys having similar starting points at the end of secondary school. Maria won the MA Thesis Award for 2004, Canadian Society for the Study of Higher Education.

Lesley Andres is an Associate Professor in the Department of Educational Studies at the University of British Columbia. She is also the principal investigator of the Paths on Life's Way Project, a fifteen-year longitudinal study of BC young adults. Her research and teaching interests include the sociology of education; foundations of higher education; issues of inequality and access; the transition from high school to post-secondary education and to work; life course research; and quantitative and qualitative research methods. Her research focuses on the intersecting domains of participation in post-secondary education, equality of educational opportunity, and the relationship between institutional structures and individuals as agents. She is the author of numerous articles, book chapters, and research reports that focus on issues of educational equity and life chances.

Finola Finlay is Associate Director of the BC Council on Admissions and Transfer, a provincial agency charged with responsibility for ensuring consistency and equity in transfer and admission policy and practice in the BC post-secondary system. Finola has been a Campus and Program Director at a community college, the director of a joint college-university teacher education program, and has taught at every level from elementary school to university.

She served as Co-Chair of the Advisory Committee to the BC Minister of Women's Programs. She is a recipient of the Chancellor's Distinguished Service Award from Simon Fraser University. Finola holds a BA and MA from the National University of Ireland, and has done further postgraduate work at Simon Fraser University.

Garnet Grosjean holds a PhD in Adult Education. He is Senior Research Fellow at the Centre for Policy Studies in Higher Education and Training, and Academic Coordinator for the Doctor of Leadership and Policy Program at the University of British Columbia. His research interests include experiential education, work-based learning and learning cultures, higher education and the economy, and higher education and the labour market. Garnet was the 2002 recipient of the Dissertation of the Year award by the Canadian Society for the Study of Higher Education.

Colleen Hawkey recently completed her PhD in Educational Studies at UBC. Her doctoral research focused on the meaning and experience of community for undergraduate students attending a research-intensive university. Her current research interests centre primarily on student success and educational outcomes, and include work on student health, transitions, retention and attrition, the quality of student life, and employment outcomes.

Sharon Liversidge is a faculty member in the Nursing Department of Langara College. She has taught in nursing programs at the diploma and baccalaureate levels. Her research interests include access to higher education, student-mothers, and strategies used by student-mothers to integrate family responsibilities with those of higher education. Her area of teaching expertise lies in Maternal Child Health. She currently holds a BSN and an MA in Higher Education.

Regina Lyakhovetska recently completed her MA in the Department of Educational Studies at UBC. Before coming to UBC, she was an English teacher in Ukraine and a visiting scholar at the University of Tennessee in Knoxville. She has worked as a Graduate Academic Assistant with the Centre for Policy Studies in Higher Education and Training at UBC. Her research is focused on experiences of international graduate students with curriculum, services, social life, and campus community. She is particularly interested in how federal, provincial, and institutional policies concerning international students affect their experiences, and in the role of international students in internationalization.

Michael Marker is an Associate Professor in the Department of Educational Studies and the director of Ts`kel First Nations Graduate Studies at the University of British Columbia. He has published articles on Indian-white relations in education and economic development and has worked with the Lummi tribe in Washington state. He is presently comparing Indigenous knowledge contexts and educational development in Coastal Salish communities on both sides of the Canada-US border.

Donna McGee Thompson has an MA in Adult Education from the Department of Educational Studies at UBC. She currently works in the Health, Counselling, and Career Centre at Simon Fraser University, where she is the coordinator of Learning Skills Programs. She is particularly interested in academic preparation programs and support services that help marginalized students to successfully access education. Her recent research concerns the community college Adult Basic Education experience for mothers of young children. Donna received the 2003 Coolie Verner Research Prize, an award for high academic standing and research excellence.

Gabriel Pillay has been an educator, counsellor, and advisor in the K-12 system for several years. He was also employed as a Credit Transfer Consultant with Corpus Christi College in Vancouver, BC. Currently, he is a Student Recruiter-Advisor with the University of British Columbia, where he provides a variety of recruitment and advising services to prospective students, locally, nationally, and internationally. His research interests focus on issues related to the secondary school guidance and counselling programs, transitional experiences of secondary school students to the post-secondary system, school-to-work transitions, as well as institutional structures and their role in transition. He holds an MEd in Higher Education.

Ruth Warick recently completed doctoral studies at the University of British Columbia. Her dissertation documented the experiences of university students who are hard of hearing. She is active in UBC's Institute for Hearing Accessibility Research and is a past chair of the board for the BC Family Hearing Resource Centre, which provides services for preschool children. She is also a past president of the Canadian Hard of Hearing Association and is presently Chair of the Education Commission for the International Federation of Hard of Hearing People. She is the author of *Hearing the Learning, A Postsecondary Handbook for Students Who Are Hard of Hearing* and *Hard of Hearing Youth Speak Out*, which shares results of a survey of 290 Canadian youth. Ruth works as an Advisor at the University of British Columbia's Disability Resource Centre. She has MA and MEd degrees.

Index

Printed and bound in Canada by Friesens

Set in Stone by Artegraphica Design Co. Ltd.

Copy editor: James Leahy

Proofreader: Deborah Kerr